Complexity and the Economy

Other Titles by W. Brian Arthur:

The Nature of Technology: What It Is and How It Evolves

The Economy as an Evolving Complex System II
(co-edited with D. Lane and S. Durlauf)

Increasing Returns and Path Dependence in the Economy

Complexity and the Economy

W. Brian Arthur

Oxford University Press is a department of the University of Oxford. It furthers the University's objective of excellence in research, scholarship, and education by publishing worldwide.

Oxford New York
Auckland Cape Town Dar es Salaam Hong Kong Karachi
Kuala Lumpur Madrid Melbourne Mexico City Nairobi
New Delhi Shanghai Taipei Toronto

With offices in
Argentina Austria Brazil Chile Czech Republic France Greece
Guatemala Hungary Italy Japan Poland Portugal Singapore
South Korea Switzerland Thailand Turkey Ukraine Vietnam

Published in the United States of America by
Oxford University Press
198 Madison Avenue, New York, NY 10016

Library of Congress Cataloging-in-Publication Data
Arthur, W. Brian.
Complexity and the economy / W. Brian Arthur.
pages cm
Includes bibliographical references and index.
ISBN 978-0-19-933429-2
1. Evolutionary economics. 2. Economics–Psychological aspects.
3. Economics. 4. Technological complexity. I. Title.
HB97.3.A78 2015
330.01′511352—dc23
2014012789

9 8 7 6 5 4
Printed in the United States of America
on acid-free paper

To Brid, Sean, Niamh, and Ronan

CONTENTS

Preface *ix*

Acknowledgments *xxiii*

1. Complexity Economics: A Different Framework for Economic Thought *1*
2. Inductive Reasoning and Bounded Rationality: The El Farol Problem *30*
3. Asset Pricing under Endogenous Expectations in an Artificial Stock Market *39*
   W. Brian Arthur, John H. Holland, Blake LeBaron, Richard Palmer, and Paul Tayler
4. Competing Technologies, Increasing Returns, and Lock-In by Historical Events *69*
5. Process and Emergence in the Economy *89*
   W. Brian Arthur, Steven N. Durlauf, and David A. Lane
6. All Systems Will Be Gamed: Exploitive Behavior in Economic and Social Systems *103*
7. The Evolution of Technology within a Simple Computer Model *119*
   W. Brian Arthur and Wolfgang Polak
8. The Economy Evolving as Its Technologies Evolve *134*
9. On the Evolution of Complexity *144*
10. Cognition: The Black Box of Economics *158*

11. The End of Certainty in Economics *171*

12. Complexity and the Economy *182*

An Historical Footnote *189*

Other Papers on Complexity and the Economy *193*

Index *195*

PREFACE

Every so often a discipline gets thrown into a period of upheaval where its old ideas once taken for granted seem no longer so reliable, and its practitioners search for what to put in their place. Economics is in such a period now. This is partly due to the financial crisis of 2008, but the rethinking goes back to well before this. Slowly, over the last three or more decades, a feeling has grown among economists that their key assumptions of perfect rationality, equilibrium, diminishing returns, and of independent agents always facing well-defined problems are somehow not trustworthy, too restrictive, somehow forced. Now in the air are ideas of behavioral rationality, nonequilibrium, increasing returns, and of interconnected agents facing fundamental uncertainty in problems of decision-making. Economics has opened up to other approaches besides the standard neoclassical one.

I have been heavily involved in one of the new approaches, complexity economics, so I decided this would be a good time to put together several of my earlier papers and bring them out in a collected volume. This collection, on complexity and the economy, dates from the mid-1980s to the present, and it follows my earlier one on increasing returns and path dependence in the economy.[1]

None of these "new" ideas of course are really completely that new. Separately and in various forms they have been mooted by economists for years, sometimes even for a century or more. But what has been missing was the means to handle them, not just raw techniques but the mindset that would go with them, that the world is not perfect, that it isn't machine-like, and that much of it cannot be reduced to simple equations—to variations in the number or level of entities. And missing too was a coherent framework for economics based on these new ideas.

In the last few decades this has changed. The missing pieces have begun to fill in and techniques have slowly become available that can deal with the new assumptions. Among these are nonlinear dynamics, nonlinear stochastic

1. *Increasing Returns and Path Dependence in the Economy*, W. B. Arthur, University of Michigan Press, 1994.

processes, agent-based computation, and computational theory itself. The mindset too has changed. A feeling now runs across the sciences, and economics too, that the world is not a perfectly ordered system reducible in principle to mathematical equations, but is to a large extent organic and algorithmic—it proceeds by building on what is there already and it builds and changes step by step. Slowly, as a result of these occurrences, economics is developing an approach based on these more realistic assumptions. It is developing a new framework for economic thought.

The collected papers in this book reflect my part in the development of this new framework. Taken together they view the economy as a system not necessarily in equilibrium, but as one where agents constantly change their actions and strategies in response to the outcome they mutually create, a system where agents are constantly creating an "ecology" of behaviors they must mutually adapt to. This viewpoint has roots of course in complexity thinking as it developed in the 1970s in groups in Brussels, Stuttgart, and Ann Arbor. And it has roots in the work of individual researchers in universities such as Stanford and MIT. But in its current economic form it grew largely from work at the Santa Fe Institute. In the late 1980s a small group of researchers at the nascent Santa Fe Institute began systematically to look at the economy as an evolving complex system. I headed that group for its first two years, and have been associated with it ever since, and in this collection of papers I want to show how these ideas developed and how the economics they led to came about.

The papers in this volume were not the outcome of some planned process. They arose haltingly and over several years, and were heavily influenced by my colleagues and by thinking in general at Santa Fe. Several appeared in well-known journals, others appeared in places more obscure. Many were written in Santa Fe, others were written at Stanford. The papers present finished thinking but not why or how that thinking came about, so it will be helpful to the reader to understand the background to them and the context in which they arose.

Most of them started with a single incident.

In April 1987 I was walking toward my office in Stanford when a helmeted Kenneth Arrow swung round me on his bicycle and stopped. He was putting together a group of economic theorists in September to exchange ideas with a group of scientists that his counterpart, physicist Philip Anderson, would propose. The venue would be a small institute in the Rockies just starting up. It was in Santa Fe. Would I like to come? I said yes immediately without being sure of what I was committing myself to. The idea looked promising.

The conference in Santa Fe when I got there a few months later turned out to be a more heavyweight affair than I'd imagined. Among the ten or so economists Arrow chose were Larry Summers, Tom Sargent, Jose Sheinkman, and

William (Buz) Brock. Among the ten or so scientists Phil Anderson chose were John Holland, David Ruelle, Stuart Kauffman, and David Pines. The meeting was held in the chapel of a convent the new institute was renting and there was nothing rushed about it. A participant would talk in the morning and we would discuss, another participant would talk in the afternoon and again we would discuss. We were learning not just solutions to problems in the others' disciplines, but about what each discipline saw as a problem, and how it thought about these, and what mindset it brought to bear on these problems. Questions not normally raised within economics were raised—why do you guys cling onto perfect rationality? Why do you assume so much linearity? And questions were asked of physics too. Why is a problem "solved," say in spin glasses, when it has not settled to a steady state? Chaos theory and nonlinear dynamics were discussed in both economics and physics. Modeling of positive feedbacks and of interactions, again in both disciplines, was discussed. People would meet at night in twos and threes to talk over ideas and problems.

The meeting was exhilarating—and exhausting. Nothing had quite been solved by the end of the ten days, yet the physics side was left with a respect for the sheer complicatedness of the economy—the elements in the economy (people), unlike the ions in a lattice, could decide what to do next not just based on the current situation of themselves and other elements, but on what they thought those other elements might do given what *they* might do. And the economists were left with a feeling for modern physics, for its interactions and nonlinearities, its multiple possible end states, its lack of predictability—indeed for its complicatedness.

Word began to leak out after the conference that something interesting had happened at Santa Fe and the new institute's Science Board decided it would follow the conference up by initiating a long-term research program on the Economy as an Evolving Complex System. John Holland and I were asked to come to Santa Fe the following year to head this. I had a sabbatical coming from Stanford and accepted, John found it harder to get away from Michigan and declined. So I found myself heading up the Santa Fe Institute's first research program; it would start in August the following year, 1988.

My immediate problem of course, working from Stanford, was to put together a team of first-rate people for the new program and to decide its direction. Some people I already knew from the conference. John Holland promised to come for a couple of months, and the physicist Richard Palmer for much longer than that. Stuart Kauffman would be in residence. From my own network I was able to bring in David Lane and Yuri Ermoliev, both excellent probability theorists. Arrow and Anderson helped greatly. Where I found it hard to cajole people to join in, Arrow or Anderson, both Nobel Prize winners, could simply lift the phone and quickly get people to join us. As to direction I was less sure. Early on, the physicist Murray Gell-Mann suggested to me that we come up with a manifesto for doing economics differently. I didn't quite have the confidence for that; in fact I didn't yet know what topics we would go after. I had done quite a bit of work already on complexity and the economy, but now we had a much broader reach in what topics we might research. From the conference it was assumed that chaos theory would be central, but the idea somehow didn't appeal to me. Vaguely I thought that we should look at increasing returns problems, which I was more than familiar with, at how some of the physics methods could be transferred into economics, and at nonlinear dynamics in the economy. Also we might be able to do something interesting with computation in economics.

When the program opened finally in 1988 we discussed directions further, still groping for a way forward. I phoned Ken Arrow from Santa Fe and asked for his advice and Phil Anderson's. They got in touch with the funder of the program, John Reed of Citibank, and the word came back: Do what you want, providing it deals with the foundations of economics, and is not conventional. For me and the others on the team, this directive seemed like a dream. We had carte blanche to do what we wanted, and at Santa Fe we wouldn't have colleagues from the discipline looking at us and asking why we were doing things differently.

In fact, outside our small team the few colleagues we did have were from physics or theoretical biology. Stuart Kauffman was one, and we immediately included him in the program. There was little else in the way of researchers the new institute could offer. It was in its earliest days and was all but unknown, an experiment, a small startup in the Rockies set up to have no students, no classes, no departments, and no disciplines—no discipline, the wags said.

We had discussions, mainly in the convent's kitchen, and I remember in an early one Kauffman said, Why do you guys do everything at equilibrium? What would it be like to do economics out of equilibrium? Like all economists I had thought about that, but not seriously. In fact the question took me aback, and it did so with the other economists. I had no good answer. It fell into the category of questions such as what would physics be like if the gravitational force were suspended, something that seemed perfectly thinkable as a thought experiment, but strange. And yet Kauffman's question stuck. We retained the question but we were still looking for a direction ahead.

One of the directions that interested me was still half formed. It had come out of the conference the previous year. In an after-lunch talk the first day of that conference, John Holland had described his work on classifier systems, basically systems that are concatenations of condition-action rules. One rule might say that *if* the system's environment fulfills condition *A*, *then* execute action *R*. Another might say, *if* it fulfills condition *D*, execute action *T*. A third might say that *if A* is true, *and R*-being-executed is not true, *then* execute action *Z*. And so on. The actions taken would change the environment, the overall state of the system. In this way you could string such if-then rules together to get a system to "recognize" its environment and execute actions appropriately, much as an *E. coli* bacterium "recognizes" a glucose gradient in its environment and swims in an appropriate direction. Moreover, you could allow the system to start with not-so-good rules and replace these with better ones it discovered over time. The system could learn and evolve.

As Holland talked about this I found myself deeply excited, and I checked the room to see if other economists were similarly taken with these ideas. There was no evidence; in fact one of them was taking a post-lunch nap. A feeling grew in me that somehow, in some way, this was an answer and all we had to do was find the question. Somehow Holland was describing a method whereby "intelligence" or appropriate action could automatically evolve within systems. I quizzed John later about his ideas. We were sharing a house in Santa Fe for two months at that time in 1987, but in several conversations neither of us could work out what these ideas might directly have to do with economics.

I had gone back to Stanford, where I was teaching a course in economic development. It occurred to me, gradually at first, that John and I could design a primitive artificial economy that would execute on my computer, and use his learning system to generate increasing sophisticated action rules that would build on each other and thus emulate how an economy bootstraps its way up from raw simplicity to modern complication. In my mind I pictured this miniature economy with its little agents as sitting in a computer in the corner of my office. I would hit the return button to start and come back a few hours later to peer in and say, oh look, they are trading sheep fleeces for obsidian. A day later as the computation ran, I would look again and see that a currency had evolved for trading, and with it some primitive banking. Still later, joint stock companies would emerge. Later still, we would see central banking, and labor unions with workers occasionally striking, and insurance companies, and a few days later, options trading. The idea was ambitious and I told Holland about it over the phone. He was interested, but neither he nor I could see how to get it to work.

That was still the status the following summer in June 1988 when Holland and I met again in Santa Fe shortly before the program was to start. I was keen to have some form of this self-evolving economy to work with. Over lunch at a restaurant called Babe's on Canyon Road, John asked how the idea was coming. I told him I found it difficult, but I had a simpler idea that might be feasible. Instead of simulating the full development of an economy, we could simulate a stock market. The market would be completely stand-alone. It would exist on a computer and would have little agents—computerized investors that would each be individual computer programs—who would buy and sell stock, try to spot trends, and even speculate. We could start with simple agents and allow them to get smart by using John's evolving condition-action rules, and we could study the results and compare these with real markets. John liked the idea.

We began in the fall, with the program now started, to build a computer-based model of the stock market. Our "investors," we had decided, would be individual computer programs that could react and evolve within a computer that sat on my desk. That much was clear, but we had little success in reducing the market to a set of condition-action rules, despite a number of attempts. The model was too ad-hoc, I thought—it wasn't clean. Tom Sargent happened to be visiting from Stanford and he suggested that we simply use Robert Lucas's classic 1978 model of the stock market as a basis for what we were doing. This worked. It was both clean and doable. Lucas's model of course was mathematical; it was expressed in equations. For ease of analysis, his investors had been identical; they responded to market signals all in the same way and on average correctly, and Lucas had managed to show mathematically how a stock's price over time would vary with its recent sequence of earnings.

Our investors, by contrast, would potentially differ in their ideas of the market and they would have to learn what worked in the market and what didn't. We could use John's methods to do this. The artificial investors would develop their own condition/forecast rules (e.g., if prices have risen in the last 3 periods *and* volume is down more than 10%, *then* forecast tomorrow's price will be 1.35% higher). We would also allow our investors to have several such rules that might apply—multiple hypotheses—and at any time they would act on the one that had proved recently most accurate of these. Rules or hypotheses would of course differ from investor to investor; they would start off chosen randomly and would be jettisoned if useless or recombined to generate potential new rules if successful. Our investors might start off not very intelligently, but over time they would discover what worked and would get smarter. And of course this would change the market; they might have to keep adjusting and discovering indefinitely.

We programmed the initial version in Basic on a Macintosh with physicist Richard Palmer doing the coding. Initially our effort was to get the system to work, to get our artificial investors to bid and offer on the basis of their current understandings of the market and to get the market to clear properly, but when all this worked we saw little at first sight that was different from the standard economic outcome. But then looking more closely, we noticed the emergence of real market phenomena: small bubbles and crashes were present, as were correlations in prices and volume, and periods of high volatility followed by periods of quiescence. Our artificial market was showing real-world phenomena that standard economics with its insistence on identical agents using rational expectations could not show.

I found it exciting that we could reproduce real phenomena that the standard theory could not. We were aware at the time that we were doing something different. We were simulating a market in which individual behavior competed and evolved in an "ecology" that these behaviors mutually created. This was something that couldn't easily be done by standard equation-based methods—if forecasting rules were triggered by specific conditions and if they differed from investor to investor their implications would be too complicated to study. And it differed from other computerized rule-based models that had begun to appear from about 1986 onward. Their rules were few and were fixed—laid down in advance—and tested in competition with each other. Our rules could change, mutate, and indeed "get smart." We had a definite feeling that the computer would free us from the simplifications of standard models or standard rule-based systems. Yet we did not think of our model as computer simulation of the market. We saw it as a lab experiment where we could set up a base case and systematically make small changes to explore their consequences.

We didn't quite have a name for this sort of work—at one stage we called it element-based modeling, as opposed to equation-based modeling. About three years later, in 1991, John Holland and John Miller wrote a paper about modeling with "artificial adaptive agents."[2] Within the economics community this label morphed into "agent-based modeling" and that name stuck. We took up other problems that first year of the Economics Program. Our idea was not to try to lay out a new general method for economics, as Samuelson and others had tried to do several decades before. Rather we would take known problems, the old chestnuts of economics, and redo them from our different perspective. John Rust and Richard Palmer were looking at the double auction market this way. David Lane and I were working on information contagion, an early version of social learning, using stochastic models. I had thought that ideas of increasing returns and positive feedbacks would define the first years of the program. But they didn't. What really defined it, at least intrinsically, was John Holland's ideas of adaptation and learning. I had also thought we were going slowly and not getting much done, but at the end of our first year, in August 1989, Kenneth Arrow told us that compared with the initial years of the Cowles Foundation effort in the 1950s, our project had made faster progress and was better accepted.

I left Santa Fe and returned to Stanford in 1990 and the program passed into other hands. It continued with various directors throughout the 1990s and the early 2000s with considerable success, delving into different themes depending on the directors' interests and passing through periods of relative daring and relative orthodoxy. I returned to the Institute in 1995 and stayed with the Program for a further five years.

Most of the economic papers in this volume come out of this first decade or so of SFI's economics program. We published an early version of the stock

2. J. H. Holland and J. H. Miller, "Artificial Adaptive Agents in Economic Theory," *Amer. Econ. Assoc. Papers and Proceedings*, 81, 2, 365–370, 1991.

market paper in *Physica A* in 1992, and followed that with the version included here in 1997. The paper got considerable notice and went on to influence much further work on agent-based economics.

One other paper that was highly noticed came out in 1994, and this was my El Farol paper (included in this volume as Chapter 2). The idea had occurred to me at a bar in Santa Fe, El Farol. There was Irish music on Thursday nights and if the bar was not too full it was enjoyable, if the bar was crowded it was much less so. It occurred to me that if everyone predicted that many would come on a given night, they would not come, negating that forecast; and if everyone predicted few would come they would come, negating that forecast too. Rational forecasts—rational expectations—would be self-negating. There was no way to form properly functioning rational expectations. I was curious about what artificial agents might make of this situation and in 1993 I programmed it up and wrote a paper on it. The paper appeared in the *American Economic Review's Papers and Proceedings*, and economists didn't know at first what to make of it. But it caught the eye of Per Bak, the physicist who had originated the idea of self-organized criticality. He started to fax it to colleagues, and suddenly El Farol was well known in physics. Three years later, a game-theoretic version of the problem was introduced by the physicists Damien Challet and Yi-Cheng Zhang of the University of Freiburg as the Minority Game.[3] Now, several hundred papers later, both the Minority Game and El Farol have been heavily studied.

In 1997 my ideas took off in a different direction, one that wasn't directly related to Santa Fe's economics program. I became deeply interested in technology. The interest at first puzzled me. My early background was engineering, but still, this fascination with technology seemed to have nothing to do with my main interests in either economics or complexity. The interest had in fact been kindled years before, when I was exploring the idea of technologies competing for adoption. I had noticed that technologies—all the technologies I was looking at—had not come into being out of inspiration alone. They were all combinations of technologies that already existed. The laser printer had been put together from—was a combination of—a computer processor, a laser, and xerography: the processor would direct the laser to "paint" letters or images on a copier drum, and the rest was copying.

I had realized something else as well. In 1992 I had been exploring jet engines out of curiosity and I wondered why they had started off so simple yet within two or three decades had become so complicated. I had been learning C programming at the time, and it occurred to me that C programs were structured in basically the same way as jet engines, and as all technologies for

3. D. Challet and Y-C. Zhang, "Emergence of Cooperation and Organization in an Evolutionary Game," *Physica A* 246: 407–418, 1997.

that matter. They had a central functioning module, and other sub-modules hung off this to set it up properly and to manage it properly. Over time with a given technology, the central module could be squeezed to deliver more performance if sub-technologies were added to get past physical limits or to work around problems, and so a technology would start off simple, but would add pieces and parts as it evolved. I wrote an essay in *Scientific American* in 1993 about why systems tended to elaborate.[4]

Somehow in all this I felt there was something general to say about technology—a general theory of technology was possible. I had started to read widely on technology, and decided I would study and know very well several particular technologies, somewhere between a dozen and twenty. In the end these included not just jet engines, but early radio, radar, steam engines, packet switching, the transistor, masers, computation, and even oddball "technologies" such as penicillin. Much of this study I did in St. John's College library in Santa Fe, some also in Xerox Parc where I was now working. I began to see common patterns emerging in how technologies had formed and come into being. They all captured and used phenomena: ultimately technologies are phenomena used for human purposes. And phenomena came along in families—the chemical ones, the electronic ones, the genomic ones—so that technologies formed into groups: industrial chemistry, electronics, biotechnology.

What became clear overall was that it wasn't just that individual technologies such as the jet engine evolved over their lifetimes. Technology—the whole collection of individual technologies—evolved in the sense that *all* technologies at any time, like all species, could trace a line of ancestry back to earlier technologies. But the base mechanism was not Darwinian. Novel technologies did not come into existence by the cumulation of small changes in earlier technologies: the jet engine certainly did not emerge from small changes in air piston engines. Novel technologies sprung from combining or integrating earlier technologies, albeit with human imagination and ingenuity. The result was a mechanism for evolution different from Darwin's. I called it Evolution by Combination, or Combinatorial Evolution.

This mechanism exists of course also in biological evolution. The major transitions in evolution are mostly combinations. Unicellular organisms became multicellular organisms by combination, and prokaryotes became eukaryotes by combination. But the occurrence of such events is rare, every few hundred million years at best. The day-to-day evolutionary mechanism in biology is Darwinian accumulation of small changes and differential selection of these. By contrast, in technology the standard evolutionary mechanism is combination, with Darwinian small changes following once a new technology exists.

4. W. B. Arthur, "Why Do Things Become More Complex?" *Scientific American*, May 1993.

I felt I now understood how technologies came into existence, and how the collection of technology evolved. I wanted to see if I could make such evolution work in the lab or on a computer. Around 2005 I was working at FXPAL, Fuji Xerox's think tank in Palo Alto, and I had met the computer scientist Wolfgang Polak. Could we create a computer experiment in which a soup of primitive technologies could be combined at random and the resulting combination—a potential new technology—tossed out if not useful but retained if useful and added to the soup for further combination? Would such a system creating successive integrations in this way bootstrap its way from simplicity to sophistication? We experimented with several systems, to no avail. Then we came across a beautiful paper by Richard Lenski in *Nature*,[5] where he and his colleagues had used the genetic algorithm to evolve digital circuits. Digital technologies seemed a natural medium to work in: if you combined two digital circuits you got another digital circuit; and the new circuit might do something useful or it might not.

Getting our experiment to work wasn't easy, but after a couple of months Polak got the system running and it began to "create" novel circuits from simple ones. Beginning with a soup of simple 2-bit *nand* circuits, the basic building block in digital circuits, we could press the return button to start the experiment and examine what had been created 20 hours later. We found circuits of all kinds. Elementary ones had formed first, then ones of intermediate complication such as a 4-bit *equals*, or 3-bit *less than*. By the end an 8-bit *exclusive-or*, 8-bit *and*, and an 8-bit *adder* had formed. Casually this may not seem that significant. But an 8-bit *adder* that works correctly (adding 8 bits of x to 8 bits of y to yield 9 bits for the result, z) is one of over $10^{177,554}$ circuits with 16 inputs and 9 outputs, and the chance of finding that randomly in 250,000 steps is negligible. Our successive integration process, of combining primitive building blocks to yield useful simple building blocks, and combining these again to create further building blocks, we realized was powerful. And actual technology had evolved in this way. It had bootstrapped its way from few technologies to many, and from primitive ones to highly complicated ones.

We published our experiment in *Complexity* but strange to say it was little noticed or commented on. My guess is that it fell between cracks. It wasn't biological evolution, it wasn't the genetic algorithm, it wasn't pure technology, and it wasn't economics. And the experiment didn't solve a particular problem. It yielded a toolbox or library of useful circuits, much like the library of useful functions that programming language designers provide. But it yielded this purely by evolution, and I found this a wonder. I have a degree in electrical engineering and Polak has one in computer science, but if you asked

5. Lenski, R., C. Ofria, R. Pennock, and C. Adami, "The Evolutionary Origin of Complex Features, *Nature*, 423, 139–443, 2003.

either of us to design an 8-bit *adder* we'd have to bone up on digital electronics and do this from scratch. Yet we had designed an algorithm that could design such circuits automatically by evolution. I found the idea of this remarkable, and of the papers assembled here this is one I am greatly taken by. It demonstrated evolution in action, and evolution by a different mechanism—by combination, or successive integration.

Somehow, I thought, all this had to fit with how an economy evolves, indeed how an economy forms in this first place. As I worked on technology, I realized that while the economy creates technology, more important, technology (the collective of technologies we use to meet our human needs) creates the economy. So the economy is not just a container for its technologies, it is an *expression* of them. As these technologies changed, and as whole new bodies of technology entered, the economy changed. It changed in what it did and how it did it, and it changed in the arrangements and institutions that fitted to the new ways of doing things. The economy, in other words, changed in structure.

I wrote all of these findings up in a book, *The Nature of Technology: What It Is and How It Evolves*, that appeared in 2009. It was well received, particularly by professional engineers, and has gone into several languages. Some of the papers collected here were way stations on the path to this book and one was directly part of it. This work on technology took me 12 years from inception to completion, and I found it fascinating. Of particular wonder were the mechanisms by which the collective of technology evolved, and the realization that technology is a thing with considerable logical structure. Technology, I believe, studied in itself, is every bit as complicated and structured as the economy, or the legal system. And it is an object of considerable beauty.

The various lines of research that have made up this intellectual journey seemed to me at the time disparate and unconnected. But if I look back on them now, and on the work of other colleagues at Santa Fe and elsewhere, I see that what was forming from all this slowly and gradually was an approach to economics. I'd summed up my earlier understanding in a 1999 article in *Science*,[6] and the editor insisted I give this different approach a name. I called it "complexity economics." Looking back now, the features of complexity economics are clear. The economy is not necessarily in equilibrium; in fact it is usually in nonequilibrium. Agents are not all knowing and perfectly rational; they must make sense of the situations they are in and explore strategies as they do this. The economy is not given, not a simple container of its technologies; it forms from them and changes in structure as this happens. In this way the economy is organic, one layer forms on top of the previous ones; it is ever changing, it shows perpetual novelty; and structures within it appear, persist

6. W. B. Arthur, "Complexity and the Economy," *Science*, April 2, 1999, 284, 107–109.

for a while, and melt back into it again. All this is not just a more poetic, humanistic view of the economy. It can be rigorously defined, and precisely probed and analyzed.

I'm often asked how this new approach fits with standard economics. Isn't it simply a variation of standard economics? And won't it be absorbed seamlessly into—"bolted on" to (in economist Richard Bronk's phrase)—the neoclassical framework? My answer on both counts is no. This different approach is not just the use of computers to do agent-based modeling, nor of adding a deeper understanding of technology change to endogenous growth models. It is economics done differently, economics based on different concerns—particularly on how nonequilibrium works—an economics where the problems are different and the very idea of a solution is also different.

One way to see this is to recognize that standard neoclassical economics comes out of a particular way of looking at the world. Neoclassical economics inherited the Enlightenment view that behind the seeming disorder of the world lay Order and Reason and Perfection. And it inherited much from the physics of the late 1800s, in particular the idea that large numbers of interacting identical elements could be analyzed collectively via simple mathematical equations. By the mid-1900s this led in turn to a hope that the core of economic theory could be captured in simple mathematically expressed principles and thereby axiomatized. Some parts, such as macroeconomics or the theory of institutions, might have to be left out, but the core of the field could be ordered and tamed, and reduced to mathematics.

That program was at best only partially successful. It certainly cleaned up much of the sloppy logic that had passed as theory before, and led to a fresh respect for the workings of markets and for the inherent advantages of the capitalist system. But it also, I believe, led to a stiffness in thinking, to a righteousness in what was permitted as economic theory and what was not, and to a closedness to other ideas. Shut out were the effects on the economy of politics, of power, of class, of society, of fundamental uncertainty, and of formation and creation and development. In the end it could be argued that the program—at least the extreme hyper-rational version of it—failed. If it needed Popperian testing, its ideas were falsified spectacularly in 2008 and the aftermath of the financial meltdown. Nobody could claim that the market had lost half of its worth in a short time because companies had suddenly lost half of their usefulness; the companies were much as before. And nobody could claim either that unemployment rates of 20% and upward in some of the European economies were due to the suddenly changed preferences of the labor force; people wanted jobs just as before. In 2009 the *Economist* magazine noted wryly that Wall Street was not the only victim of the financial crash, standard neoclassical economics had collapsed along with it.

On reflection, it shouldn't be surprising that this highly purified form of economic thinking ran into difficulties. One lesson Western thought has had to learn slowly in modern times is that if we try hard enough to reduce anything to pure logic—for example if we try to pin down a final meaning of such concepts as Truth, or Being, or Life, or if we try to reduce some field such as philosophy or mathematics (or economics for that matter) to a narrow set of axioms—such attempts founder. The world cannot be reduced to pure logic and caged within it. Sooner or later it slips out to reveal its true messiness, and all such projects fail.

Slowly replacing the pure order of neoclassical economics is a new respect for reality, shared by many researchers in economics. Behavioral economics is one such approach being pressed forward; the psychology of markets is another. So too are theories of development that rely increasingly on understanding institutions and the workings of technology. And so too is the approach offered here which now has very many practitioners besides our initial group at Santa Fe.

One of things that has surprised me, and pleased me enormously, was that many of the "modern" themes in this approach fit well with ideas in Schumpeter, and Smith, and Mill, and Marx, and Keynes, and with the ideas of the institutionalists and political economists that followed. They too saw the economy as emerging from its technologies, as changing structurally, as not necessarily being in equilibrium, and with its decision-makers facing fundamental uncertainty. These connections have not yet been formally made; they are more like threads of thought that link these new ideas with ones discussed in the past. But they do show economics rediscovering some of what it lost. We are beginning to have a theoretical picture of the economy in formation and in nonequilibrium.

The papers collected here were written from when I first went to Santa Fe in 1987 until the present day. There is some overlap among them; but that is inevitable. Several of the papers were written to make the main ideas available to wider audiences; and also to explore these ideas from different viewpoints. The papers build on the work of many other people in economics, complexity, and other fields, in particular my Santa Fe colleagues John Holland, Stuart Kauffman, David Lane, and Richard Palmer. And they build also on the work of people not closely connected with our original Santa Fe group: in particular, Peter Allen, Rob Axtell, Josh Epstein, Alan Kirman, and Lee Tesfatsion, who all have contributed to this new approach. The papers here owe a great deal to the neoclassical formulation—that's after all what I was trained in. Many are full-blown analyses, others are essays. They are arranged more or less by theme rather than by when they were written, but the research papers are mostly in the first half of the book and the essays in the second. They can be read in any order and I encourage readers to follow whatever sequence appeals to them—and certainly to reach out to the work of others in this area.

Taken together, a theme or framework for thinking emerges from the papers here. In the place of agents in well-defined problems with well-defined probabilistic outcomes using perfect deductive reasoning and thereby arriving at an equilibrium, we have agents who must make sense out of the situation they face, who need to explore choices using whatever reasoning is at hand, and who live with and must adjust to an outcome that their very adjustments may cause perpetually to change.

In 1996 the historian of economic thought David Colander put forward an allegory in which economists a century ago stood at the base of two mountains whose peaks were hidden in the clouds. They wanted to climb the higher peak and had to choose one of the two. They chose the mountain of well-definedness and mathematical order, only to see when they had worked their way up and finally got above the clouds that the other mountain, the one of process and organicism, was far higher.

Many economists have started to climb that other mountain in the last few years. I will be interested to see what we will find along the way.

W. Brian Arthur
Palo Alto, California
January 2014

ACKNOWLEDGMENTS

Many people have heavily influenced the ideas here. I thank in particular John Holland, Stuart Kauffman, David Lane, and Richard Palmer—the core of our team on the Economy as an Evolving Complex System Program in 1988–1990 at the Santa Fe Institute—from whom I learned so much and with whom I greatly enjoyed myself. I have also learned much over the years from a wide cluster of practitioners in several fields: complexity, economics, biology, physics, mathematics, and computation. It's impossible to mention them all, but to single out a few, I'd like to thank Peter Allen, Ken Arrow, Rob Axtell, Chris Barrett, Eric Beinhocker, Larry Blume, Buz Brock, Richard Bronk, David Colander, Steven Durlauf, Josh Epstein, Yuri Ermoliev, Doug Erwin, Doyne Farmer, Magda Fontana, Walter Fontana, John Geanakoplos, Herb Gintis, Yuri Kaniovski, Alan Kirman, Roger Koppl, Chris Langton, Steve Lansing, Blake LeBaron, Sander van der Leeuw, Phil Mirowski, Melanie Mitchell, Wolfgang Polak, David Reisman, Nate Rosenberg, Daria Roithmayr, John Rust, Tom Sargent, Lee Smolin, Martin Shubik, William Tabb, Paul Tayler, and Leigh Tesfatsion—all of whom have influenced me.

None of our early work at Santa Fe would have happened without the help and backing of Kenneth Arrow, Philip Anderson, George Cowan, Murray Gell-Mann, and David Pines. And at Santa Fe, Ronda Butler-Villa, Ellen Goldberg, Ginger Richardson, Geoffrey West, and Chris Wood have been of constant help and encouragement.

Most of papers here were written when I was at Stanford or the Santa Fe Institute. Others were written under the auspices of PARC (formerly Xerox Parc), IBM Almaden, and Fuji Xerox Palo Alto Lab (FXPAL). For financial support, or simply for access to facilities where I could chew the end of a pencil and think and write, I'm grateful to several people and sources: John Reed and Henry Lichstein of Citibank; Ernesto and Andrea Illy of IllyCaffè; Andy Grove and Les Vadasz of Intel; Bill Miller and Michael Mauboussin of Legg Mason Capital Management; the Sloan Foundation; John Seeley Brown and Walt Johnson of PARC; Jim Baker of FXPAL; Paul Maglio and Jim Spohrer of IBM Almaden; Bertil Andersson, Jitendra Singh, Guaning Su, and Jan Vasbinder of Nanyang Technological University; Mike Keller of Stanford University

Library, and the excellent staff of St John's College Library at Santa Fe. I also thank James Bailey, Randy Burge, John Chisholm, Mick Costigan, Bo Ekman, Richard Rhodes, and Paul Saffo for much help and cheerful encouragement. Naturally, I take responsibility for all the ideas here; no intellectual transgressions should be attributed to any people or institutions named on this page.

It has been a pleasure to work with my son Ronan Arthur who read and commented on several of the papers, and my editors, Joan Bossert and Louis Gulino at Oxford, who did much to make this book a reality. Finally, for support, advice, and simple good fellowship over the years, I thank my friends David Lane, Cormac McCarthy, Jim Newcomb, and Martin Shubik.

CHAPTER 1

Complexity Economics

A Different Framework for Economic Thought

W. BRIAN ARTHUR[1]

This paper serves as an introduction to many of the themes that follow; it provides a framework for complexity economics. Complexity economics builds on the proposition that the economy is not necessarily in equilibrium: economic agents (firms, consumers, investors) constantly change their actions and strategies in response to the outcome they mutually create. This further changes the outcome, which requires them to adjust afresh. Agents thus live in a world where their beliefs and strategies are constantly being "tested" for survival within an outcome or "ecology" these beliefs and strategies together create.

Economics has largely avoided this nonequilibrium view in the past, but if we allow it, we see patterns or phenomena not visible to equilibrium analysis. These emerge probabilistically, last for some time and dissipate, and act at the "meso-level" of the economy (between the micro- and macro-levels). We also see the economy not as something given and existing but forming from a constantly developing set of technological innovations, institutions, and arrangements that draw forth further innovations, institutions, and arrangements. Complexity economics thus sees the economy as in motion, perpetually "computing" itself—perpetually constructing itself anew. Where equilibrium economics emphasizes order, determinacy, deduction, and stasis, complexity economics emphasizes contingency, indeterminacy, sense-making, and openness to change.

The paper was written especially for this volume. It builds on a 1999 essay of mine in *Science* on complexity and the economy (Chapter 12 here).

1. Intelligent Systems Lab, PARC, and External Professor, Santa Fe Institute. I thank Ronan Arthur, Richard Bronk, David Colander, Doyne Farmer, Magda Fontana, Ole Peters, David Reisman, and William Tabb for valuable comments.

Over the past twenty-five years, a different approach to economics has been slowly birthing, and slowly growing—*complexity economics*. Complexity economics holds that the economy is not necessarily in equilibrium, that computation as well as mathematics is useful in economics, that increasing as well as diminishing returns may be present in an economic situation, and that the economy is not something given and existing but forms from a constantly developing set of institutions, arrangements, and technological innovations. The approach got its start largely at the Santa Fe Institute in the late 1980s but now has many practitioners,[2] and it raises several questions. What does this different way of thinking about the economy offer? How exactly does it work and where does it fit in? Will it replace neoclassical economics, or be subsumed into neoclassical economics? And under what logic, if any, does it operate?

My purpose in this paper is to answer these questions, especially the last one. In doing so I will not attempt to provide a survey or guided tour, rather I want to provide a framework—a coherent logic—for thinking about this new approach. I will argue from first principles and will build from two earlier essays of mine (Arthur 1999, 2006) as well as the work of many other people to illustrate the key points.[3]

I will argue that this new approach is not just an extension of standard economics, nor does it consist of adding agent-based behavior to standard models. It is a different way of seeing the economy. It gives a different view, one where actions and strategies constantly evolve, where time becomes important, where structures constantly form and re-form, where phenomena appear that are not visible to standard equilibrium analysis, and where a meso-layer between the micro and the macro becomes important. This view, in other words, gives us a world closer to that of political economy than to neoclassical theory, a world that is organic, evolutionary, and historically contingent.

THE ECONOMY AND COMPLEXITY

Let me begin with the economy itself. The economy is a vast and complicated set of arrangements and actions wherein agents—consumers, firms, banks,

2. See *The Economy as an Evolving Complex System* volumes edited by: Arrow, Anderson and Pines (1988); Arthur, Durlauf and Lane (1997); and Blume and Durlauf (2006). For history of the ideas see Fontana (2010), Arthur (2010b), and the popular accounts of Waldrop (1992) and Beinhocker (2006). Variants of complexity economics include generative economics, interactive-agent economics, agent-based computational economics, (see Epstein, 2006a; Miller and Page, 2007; Tesfatsion and Judd, 2006).

3. For other essays on this general approach see Axtell (2007), Colander (2000, 2012), Epstein (2006), Farmer (2012), Judd (2006), Kirman (2011), Rosser (1999), and Tesfatsion (2006). The term "complexity economics" was first used in Arthur (1999).

investors, government agencies—buy and sell, speculate, trade, oversee, bring products into being, offer services, invest in companies, strategize, explore, forecast, compete, learn, innovate, and adapt. In modern parlance we would say it is a massively parallel system of concurrent behavior. And from all this concurrent behavior markets form, prices form, trading arrangements form, institutions and industries form. Aggregate patterns form.

One of the earliest insights of economics—it certainly goes back to Smith—is that these aggregate patterns form from individual behavior, and individual behavior in turn responds to these aggregate patterns: there is a recursive loop. It is this recursive loop that connects with complexity. Complexity is not a theory but a movement in the sciences that studies how the interacting elements in a system create overall patterns, and how these overall patterns in turn cause the interacting elements to change or adapt. It might study how individual cars together act to form patterns in traffic, and how these patterns in turn cause the cars to alter their position. Complexity is about formation—the formation of structures—and how this formation affects the objects causing it.

To look at the economy, or areas within the economy, from a complexity viewpoint then would mean asking how it evolves, and this means examining in detail how individual agents' behaviors together form some outcome and how this might in turn alter their behavior as a result. Complexity, in other words, asks how individual behaviors might *react to* the pattern they together create, and how that pattern would alter itself as a result. This is often a difficult question; we are asking how a process is created from the purposed actions of multiple agents. And so economics early in its history took a simpler approach, one more amenable to mathematical analysis. It asked not how agents' behaviors would *react to* the aggregate patterns these created, but what behaviors (actions, strategies, expectations) would be upheld by—would be *consistent with*—the aggregate patterns these caused. It asked, in other words, what patterns would call for no changes in micro-behavior, and would therefore be in stasis, or equilibrium. (General equilibrium theory thus asked what prices and quantities of goods produced and consumed would be consistent with—would pose no incentives for change to—the overall pattern of prices and quantities in the economy's markets. Classical game theory asked what strategies, moves, or allocations would be consistent with—would be the best course of action for an agent (under some criterion)—given the strategies, moves, allocations his rivals might choose. And rational expectations economics asked what expectations would be consistent with—would on average be validated by—the outcomes these expectations together created.)

This equilibrium shortcut was a natural way to examine patterns in the economy and render them open to mathematical analysis. It was an understandable—even proper—way to push economics forward. And it achieved a great deal. Its central construct, general equilibrium theory, is not just mathematically elegant; in modeling the economy it re-composes it in our minds, gives us a way to picture it, a way to comprehend the economy in its wholeness. This is extremely valuable, and the same can be said for other equilibrium modelings: of the theory of the firm, of international trade, of financial markets.

But there has been a price for this equilibrium finesse. Economists have objected to it—to the neoclassical construction it has brought about—on the grounds that it posits an idealized, rationalized world that distorts reality, one whose underlying assumptions are often chosen for analytical convenience.[4] I share these objections. Like many economists I admire the beauty of the neoclassical economy; but for me the construct is too pure, too brittle—too bled of reality. It lives in a Platonic world of order, stasis, knowableness, and perfection. Absent from it is the ambiguous, the messy, the real.

Good economists of course have always harbored a richer view of the economy than this (Colander and Kupers, 2012; Louça, 2010), so perhaps we could stick with equilibrium as the basis of our thinking, allowing that experience and intuition can fill out the realities. But this still is not satisfactory. If we assume equilibrium we place a very strong filter on what we can see in the economy. Under equilibrium by definition there is no scope for improvement or further adjustment, no scope for exploration, no scope for creation, no scope for transitory phenomena, so anything in the economy that takes adjustment—adaptation, innovation, structural change, history itself—must be bypassed or dropped from theory. The result may be a beautiful structure, but it is one that lacks authenticity, aliveness, and creation.

What if economics allowed the wider possibility and asked how agents in the economy might react to the patterns they together create? Would this make a difference? What would we see then?

ENDOGENOUSLY GENERATED NONEQUILIBRIUM

The first thing to observe is that in asking "how agents might react to," we are implicitly assuming nonequilibrium, for if novel reactions are possible they will alter the outcome, so by definition it cannot be an equilibrium. A well-trained economist might object to this assumption of nonequilibrium; standard doctrine holds that nonequilibrium cannot be important in the economy. "[P]ositions of unstable equilibrium," said Samuelson (1983), "even

4. Blaug (2003), Bronk (2009, 2011), Cassidy (2009), Colander et al. (2009), Davis (2007), Farmer and Geanakoplos, (2008), Kirman (2010), Koppl and Luther (2010), Krugman (2009), Mirowski (2002), Simpson (2002).

if they exist, are transient, non-persistent states. . . . How many times has the reader seen an egg standing on its end?"[5]

Equilibrium, we are assured, is the natural state of the economy.

I want to argue that this is not the case, emphatically not the case, that nonequilibrium is the natural state of the economy, and therefore the economy is always open to reaction. This isn't merely because of outside shocks or external influences, but because nonequilibrium arises endogenously in the economy. There are two main reasons for this. One is fundamental (or Knightian) uncertainty, the other is technological innovation. Let me take each in turn.

First, fundamental uncertainty. All problems of choice in the economy involve something that takes place in the future, perhaps almost immediately, perhaps at some distance of time. Therefore they involve some degree of not knowing. In some cases agents are well informed, or can put realistic probability distributions over events that might happen; but in many other cases—in fact in most cases—they have no basis to do this, they simply do not know.[6] I may be choosing to put venture capital into a new technology, but my startup may simply not know how well the technology will work, how the public will receive it, how the government will choose to regulate it, or who will enter the space with a competing product. I must make a move but I have genuine not-knowingness—fundamental uncertainty. There is no "optimal" move. Things worsen when other agents are involved; such uncertainty then becomes self-reinforcing. If I cannot know exactly what the situation is, I can take it that other agents cannot know either. Not only will I have to form subjective beliefs, but I will have to form subjective beliefs about subjective beliefs. And other agents must do the same. Uncertainty engenders further uncertainty.[7]

This observation of course is not new. Other economists, Shackle in particular (1955, 1992), have written much about this. But it has an important consequence for theorizing. To the degree that outcomes are unknowable, the decision problems they pose are not well-defined. It follows that rationality—pure deductive rationality—is not well-defined either, for the simple reason that there cannot be a logical solution to a problem that is not logically defined. It follows that in such situations deductive rationality is not just a

5. Walras expressed a similar thought in a 1909 conversation with Schumpeter, "life is essentially passive and merely adapts itself to the natural and social influences which may be acting on it, so that the theory of a stationary process constitutes really the whole of theoretical economics. . . ." (Tabb, 1999; Reisman, 2004).

6. As Keynes (1937) puts it: "the prospect of a European war . . . the price of copper . . . the rate of interest twenty years hence. . . . About these matters there is no scientific basis on which to form any calculable probability whatever. We simply do not know."

7. Soros (1987) calls this the principle of *reflexivity*.

bad assumption; it cannot exist. There might be intelligent behavior, there might be sensible behavior, there might be farsighted behavior, but rigorously speaking there cannot be deductively rational behavior. Therefore we cannot assume it.

None of this means that people cannot proceed in the economy, or that they do not choose to act. Behavioral economics tells us that often the context determines how people decide, and certainly we can use its findings. And cognitive science tells us that if a decision is important, people may stand back from the situation and attempt to make sense out of it by surmising, making guesses, using past knowledge and experience. They use their imaginations to try to come up with some picture of the future and proceed on this (Bronk, 2009, 2014). Indeed, as Shackle (1992) puts it, "The future is imagined by each man for himself and this process of the imagination is a vital part of the process of decision." One way to model this is to suppose economic agents form individual beliefs (possibly several) or hypotheses—internal models—about the situation they are in and continually update these, which means they constantly adapt or discard and replace the actions or strategies based on these as they explore.[8] They proceed in other words by induction (Holland et al., 1986; Sargent, 1993; Arthur, 1994a).[9]

This ongoing materialization of exploratory actions causes an always-present Brownian motion within the economy. The economy is permanently in disruptive motion as agents explore, learn, and adapt. These disruptions, as we will see, can get magnified into larger phenomena.

The other driver of disruption is technological change. About a hundred years ago, Schumpeter (1912) famously pointed out that there is "a source of energy within the economic system which would of itself disrupt any equilibrium that might be attained." That source was "new combinations of productive means." (Nowadays we would say new combinations of technology.) Economics does not deny this, but incorporates it by allowing that from time to time its equilibria must adjust to such outside changes.

But this technology force is more disruptive than Schumpeter allowed. Novel technologies call forth further novel technologies: when computers arrive, they call forth or "demand" the further technologies of data storage, computer languages, computational algorithms, and solid-state switching devices. And novel technologies make possible other novel technologies: when the vacuum tube arrives, it makes possible or "supplies" the further technologies

8. A standard objection is that allowing agents to reason non-deductively admits arbitrariness. What prevents such beliefs or behaviors from being chosen ad-hoc to yield some favored outcome? Certainly this is possible, but that doesn't justify retreating to unrealistic "rational" models of behavior. The idea is not to assume behavior that makes analysis simple, but behavior that makes models realistic.

9. Calling this "bounded rationality" is a misnomer. It implies that agents do not use all reasoning powers at their disposal, which under uncertainly may often be false.

of radio transmission and receiving, broadcasting, relay circuits, early computation, and radar. And these novel technologies in turn demand and supply yet further technologies. It follows that a novel technology is not just a one-time disruption to equilibrium, it is a permanent ongoing generator and demander of further technologies that themselves generate and demand still further technologies (Arthur, 2009). Notice again the self-reinforcing nature of this process. The result is not occasional disruption but ongoing waves of disruption causing disruptions, acting in parallel across the economy and at all scales within the economy. Technology change breeds further change endogenously and continually, and this throws the economy into a permanent state of disruption.

Technological disruption acts on a somewhat slower timescale than the Brownian motion of uncertainty. But if anything it causes larger upheavals. And by itself it induces further uncertainty: businesses and industries simply do not know what technologies will enter their space next. Both uncertainty and technology then give us an economy where agents have no determinate means to make decisions.

A picture is now emerging of the economy different from the standard equilibrium one. To the degree that uncertainty and technological changes are present in the economy—and certainly both are pervasive at all levels—agents must explore their way forward, must "learn" about the decision problem they are in, must respond to the opportunities confronting them. We are in a world where beliefs, strategies, and actions of agents are being "tested" for survival within a situation or outcome or "ecology" that these beliefs, strategies, and actions together create. Further, and more subtly, these very explorations alter the economy itself and the situation agents encounter. So agents are not just reacting to a problem they are trying to make sense of; their very actions in doing so collectively re-form the current outcome, which requires them to adjust afresh. We are, in other words, in a world of complexity, a complexity closely associated with nonequilibrium.

THEORIZING UNDER NONEQUILIBRIUM

Where does this leave us? If the economy is large and constantly aboil with activity, then we would seem to be dealing here (to borrow a phrase from Schumpeter, 1954) with "a chaos that is not in analytical control." Faced with this prospect in the past, economics has metaphorically thrown up its hands and backed away. But what if we don't do this, what if we stand our ground and take nonequilibrium seriously, how then can we proceed? Can we say anything useful? What would we see? And above all, what would it mean to do theory under nonequilibrium?

Certainly, many parts of the economy could still be treated as approximately at equilibrium, and standard theory would still be valid here. And other parts could be treated as temporarily diverging from strong attracting states, and we could study convergence here. But this would still be seeing the economy as a well-balanced machine temporarily prone to getting out of adjustment; and that neither gets us to the heart of seeing how the economy behaves out of equilibrium nor captures the creative side of nonequilibrium.

A better way forward is to observe that in the economy, current circumstances form the conditions that will determine what comes next. The economy is a system whose elements are constantly updating their behavior based on the present situation.[10] To state this in another way, formally, we can say that the economy is an ongoing *computation*—a vast, distributed, massively parallel, stochastic one.[11] Viewed this way, the economy becomes a system that evolves procedurally in a series of events; it becomes algorithmic.

There is a danger that seeing the economy this way is merely bowing to a current fashion in science, but the idea allows me to make an important point. Suppose for a moment that we—or better, Laplace or "God"—know the algorithm[12] behind the computation (the large but finite set of detailed mechanisms by which the economy, or the part of it that interests us, makes its next move). A fundamental theorem in computation (Turing, 1936) tells us that in general (if we choose an algorithm randomly) there is no way—no systematic analytical method—to tell in advance whether that algorithm or computer program will halt (as opposed to going on forever, or cycling). Since we could arrange that an algorithm halt if its output fulfilled some particular set of mathematical conditions or reached a given "solution," in general we cannot tell that that will be the case either. In other words there is no analytical method to decide in advance what a given algorithm will do.[13] All we can do is follow the computation and see what it brings. Of course, with simple algorithms we can often see they will settle down to a given outcome. But algorithms don't have to be particularly complicated before we cannot decide their outcomes (Wolfram, 2002).

So we need to be cautious. For highly interconnected systems, equilibrium and closed-form solutions are not the default outcomes; if they exist

10. Current circumstances would of course include relevant past history or memory of past history.

11. Modern computational thinking sees computation as ongoing, concurrent (parallel), distributed, and often probabilistic. See the 2010 ACM Ubiquity Symposium *What Is Computation?* See also Beinhocker (2011).

12. Earlier I argued that the economy's future is indeterminate, so strictly speaking the economy is not perfectly algorithmic. Hence for this thought experiment I posit a "God" who can determine how each agent would react in all circumstances.

13. Including whether it converges (or stays within a given neighborhood of some limit forever).

they require justification. And computation for such systems should not be regarded as the avoidance of analytical thinking; rigorously speaking, it may be completely necessary. We can often do much useful pre-analysis of the qualitative properties of nonequilibrium systems, and understand the mechanisms behind these; still, in general the only precise way to study their outcomes is by computation itself.

Of course the algorithm behind the actual economy is not randomly chosen, it is highly structured, so it may be that the actual economy's "computations" always have simple outcomes. Or it may equally be that the economy's computations are always unordered and amorphous. Usually in the parts of the economy we study, neither is the case. Often, especially when there are strong countervailing forces at work, we see large structures—regions of attraction that correspond loosely to equilibria. And within these (or in their absence) we also see mechanisms that cause phenomena or sub-patterns or sub-structures to appear and disappear randomly from time to time. To give a physical analogy, consider the sun. From afar it appears to be a large gaseous ball in uniform spherical equilibrium. But within this "equilibrium," powerful mechanisms cause dynamic phenomena such as gigantic magnetic loops and arches, coronal holes, X-ray bright spots, and mass plasma ejections moving at up to 2,000 kilometers per second. The gaseous ball indeed displays a loose spherical shape, but it is never at equilibrium. Rather it is seething with activity that disrupts the possibility of equilibrium and builds from earlier disruptions. These phenomena are localized and can act at many scales. And they are transitory or temporal—they appear, disappear, and interact, seemingly randomly in time.

We will find a similar situation frequently in the economy. Theorizing in nonequilibrium then would mean uncovering large attractors at work (if indeed there are any), but also studying other sub-structures or phenomena that might be present for their properties and behavior. We can use carefully designed computer experiments to do this, often using statistics on the results to isolate phenomena and the mechanisms that cause these. And in many cases we can construct simpler toy models of a phenomenon that capture its essential features and allow us to use mathematics or stochastic theory to study it. The objective, we should remember, is not necessarily to formulate equations or to arrive at necessary conditions. The objective, as it is with all theory, is to obtain general insights.

Let us put some of these ideas together by looking at an actual nonequilibrium study performed computationally. Here is a classic example.

In 1991 Kristian Lindgren constructed a computerized tournament where strategies competed in randomly chosen pairs to play a repeated prisoner's dilemma game. (The details of the prisoner's dilemma needn't concern us; think of this as simply a game played by a specified current set of strategies.) The strategies consisted of instructions for how to move given the opponent's immediate past moves. If strategies did well they replicated and mutated, if they did badly they were removed. Lindgren allowed that strategies could "deepen" by using deeper memory of their opponent's immediate past moves and their own. So in our language we can think of such strategies as "exploring" strategy space: they change and adapt if they are not successful. Lindgren found that at the start of his tournament, simple strategies such as Tit-for-Tat dominated, but over time, deeper strategies appeared that exploited the simple ones. In time, further deeper strategies emerged to take advantage of these with periods of relative stasis alternating with dynamic instability (Figure 1).

The dynamics are simple enough that Lindgren could write them as stochastic equations, yet these give far from a full picture; we really need computation to see what is going on. What emerges computationally is an *ecology*—an ecology of strategies, each attempting to exploit and survive within an environment created by itself and other strategies attempting to exploit and survive. This ecology is a miniature biosphere where novel species (strategies) continually appear, exploit the environment created by existing species, and do not survive if they fail. Notice that evolution has entered, but it hasn't been brought in from outside, it has arisen in the natural tendency of strategies to compete for survival. The point is general in this type of economics. What constitutes a "solution" is typically an ecology where strategies, or actions, or beliefs compete; an ecology that may not settle down, that has its own characteristic properties and can be studied qualitatively and statistically.[14]

In Lindgren's study, the outcome differs from one run of the computation to another. In many runs an evolutionary stable strategy appears, a complicated one that relies on four periods of memory of past actions. In other runs the system continues to evolve. In some runs we see the quick emergence of complicated strategies, in others these appear later on. And yet there are constants: phenomena such as coexistence among strategies, exploitation, the spontaneous emergence of mutualism, sudden collapses, periods of stasis and unstable change. The picture resembles paleozoology more than anything else.

I have put forward Lindgren's study as an example of doing nonequilibrium economics and the reader may be wondering how the study of such computer-based worlds can qualify as economics, or what relationship this might have to doing theory—it certainly doesn't look very mathematical. My answer is that theory does not consist of mathematics. Mathematics is a technique, a tool, albeit a sophisticated one. Theory is something different. Theory lies in the discovery, understanding, and explaining of phenomena present in the world. Mathematics facilitates this—enormously—but then so does

14. In the well-known El Farol problem (Arthur, 1994a) an ecology of ever-changing individual forecasts emerges, along with an overall equilibrium attractor state. Metaphorically the individual trees change, but the shape of the forest persists.

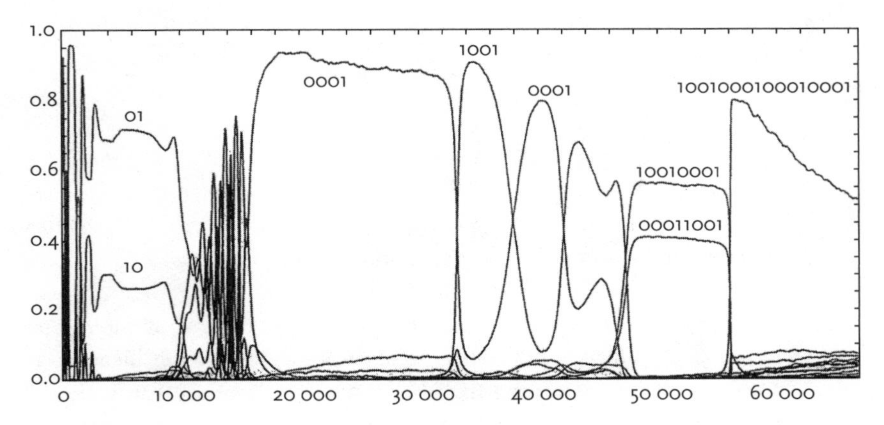

Figure 1:
Strategies in Lindgren's computerized tournament. The horizontal axis denotes time, the vertical axis numbers using a particular strategy, the labels code for the memory-depth of strategies.

computation. Naturally, there is a difference. Working with equations allows us to follow an argument step by step and reveals conditions a solution must adhere to, whereas computation does not.[15] But computation—and this more than compensates—allows us to see phenomena that equilibrium mathematics does not. It allows us to rerun results under different conditions, exploring when structures appear and don't appear, isolating underlying mechanisms, and simplifying again and again to extract the bones of a phenomenon. Computation in other words is an aid to thought, and it joins earlier aids in economics—algebra, calculus, statistics, topology, stochastic processes—each of which was resisted in its time. The computer is an exploratory lab for economics, and used skillfully, a powerful generator for theory.[16]

All this suggests a way forward for our nonequilibrium way of looking at the economy. We can see the economy, or the parts of it that interest us, as the ever-changing outcome of agents' strategies, forecasts, and behaviors. And we can investigate these parts, and also classic problems within economics—intergenerational transfers, asset pricing, international trade, financial transactions, banking—by constructing models where responses are specified not just at equilibrium but in all circumstances. Sometimes our models will be amenable to mathematical analysis, sometimes only to computation, sometimes to both. What we can seek is not just equilibrium conditions, but

15. Note that we can always rewrite any algorithmic model in equation form (any computation by a Turing machine can be represented in equation form) so that, rigorously speaking, computation-based analysis is as mathematical as standard analysis. See Epstein (2006).

16. For computation's role in theorizing in mathematics, physics, biology, and earth-sciences, see Robertson (2003). See also Bailey (2010) and Chaitin (2006).

understandings of the formation of outcomes and their further unfolding, and of any dynamic phenomena that appear.

PHENOMENA AND THE MESO LEVEL

What dynamic phenomena then appear under nonequilibrium? And how do these, and nonequilibrium, connect with complexity? I will take these two questions in succession. To look at what patterns or structures might appear in the economy under nonequilibrium, we can begin by looking at the difference the filter of equilibrium makes to the patterns we see. To set ideas, consider a simple model of something slightly outside the economy, traffic flow.

A typical model would acknowledge that at close separation from cars in front, cars lower their speed, and at wide separation they raise it. A given high density of traffic of *N* cars per mile would imply a certain average separation, and cars would slow or accelerate to a speed that corresponds. Trivially, an equilibrium speed emerges, and if we were restricting solutions to equilibrium that is all we would see. But in practice at high density, a nonequilibrium phenomenon occurs. Some car may slow down—its driver may lose concentration or get distracted—and this might cause cars behind to slow down. This immediately compresses the flow, which causes further slowing of the cars behind. The compression propagates backwards, traffic backs up, and a jam emerges. In due course the jam clears. But notice three things. The phenomenon's onset is spontaneous; each instance of it is unique in time of appearance, length of propagation, and time of clearing. It is therefore not easily captured by closed-form solutions, but best studied by probabilistic or statistical methods. Second, the phenomenon is *temporal*, it emerges or happens within time, and cannot appear if we insist on equilibrium.[17] And third, the phenomenon occurs neither at the micro-level (individual car level) nor at the macro-level (overall flow on the road) but at a level in between—the *meso-level*.

What about the economy more generally? If we are willing to take away the equilibrium filter, what phenomena might we see there and how will these operate? I will mention three.

17. We could of course model this as a stationary stochastic process that includes jams, and artificially call this an "equilibrium" process. Some neoclassical models do this (e.g. Angeletos and La'O, 2011), which would seem to negate my claim that standard economics doesn't handle nonequilibrium. But closer scrutiny shows that such nonequilibrium behavior is always contained within an overall equilibrium wrapper, typically within some overall stochastic process that remains stationary (and hence "in equilibrium"). Such models stretch the neoclassical paradigm by appearing to be "in equilibrium," but at their core are nonequilibrium processes, so I include them as such under the argument here.

The first is *self-reinforcing asset-price changes,* or in the vernacular, bubbles and crashes. To see how these are generated consider the Santa Fe artificial stock market (Palmer et al., 1994; Arthur et al., 1997). In this computer-based model the "investors" are artificially intelligent computer programs, who for the reasons given earlier, cannot simply assume or deduce a given "rational" forecasting model, but must individually discover expectations (forecasting models) that work well. The investors randomly generate (or discover) their own forecasting methods, try out promising ones, drop those that don't work, and periodically generate new ones to replace them. The stock price forms from their bids and offers, and thus ultimately from agents' forecasts. Our market becomes an ecology of forecasting methods that either succeed or are winnowed out, an ecology that perpetually changes as this happens.[18] And we see several phenomena, chief among them, spontaneous bubbles and crashes.

To see how these appear, we can extract a simple version of the mechanism from our experiment. Suppose some of our investors "discover" a class of trading forecast that essentially says "If the price has risen in the last k periods, expect it to increase by $x\%$ next period." Suppose also, some investors (they could even be the same investors) "discover" forecasts of the type: "If the current price is more than y times fundamental earnings (or dividend) value, expect it to fall by $z\%$." The first forecasts cause bubble behavior: if the price rises for a while, investors will buy in, thus validating it, which may cause a further rise. Eventually this drives the price high enough to trigger the second type of forecast. Investors holding these sell, the price drops, which switches off the upward forecasts, causing other investors to sell too, and a crash ensues. The scale and duration of such disruptions vary, they happen randomly in time, so they cannot be predicted. What *can* be predicted is that such phenomena will occur, and will have certain probability distributions of size and scale.

A second temporal phenomenon is *clustered volatility*. This is the appearance of random periods of low activity followed by periods of high activity. In our artificial market these show up as periods of low and high price volatility. Low volatility reigns when agents' forecasts are working reasonably well mutually; then there is little incentive to change them or the results they produce. High volatility happens when some agent or group of agents "discover" better predictors. This perturbs the overall pattern, so that other investors have to change *their* predictors to readapt, causing further perturbation and further re-adaptation. (This pattern is clearly visible in Lindgren's study, Figure 1.) The result is a period of intense readjustment or volatility. Such random periods of low volatility alternating with high volatility show up in actual financial market data, where they are called GARCH behavior.

18. Cf. Soros's (1987) observation that "stock markets are places where different propositions are tested."

A third phenomenon, more to do with space than with time, we can call *sudden percolation*. When a transmissible change happens somewhere in a network, if the network is sparsely connected the change will sooner or later peter out for lack of onward connections. If the network is densely connected, the change will propagate and continue to propagate. In a network of banks, an individual bank might discover it holds distressed assets. It then comes under pressure to increase its liquidity and calls on its counterparty banks. These in turn come under pressure to increase their liquidity and call on *their* counterparties, and so the distress cascades across the network (Haldane, 2009). Such events can cause serious damage. They peter out in a low-connection network, but propagate—or percolate—for long periods as the degree of connection passes some point and gets large (Watts, 2002).[19]

This last example brings us to a general property. Generally in complex systems, phenomena do not appear until some underlying parameter of the model that depicts the intensity of adjustment or the degree of connection passes some point and reaches some critical level. The overall behavior then undergoes a *phase transition*. In our artificial stock market at low rates of investors' exploring new forecasts, the market behavior collapses to a rational expectations equilibrium (agents make identical forecasts that produce price changes that on average validate those forecasts): simple behavior reigns. But if our investors explore at a faster, more realistic rate, the market develops a "rich psychology" of differing forecasting beliefs and starts to display temporal phenomena: complex behavior reigns. If we tune the rate of exploration still higher, individual behavior cannot adjust usefully to the rapidly changing behaviors of others, and chaotic behavior reigns. Other studies (e.g. Hommes, 2009; Kopel, 2009; LeBaron et al., 1999) have found similar regime transitions from equilibrium to complexity to chaos, or from equilibrium to complexity to multiple equilibria (Galla and Farmer, 2012). Such transitions I believe will be general in nonequilibrium models.

We can now begin to see how such phenomena—or order, or structures, if you like—connect with complexity. Complexity, as I said, is the study of the consequences of interactions; it studies patterns, or structures, or phenomena, that emerge from interactions among elements—particles, or cells, or dipoles, or agents, or firms. It's obvious that interaction takes place in our network example, but in our stock market, interaction is more subtle. If one of our investors buys or sells, this changes the price, perhaps slightly, and the

19. The literature on networks is large: see for example Albert et al. (2000), Allen and Gale (2000), May et al. (2008), Newman et al. (2006). Networks can be mutually stabilizing (as with banks providing insurance to other banks), but they can also be mutually destabilizing (as when losses cascade across financial institutions). And the topology of the network matters to how swiftly events propagate and to whether connectedness enhances stability or not (Scheffer et al., 2012).

others may react to this change. In all three examples, changes can propagate through the system.

Complexity studies how such changes play out. Or, to put it another way, complexity studies the propagation of change through interconnected behavior. When a bank comes under stress, it may pass this change to its connected neighbors, which may pass it to their neighbors, which may pass it to *theirs*. An event occurring at one node will cause a cascade of events: often this cascade or avalanche propagates to affect only one or two further elements, occasionally it affects more, and more rarely it affects many. The mathematical theory of this—which is very much part of complexity theory—shows that propagations of events causing further events show characteristic properties such as power laws (caused by many and frequent small propagations, few and infrequent large ones), heavy tailed probability distributions (lengthy propagations though rare appear more frequently than normal distributions would predict),[20] and long correlations (events can and do propagate for long distances and times). Such features occur in all systems—physical, chemical, biological, geological—in which events propagate, so it is not surprising that they occur in our economic examples where propagation is important.[21] They also show up tellingly in actual economic data (Brock et al. 1992; LeBaron et al., 1999).

And we can see something else. If the degree of interaction in such a system is changed from outside (the probability of events causing further events is increased, say, or more linkages are added), the system will go from few if any consequences to many, and from that to undying-out consequences. It will go through a phase change. All these properties are hallmarks of complexity.

We can now say why nonequilibrium connects with complexity. Nonequilibrium in the economy forces us to study the propagation of the changes it causes; and complexity is very much the study of such propagations. It follows that this type of economics properly lies within the purview of complexity.[22]

One further comment. The phenomena I've illustrated appear and disappear very much in distinct historical time or space, so we will not see them if we insist on equilibrium. And they are localized: they appear in one part of the network or the stock market, possibly to diffuse from there. They operate typically at all scales—network events can involve just a few individual nodes

20. Their probabilities are proportional to $\exp(-|\text{propagation-length}|)$ rather than to the $\exp(-(\text{propagation-length})^2)$ of large normal deviations.

21. The reason these properties do not appear in standard economics is because it assumes that agents react to a *given* equilibrium price, not to one that fluctuates due to other agents' behaviors; so random changes individual agents make are independent and can be added together. They therefore result in normal distributions.

22. Hence this form of economics is properly called complexity economics.

or they can be felt right across the economy. But usually they take place in between the micro and macro, so we can rightly call them *meso-phenomena*.[23] They are properties of the *meso-economy*.

It could still be objected that such phenomena make little difference. The standard equilibrium solution after all lies beneath and still has first-order validity. This is certainly true with our stock market model; no stock will stay at 100 times earnings for long.[24] But—and this is an important "but"—the interesting things in markets happen because of their temporal phenomena, they happen within departures from equilibrium. That, after all, is where the money is made. We could similarly say that in an ocean under the undeniable force of gravity an approximately equilibrium sea level has first-order validity. And this is certainly true. But, as with markets, in the ocean the interesting things happen not at the equilibrium sea level which is seldom realized, they happen on the surface where ever-present disturbances cause further disturbances. That, after all, is where the boats are.

I have used three fairly well-known phenomena in this section as illustration. Other phenomena have been noticed and no doubt others remain to be discovered. Exactly what these might be, what their characteristics are, and how they might interact are important questions for future work. But most important, our argument tells us that we need to pay attention to a new level in the economy, the meso-level, where events can trigger other events at all scales. The economy has a middle or meso layer, and in this layer phenomena arrive, last for a while, and dissipate.

POSITIVE FEEDBACKS

I want to point out a further thing about the mechanisms we've been looking at. They arise from self-reinforcing behavior in the interactions. Agents buy into a stock, or disturb a market slightly, or propagate some change, and this causes further buying in, or further disturbance, or further propagation of change. Or as we saw earlier, agents show uncertainty in choice and this causes further uncertainty, or bring on some novel technology and this calls for further novel technologies. Such positive feedbacks disturb the status quo, they cause nonequilibrium. And they cause structures to appear. A small backup in traffic causes further backup and a structure forms, in this case a traffic jam. This is where the Brownian motion I alluded to comes in; it brings

23. For earlier uses of "meso" in economics, see Dopfer (2007) and Elsner and Heinrich (2009).

24. But it is not true in general: many economic situations do not have forces leading to any equilibrium attractor.

perturbations around which small movements nucleate; positive feedback magnifies them and they "lock in," in time eventually to dissipate.

Positive feedbacks in fact are very much a defining property of complex systems—or I should say more accurately, the presence of positive and negative feedbacks acting together is. If a system contains only negative feedbacks (in economics, diminishing returns) it quickly converges to equilibrium and shows "dead" behavior. If it contains only positive feedbacks, it runs away and shows explosive behavior. With a mixture of both it shows "interesting" or "complex" behavior. With positive feedback interactions add to each other and cause structure, in time to be offset by negative forces and dissipate. Structures then come and go, some stay to be further built on and some lead to further structures. The system is "alive."

These observations add to the earlier literature in economics on positive feedbacks or increasing returns. Here, if a firm (or product or technology or geographical region) gets ahead, possibly by small chance events, given increasing returns it will gain further advantage and get further ahead; it may then subsequently go on to dominate the outcome (Arthur, 1989, 1994b). If N firms compete there are N possible outcomes, but N need not be small. In the late 1800s, typewriter keyboard layouts "competed" for use, and only the one we use today became a standard. But a simple calculation shows there were more than 10^{54} outcomes possible, and this is a large number by any measure.

The process that increasing returns bring into being is by now well known. What I would add is that positive feedbacks are present more widely in the economy than we previously thought: they show up not just with firms or products, but in small mechanisms and large, in decision behavior, market behavior, financial behavior, and network dynamics. They act at all scales to destabilize the economy, even the macro-scale (Keynes' theory can be seen as positive feedbacks temporarily locking in one of two possible states: full employment and unemployment). And they lead to a set of characteristic properties: multiple attractors, unpredictability, lock-in, possible inefficiencies, and path-dependence. Their counterparts in physics are multiple metastable states, unpredictability, phase- or mode-locking, high-energy ground states, and non-ergodicity. Once again these are properties we associate with formal complexity.

THE ECONOMY IN FORMATION

I want to turn now to a very different topic, one that builds on our earlier issue of disruption by technologies. Until now, we have seen *given* elements that comprise the economy reacting to the patterns they create and forming ever different patterns. But this still doesn't quite capture one fundamental feature of the economy. The economy continually creates and re-creates itself, and it does this by creating *novel* elements—often novel technologies and institutions—which produce novel structures as it evolves. How exactly does this happen? How does the economy form itself and change structurally? Schumpeter (1908) called this question "the most important of all the phenomena we seek to explain." Complexity should be able to help here; it is very much about the creation and re-creation of structure.

Let us begin by observing that if we want to look at how the economy constructs itself and changes, we need to look at technology and how *it* constructs itself and changes over time. Technology isn't the only agent of change in the economy but it is by far the main one (Solow, 1957). The standard story of economic change equates technologies with production functions and sees the economy as a container for these. As new industrial technologies enter, production functions change, output increases and labor or other resources are released; this provides further wealth that can be invested in further technologies. The economy shifts smoothly from one equilibrium to another and endogenously grows. This is fine and it fits well with equilibrium economics. But it puts the main driver, technology, in the background, with prices and quantities in the foreground. And it sees technologies as formless; they just somehow arrive, singly and randomly, with no structure to how they build out or how they change the economy in character over time.

A complexity view would put technologies in the foreground, and prices and quantities in the back.[25] It would recognize that there is considerable structure to how technologies arise and enter the economy (Arthur, 2009). In doing this it would focus directly on the collection of technologies present at any time, and ask how this collection evolves: how its members come into being, how they create and re-create a mutually supporting set, and how this alters the economy structurally over time.

To start, we can define individual technologies as means to human purposes. These would include industrial processes, machinery, medical procedures, algorithms, and business processes. And they would also include organizations, laws, and institutions—these too are means to human purposes. The significant thing about technologies is that they are constructed, put together, combined—always—from parts, assemblies, sub-assemblies. These latter are also means to purposes, so novel technologies form by combination from existing technologies.[26] The laser printer was constructed from the existing laser, digital processor, and xerography (the processor directs a highly focused laser beam to "paint" an image on a copier drum). We now have

25. For other complexity approaches to formation see Hildago and Hausmann (2009), and Lane et al. (2009). On structural change see North (1981).

26. Schumpeter (1912) cites combination as the key driving force of formation (or "development" as he called it).

a system where novel elements (technologies) constantly form from existing elements, whose existence may call forth yet further elements.

Next let us define the economy as the set of arrangements and activities by which a society fulfills its needs. These arrangements of course are the economy's technologies. This is not a familiar way to look at the economy, but it fits well with the classical economists' view of the economy as proceeding from its instruments of production. The economy we can then say *emerges* from its arrangements, its technologies: it is an *expression* of its technologies. Seen this way, the economy immediately becomes an ecology of its means of production (its technologies), one where the technologies in use need to be mutually supporting and economically consistent.

We can add one more observation. Technologies come into being only if there exists a "demand" for them. Most of this demand comes from the needs of technologies themselves. The automobile "demands" or calls forth the further technologies of oil exploration, oil drilling, oil refining, mass manufacture, gasoline distribution, and car maintenance. At any time then there is an open web of opportunities inviting further technologies and arrangements.

We now have the basic setup. To put it in motion we can ask how the collection builds out. The steps involved yield the following algorithm for the formation of the economy.

1. A novel technology appears. It is created from particular existing ones, and enters the active collection as a novel element.
2. The novel element becomes available to replace existing technologies and components in existing technologies.
3. The novel element sets up further "needs" or opportunity niches for supporting technologies and organizational arrangements.
4. If old displaced technologies fade from the collective, their ancillary needs are dropped. The opportunity niches they provide disappear with them, and the elements that in turn fill these may become inactive.
5. The novel element becomes available as a potential component in further technologies—further elements.
6. The economy—the pattern of goods and services produced and consumed—readjusts to these steps. Costs and prices (and therefore incentives for novel technologies) change accordingly.

Thus the railway locomotive was constructed from the already existing steam engine, boiler, cranks, and iron wheels. It entered the collective around 1829 (step 1); replaced existing horse-drawn trains (step 2); set up needs for the fabrication of iron rails and the organization of railways (step 3); caused the canal and horse-drayage industries to wither (step 4); became a key component in the transportation of goods (step 5); and in time caused prices and incentives across the economy to change (step 6). Such events may operate in parallel: new opportunities for example appear almost as soon as a new technology appears.

If you play the algorithm out in your mind you see something interesting. It can set in motion a sequence of happenings that never end, because each of the events may trigger a cascade of further events. A novel technology may cause further technologies to be added, by steps 3 and 5; further replacements of old technologies, by step 4; and further readjustments, by step 6. And these new technologies in turn can cause yet further opportunities, further technologies, and further replacements. The algorithm may be simple, but once set in motion it engenders rich, patterned, endlessly novel behavior.

So far this depicts the basic mechanism of formation of the economy. But there is a second layer of mechanism that adds further structure. New technologies often enter in groups (Perez, 2002; Arthur, 2009): over decades, families of technologies, the steam-driven ones, electrical ones, chemical ones, digital ones, enter. These are based on a given key technology, the steam engine say, or on families of related phenomena—chemical, electrical, genetic—that are harnessed and become available. And they build haltingly from one or two early central technologies then fill in the needed sub-technologies. These bodies of technology are not adopted within the economy, rather they are *encountered* by industries, combining with business processes that already exist and causing new activities, new incentives, new available processes, and little irruptions in the shape of little firms, a few of which go on to become large firms.

The economy—the set of arrangements and activities that satisfy our needs—builds out as a result of all this. Indeed the economy *is* the result of all this.

I have given only the bare bones of the processes by which the economy re-forms itself, and each mechanism has sub-mechanisms omitted here (see Arthur, 2009). But notice the overall theme: A few simple properties of technology yield a system of changing elements (technologies), each new element created from previous elements, each causing replacements, and all bringing on an ever-changing set of demands for further elements, the whole channeled and structured by the properties and possibilities of the dominant families of phenomena recently captured.

This overall process is a self-creating one. Novel technologies form from existing technologies, so the collective of technology is self-producing or *autopoietic*. So too is the economy. It forms from its technologies and mediates the creation of further technologies and thereby its own further formation. Here again we are very much in complexity territory.

We can now see how the economy changes structurally. As novel physical technologies enter, novel forms of organization and novel institutions are called for and come into place, and these in turn call forth further new technologies—further methods, organizations, and institutions. Structure emerges. On a longer time scale, the large bodies of technology define a thematic way by which operations in the economy are carried out. So we have the steam era, the railroad era, the digital era. They also pose characteristic or thematic challenges that call forth novel solutions; the economy changes structurally. The steam engine and early textile machinery made possible the Victorian mill-based economy, and its excesses called forth new arrangements: laws covering child safety, regulations ameliorating working conditions, and labor unions in modern form.[27] As the economy changes then, its organizations and institutions change, and these call forth yet further arrangements—further technologies—and further changes. The economy transforms structurally. We can isolate the mechanisms by which the economy renews itself, but we can't predict the exact ways these play out. The overall process (or computation, if you will) is far from determinate. And it is par excellence one of nonequilibrium.

Notice that the theory I have outlined is algorithmic: it is expressed as a set of processes triggered by other processes, not as a set of equations. The reader may again ask how this can be theory? Consider a parallel with biology. Even now, 150 years after Darwin's *Origin*, no one has succeeded in reducing to an equation-based system the process by which novel species are created, form ecologies, and bring into being whole eras dominated by characteristic species. The reason is that the evolutionary process is based on mechanisms that work in steps and trigger each other, and it continually defines new categories—new species. Equations do well with changes in number or quantities within *given* categories, but poorly with the appearance of new categories themselves. Yet we must admit that evolution's central mechanisms are deeply understood and form a coherent group of general propositions that match real world observations, so these understandings indeed constitute theory.[28] Biology then is theoretical but not mathematical; it is process-based, not quantity-based. In a word it is *procedural*. By this token, a detailed economic theory of formation and change would also be procedural.[29] It would seek to

27. Political economist William Tabb (1999), expresses structural change this way: "Technological revolutions and political upheavals condition economic possibilities, which then become the givens for sustained periods of seeming stability in which regulatory regimes designed for the conditions of the social structure of accumulation of the era lend a semblance of orderly progress. These institutional forms, appropriate to one stage of development, become a drag on the development of new forces and emergent relations of production. The vitality of market forces create in their wake social problems which, when they become severe enough need to be addressed through spirited struggle out of which new rules, regulations, and institutions form."

28. Similar observations can be made about the theories of embryological development, of biochemical pathways, of molecular genetics, and of cell biology. The process of mitosis (cell division) has no mathematics, but does have a series of well-understood, if complicated, phases or steps.

29. The reader might be tempted to translate this back into familiar terms such as capital, labor, growth, etc. That might be possible, but I prefer to see this as a different way to "image" or understand change in the economy, much as MRI scanning images organs differently than conventional x-ray scanning.

understand deeply the mechanisms that drive formation in the economy and not necessarily seek to reduce these to equations. The procedural theory I have outlined doesn't negate the standard one, but it does give an alternative that puts the emphasis squarely on the driver of change itself—on technology.

How can we study all this more deeply? The base processes are algorithmic, so certainly we can construct computer-based models of their key mechanisms.[30] Studies here are still at their beginning. The overall view we end up with is one of creative formation: of new elements forming from existing elements, new structure forming from existing structure, formation itself proceeding from earlier formation. This is very much a complexity view.

DISCUSSION

It should be clear by now that we have a different framework for thinking about the economy, one that emphasizes not the physics of goods and services, but processes of change and creation. Yet, as the reader may have surmised, this new view is not entirely new within economic thought. It links with earlier thinking in a way I want to comment on now.

There are two great problems in economics. One is *allocation* within the economy: how quantities of goods and services and their prices are determined within and across markets. This is represented by the great theories of general equilibrium, international trade, and game-theoretic analysis. The other is *formation* within the economy: how an economy emerges in the first place, and grows and changes structurally over time. This is represented by ideas about innovation, economic development, structural change, and the role of history, institutions, and governance in the economy. The allocation problem is well understood and highly mathematized, the formation one less well understood and barely mathematized.[31]

How did this come about? Until about 1870 both problems were of equal importance to the great theorists in economics. Smith, Mill, and Marx all contributed to making a rational science out of allocation, yet they equally contributed to questions of formation, governance, and history. Then in Victorian times came the great marginalist and general-equilibrium revolution that rendered the problem of allocation into algebra and calculus (given strict assumptions of rationality and equilibrium). But the problem of formation could not be so rendered. By its nature it couldn't be restricted to either

30. In 2006 Wolfgang Polak and I modeled a creation process successfully on the computer by which increasingly complicated technologies (digital logic circuits) emerged from initially simple ones via random combination of earlier combinations (circuits).

31. See Tabb (1999) for an excellent discussion of these two branches of economics. Also Bronk (2009).

stasis or rationality, and so the mathematization of economics—what came in the twentieth century to be taken as "theory"—passed it by. Formation was still studied by Marshall, Veblen, Schumpeter, Hayek, and Shackle, and by the many institutionalists and historians that followed. But the thinking was largely history-specific, particular, case-based, and intuitive—in a word, literary—and therefore held to be beyond the reach of generalizable reasoning, so in time what had come to be called political economy became pushed to the side, acknowledged as practical and useful but not always respected.

It is now clear to economists that the mathematical analysis of allocation far from covers all of economics and operates poorly with questions of formation, exploration, adaptation, and qualitative change (Tabb, 1999). Complexity economics by contrast is very much about these questions of creation and the formation of structure, and it studies the mechanisms by which these operate. So here complexity meets up with and revives the grand tradition of political economy, and the two—much to my delight—have a lot to say to each other. Complexity economics allows us to explore the world of formation theoretically and systematically; political economy allows us to explore it intuitively and empirically. The new approach will help provide a theoretical backbone for political economy. It will not and should not displace case-based historical analysis, but will deepen and develop this venerable branch of thinking. And political economy will deepen and develop complexity economics.

One of the main strengths of political economy is its sense of history, of historical time—time that makes a real, irreversible difference, and that continually creates new structures. By contrast neoclassical economics handles time poorly (Smolin, 2009, 2013). At equilibrium an outcome simply persists and so time largely disappears; or in dynamic models it becomes a parameter that can be slid back and forth reversibly to denote the current outcome (Harris, 2003). This has made many economic thinkers uncomfortable (Robinson, 1980). In 1973 Joan Robinson said famously, "Once we admit that an economy exists in time, that history goes one way, from the irrevocable past into the unknown future, the conception of equilibrium . . . becomes untenable. The whole of traditional economics needs to be thought out afresh."

Certainly, in rethinking this issue of time, complexity economics accords with political economy. In the "computation" that is the economy, large and small probabilistic events at particular non-repeatable moments determine the attractors fallen into, the temporal structures that form and die away, the technologies that are brought to life, the economic structures and institutions that result from these, the technologies and structures that in turn build upon *these*; indeed the future shape of the economy—the future path taken. The economy at all levels and at all times is path dependent. History again becomes important. And time reappears.

A natural question is whether this new approach has policy implications. Certainly, complexity teaches us that markets left to themselves possess a tendency to bubbles and crashes, induce a multiplicity of local attractor states, propagate events through financial networks, and generate a sequence of technological solutions and challenges, and this opens a role for policies of regulating excess, nudging towards favored outcomes, and judiciously fostering conditions for innovation. Colander and Kupers (2014) express this succinctly as getting meta conditions right.

This is certainly valid. But I believe we can make a stronger statement. The failures of economics in the practical world are largely due to seeing the economy in equilibrium. If we look at the economic crises of the last 25 years—the debacle that followed the freeing of markets in Russia in 1990, the extensive gaming of California's energy market after the lifting of regulations in 2000, the collapse of Iceland's banks in 2008, the ongoing Euro crisis, the Wall Street meltdown of 2008—all these were caused in no small part by the exploitation of the system by a few well-positioned players, or by markets that careened out of control (Arthur, 2010a). Equilibrium thinking cannot "see" such exploitation in advance for a subtle reason: by definition, equilibrium is a condition where no agent has any incentive to diverge from its present behavior, therefore exploitive behavior cannot happen. And it cannot see extreme market behavior easily either: divergences are quickly corrected by countervailing forces. By its base assumptions, equilibrium economics is not primed to look for exploitation of parts of the economy or for system breakdowns.

Complexity economics, by contrast, teaches us that the economy is permanently open to response and that every part of it is open to new behavior—to being exploited for gain, or to abrupt changes in structure. A complexity outlook would recommend putting carefully thought out controls in place, much as authorities put sensible building codes in place in seismic regions. But just as important, it would bring a shift in attitude in the direction of realism. The economy does not consist of a set of behaviors that have no motivation to change and collectively cause optimality; the economy is a web of incentives that always induce further behavior, invite further strategies, provide collectively "reasonable" outcomes along the way, and ever cause the system to change.

CONCLUSION

Complexity economics is neither an add-on to standard economics (see Fontana, 2010), nor does it consist of adding agent-based behavior to standard models. It is a different way of thinking about the economy. It sees the economy not as a system in equilibrium but as one in motion, perpetually "computing" itself—perpetually constructing itself anew. Where equilibrium economics emphasizes order, determinacy, deduction, and stasis, this new framework emphasizes contingency, indeterminacy, sense-making, and openness to change. There is another way to say this. Until now, economics has been a noun-based rather than verb-based science. It has pictured changes over time in the economy function as changes in levels of fixed noun-entities—employment, production, consumption, prices. Now it is shifting toward seeing these changes as a series of verb-actions—forecast, respond, innovate, replace—that cause further actions.

This shift reveals an important middle layer in the economy, the *meso-layer*. And it redefines what constitutes a solution in economics. A solution is no longer necessarily a set of mathematical conditions but a pattern, a set of emergent phenomena, a set of changes that may induce further changes, a set of existing entities creating novel entities. Theory in turn becomes not the discovery of theorems of undying generality, but the deep understanding of mechanisms that create these patterns and propagations of change.

This shift in economics is very much part of a larger shift in science itself. All the sciences are becoming more procedural, more algorithmic, more Turingesque; and less equation-based, less continuous, less Newtonian, than before. This is due both to the rise of biology as a rigorous science and to the rise of computation and computer science. Even mathematics is shifting in this direction. Gregory Chaitin (2012) speaks of a mathematics that is shifting away from continuous formulations, differential equations, and static outcomes, to one based on discrete formulations, combinatorial reasoning, and algorithmic thinking. "The computer," he says, "is not just a tremendously useful technology, it is a revolutionary new kind of mathematics with profound philosophical consequences. It reveals a new world." Science and mathematics are shedding their certainties and embracing openness and procedural thinking, and there is no reason to expect that economics will differ in this regard.

Complexity economics is not a special case of neoclassical economics. On the contrary, equilibrium economics is a special case of nonequilibrium and hence complexity economics. Complexity economics, we can say, is economics done in a more general way. Equilibrium of course will remain a useful first-order approximation, useful for situations in economics that are well-defined, rationalizable, and reasonably static, but it can no longer claim to be the center of economics. Moving steadily to the center[32] is an economics that can handle interactions more generally, that can recognize nonequilibrium phenomena, that can deal with novelty, formation and change.

Complexity economics is still in its early days and many economists are pushing its boundaries outward. It shows us an economy perpetually inventing itself, perpetually creating possibilities for exploitation, perpetually open to response. An economy that is not dead, static, timeless, and perfect, but one that is alive, ever-changing, organic, and full of messy vitality.

32. See Holt et al. (2010); Davis (2008).

REFERENCES

ACM Ubiquity Symposium: *What Is Computation?* 2010.

Angeletos, G-M., and J. La'O, "Decentralization, Communication, and the Origins of Fluctuations," NBER Working Paper 17060, NBER, Cambridge, MA, 2011.

Albert, R., H. Jeong, and A-L. Barabasi, "Attack and Error Tolerance of Complex Networks," *Nature,* 406, 379–382, 2000.

Allen, F., and D. Gale, "Financial Contagion," *Journal of Political Economy*, 108, 1, 1–33, 2000.

Arrow, K., P. Anderson, and D. Pines, *The Economy as an Evolving Complex System*, Addison-Wesley, Reading, MA, 1988.

Arthur, W. B., "Competing Technologies, Increasing Returns, and Lock-In by Historical Events," *Economic Journal*, 99, 116–131, 1989.

Arthur, W. B., "Bounded Rationality and Inductive Behavior (the El Farol problem)," *American Economic Review Papers and Proceedings*, 84, 406–411, 1994a.

Arthur, W. B., *Increasing Returns and Path Dependence in the Economy*, University of Michigan Press, Ann Arbor, MI, 1994b.

Arthur, W. B., S. Durlauf, and D. Lane, eds. *The Economy as an Evolving Complex System II*, Addison-Wesley, Reading, MA, 1997.

Arthur, W. B., J. H. Holland, B. LeBaron, R. Palmer, and P. Tayler, "Asset Pricing under Endogenous Expectations in an Artificial Stock Market," in *The Economy as an Evolving Complex System II*, (*op. cit.*), 1997.

Arthur, W. B., "Complexity and the Economy," *Science*, 284, 107–109, 1999.

Arthur, W. B., "Out-of-equilibrium Economics and Agent-based Modeling," in L. Tesfatsion and K. Judd, (*op. cit.* below), 2006.

Arthur, W. B., and W. Polak, "The Evolution of Technology in a Simple Computer Model," *Complexity*, 11, 5, 2006.

Arthur, W. B., *The Nature of Technology: What It Is and How It Evolves,* The Free Press, New York, 2009.

Arthur, W. B., "Exploitive Behavior in Policy Systems," Mss., IBM Almaden, 2010a.

Arthur, W. B., "Complexity, the Santa Fe Approach, and Nonequilibrium Economics," *Hist. Econ. Ideas,* 18, 2, 149–166, 2010b.

Axtell, R., "What Economic Agents Do: How Cognition and Interaction Lead to Emergence and Complexity," *Rev. Austrian Econ.*, 20, 105–122, 2007.

Bailey, J., *Emerge: The Data-Rich Mathematical Infinitesimals of Life, MAPematics*, The Mapematics Institute, 2010.

Beinhocker, E., *The Origin of Wealth: Evolution, Complexity, and the Radical Remaking of Economics*, Harvard Business School Press, Cambridge, MA, 2006.

Beinhocker, E., "Evolution as Computation: Integrating Self-Organization with Generalized Darwinism," *J. Inst. Econ.*, 7, 3, 393–423, 2011.

Blaug, M., "The Formalist Revolution of the 1950s," *J. History of Economic Thought*, 25, 2, 145–156, 2003.

Blume, L., and S. Durlauf, *The Economy as an Evolving Complex System III*, Oxford University Press, New York, 2006.

Brock, W. A., J. Lakonishok, and B. LeBaron, "Simple Technical Trading Rules and the Stochastic Properties of Stock Returns," *Journal of Finance,* 47, 1731–1764, 1992.

Bronk, R., *The Romantic Economist: Imagination in Economics*, Cambridge University Press, Cambridge, UK, 2009.

Bronk, R., "Epistemological Difficulties with Neoclassical Economics," *Rev. Austrian Economics*, 2014.
Cassidy, J., *How Markets Fail: The Logic of Economic Calamities*, Farrar, Straus and Giroux, New York, 2009.
Chaitin, G., *Meta Math! The Quest for Omega*, Vintage Books, New York, 2006.
Chaitin, G., *Proving Darwin: Making Biology Mathematical*, Pantheon Books, New York, 2012.
Colander, D., and R. Kupers. *Laissez-Faire Activism: The Complexity Frame for Policy*, Princeton University Press, Princeton, NJ, 2014.
Colander, D. (ed.), *The Complexity Vision and the Teaching of Economics*, E. Elgar, Cheltenham, UK, 2000.
Colander, D., M. Goldberg, A. Haas, K. Juselius, T. Lux, H. Föllmer, A. Kirman, and B. Sloth, "The Financial Crisis and the Systemic Failure of the Economics Profession," *Critical Rev.*, 21, 2, 2009.
Davis, J., "The Turn in Recent Economics and Return of Orthodoxy," *Cambridge J. Econ.*, 32, 349–366, 2008.
Dopfer, K., "The Pillars of Schumpeter's Economics: Micro, Meso, Macro," in Hanusch and Pyka, eds., *Elgar Companion to Neo-Schumpeterian Economics*. E. Elgar, Cheltenham, UK, 2007.
Elsner, W., and T. Heinrich, "A Simple Theory of 'Meso:' On the Co-evolution of Institutions and Platform Size," in *Journal of Socio-Economics*, 38, 843–858, 2009.
Epstein J., *Generative Social Science*, Princeton University Press, Princeton, NJ, 2006a.
Epstein, J., "Remarks on the Foundations of Agent-based Generative Social Science," in Tesfatsion and Judd, eds., *op. cit.* (below), 2006b.
Farmer, J. D., and J. Geanakoplos, "The Virtues and Vices of Equilibrium and the Future of Financial Economics," *Complexity*, 14, 8, 11–38, 2008.
Farmer, J. D., "Economics Needs to Treat the Economy as a Complex System," Mss., 2012.
Fontana, M., "Can Neoclassical Economics Handle Complexity? The Fallacy of the Oil Spot Dynamic," *J. Economic Behavior & Organization*, 76, 584–596, 2010.
Fontana, M. "The Santa Fe Perspective on Economics," *Hist. Econ. Ideas*, 18, 2, 167–196, 2010.
Galla, T., and J. D. Farmer, "Complex Dynamics in Learning Complicated Games," Mss., 2012.
Haldane, A. G., "Rethinking the Financial Network," Speech at Financial Student Assoc., Amsterdam. Bank of England, 2009.
Harris, D. J., "Joan Robinson on 'History versus Equilibrium,'" J. Robinson Centennial Conference, Burlington, VT, 2003.
Hildago, C. A., and R. Hausmann, "The Building Blocks of Economic Complexity," *Proc. Nat. Acad. Sci.*, 106, 26, 10570–10575, 2009.
Holland, J., K. Holyoak, R. Nisbett, and P. Thagard, *Induction*, MIT Press, Cambridge, MA, 1986.
Holt R., J. Rosser, and D. Colander, "The Complexity Era in Economics," Middlebury College, 2010.
Hommes, C. H. "Bounded Rationality and Learning in Complex Markets," in Rosser, J. B., (*op. cit.* below), 2009.
Judd, K., "Computationally Intensive Analyses in Economics," in Tesfatsion and Judd, eds., (*op. cit.* below), 2006.

Keynes, J. M., "The General Theory of Employment," *Quarterly Journal of Economics*, 51, 209–233, 1937.

Kirman, A., *Complex Economics*, Routledge, New York, 2011.

Kirman, A., "The Economic Crisis Is a Crisis for Economic Theory," *CESifo Economic Studies*, 56, 4, 498–535, 2010.

Kopel, M., "Oligopoly Dynamics," in Rosser, J. B., (*op. cit.* below), 2009.

Koppl, R., and W. Luther, "BRACE for a New Interventionist Economics," Fairleigh Dickinson University, 2010.

Krugman, P., "How Did Economists Get It So Wrong?" *New York Times*, Sept. 6, 2009.

Lane, D., D. Pumain, S. van der Leeuw, and G. West (eds.), *Complexity Perspectives in Innovation and Social Change*, Springer, Berlin, 2009.

LeBaron, B., W. B. Arthur, and R. Palmer, "Time Series Properties of an Artificial Stock Market, *Journal of Econ. Dynamics and Control*, 23, 1487–1516, 1999.

Lindgren, K., "Evolutionary Phenomena in Simple Dynamics," in C. Langton, C. Taylor, J. D. Farmer, and S. Rasmussen, eds, *Artificial Life II*, Addison-Wesley, Reading, MA, 1991.

Louça, F., "Bounded Heresies: Early Intuitions of Complexity in Economics." *Hist. Econ. Ideas*, 18, 2, 77–113, 2010.

May, R., S. Levin, G. Sugihara, "Complex Systems: Ecology for Bankers," *Nature*, 451, 893–895, 2008.

Miller, J., and S. Page, *Complex Adaptive Systems: An Introduction to Computational Models of Social Life*, Princeton University Press, Princeton, NJ, 2007.

Mirowski, P., *Machine Dreams: Economics Becomes a Cyborg Science*, Cambridge University Press, Cambridge, UK, 2002.

Newman, M., A-L. Barabasi, and D. Watts (eds.). *The Structure and Dynamics of Networks*, Princeton University Press, Princeton, NJ, 2006.

North, D., *Structure and Change in Economic Theory*, Norton, New York, 1981.

Palmer, R. G., W. B. Arthur, J. Holland, B. LeBaron, P. Tayler, "Artificial Economic Life: A Simple Model of a Stock Market," *Physica D*, 75, 264–274, 1994.

Perez, C., *Technological Revolutions and Financial Capital*, E. Elgar, Cheltenham, UK, 2002.

Reisman, D., *Schumpeter's Market: Enterprise and Evolution*, E. Elgar, Cheltenham, UK, 2004.

Robinson, J., "Time in Economic Theory," *Kyklos*, 33, 2, 219–229, 1980.

Robinson, J., "What Has Become of the Keynesian Revolution?" in J. Robinson, ed. *After Keynes*, Basil Blackwell, Oxford, 1973.

Robertson, D. S. *Phase Change: The Computer Revolution in Science and Mathematics*, Oxford, New York, 2003.

Rosser, J. B., "On the Complexities of Complex Economic Dynamics," *J. Econ. Perspectives*, 13, 4, 1999.

Rosser, J. B., ed. *Handbook of Research on Complexity*, E. Elgar, Cheltenham, UK, 2009.

Samuelson, P. A., *Foundations of Economic Analysis*, Harvard University Press, Cambridge, MA, 1983 (originally 1947).

Sargent T. J., *Bounded Rationality in Macroeconomics*, Clarendon Press, Oxford, UK, 1993.

Scheffer, M., S. Carpenter, T. Lenton, J. Bascompte, W. Brock, V. Dakos, J. van de Koppel, I. van de Leemput, S. Levin, E. van Nes, M. Pascual, and J. Vandermeer, "Anticipating Critical Transitions," *Science*, 338, 19 Oct. 2012.

Schumpeter, J. A., *Das Wesen und der Hauptinhalt der theoretischen Nationalökonomie*. Dunker & Humbolt, Leipzig, 1908.

Schumpeter, J. A., *The Theory of Economic Development* (1912), Oxford University Press, London, 1961.
Schumpeter, J. A., *History of Economic Analysis*, Allen and Unwin, London, 1954.
Shackle, G. L. S., *Uncertainty in Economics*, Cambridge University Press, Cambridge, UK, 1955.
Shackle, G. L. S., *Epistemics and Economics*, Transaction Publishers, Piscataway, NJ, 1992.
Simpson, D., *Rethinking Economic Behaviour*, St. Martin's Press, New York, 2002.
Smolin, L., "Time and Symmetry in Models of Economic Markets," Mss., Feb 2009.
Smolin, L., *Time Reborn*. Houghton, Mifflin, Harcourt, New York, 2013.
Solow, R., "Technical Change and the Aggregate Production Function," *Rev. Economics and Statistics*, 39, 312–320, 1957.
Soros, G., *The Alchemy of Finance*, Simon & Schuster, New York, 1987.
Tabb, W., *Reconstructing Political Economy*, Routledge, New York, 1999.
Tesfatsion, L., and K. L. Judd, eds., *Handbook of Computational Economics: Vol. 2. Agent-Based Computational Economics*, North-Holland Elsevier, New York, 2006.
Tesfatsion, L., "Agent-Based Computational Economics: A Constructive Approach to Economic Theory," in Tesfatsion and Judd, *op. cit.*, 2006.
Turing, A. M., "On Computable Numbers, with an Application to the Entscheidungsproblem," *Proc. London Math. Society*, Series 2, 42, 1936.
Waldrop, M., *Complexity*, Simon & Schuster, New York, 1992.
Watts, D., "A Simple Model of Global Cascades on Random Networks," *PNAS*, 9, 5766–5771, 2002.
Wolfram, S., *A New Kind of Science*, Wolfram Media, Champaign, IL, 2002.

CHAPTER 2
Inductive Reasoning and Bounded Rationality
The El Farol Problem

W. BRIAN ARTHUR*

In 1993 I was experimenting with ways to model inductive choice behavior in the economy and came upon a seeming paradox. There was a bar in Santa Fe, El Farol on Canyon Road, to which people would go on a Thursday night if they expected few people to be there, but would avoid if they expected it to be crowded. I realized this represented a decision problem where expectations (forecasts) that many would attend would lead to few attending, and expectations that few would attend would lead to many attending: expectations would lead to outcomes that would negate these expectations. In particular, rational expectations (by definition forecasts that are on average correct or valid) would lead to their own incorrectness—a logical self-contradiction not unlike the Liar's Paradox.

The paper was taken up by physicists and became well known in complexity circles; later it was generalized and put into game form by Zhang and Challet as the Minority Game. In its original and minority game versions it has spawned very many "solutions," variants, and further papers. The paper appeared in the *American Economic Review Papers & Proceedings*, 84, 406–411, 1994.

* Santa Fe Institute, 1660 Old Pecos Trail, Santa Fe, NM 87501, and Stanford University. I thank particularly John Holland, whose work inspired many of the ideas here. I also thank Kenneth Arrow, David Lane, David Rumelhart, Roger Shepard, Glen Swindle, Nick Vriend, and colleagues at Santa Fe and Stanford for discussions. A lengthier version is given in Arthur (1992). For parallel work on bounded rationality and induction, but applied to macroeconomics, see Thomas J. Sargent (1994).

The type of rationality assumed in economics—perfect, logical, deductive rationality—is extremely useful in generating solutions to theoretical problems. But it demands much of human behavior, much more in fact than it can usually deliver. If one were to imagine the vast collection of decision problems economic agents might conceivably deal with as a sea or an ocean, with the easier problems on top and more complicated ones at increasing depth, then deductive rationality would describe human behavior accurately only within a few feet of the surface. For example, the game tic-tac-toe is simple, and one can readily find a perfectly rational, minimax solution to it; but rational "solutions" are not found at the depth of checkers; and certainly not at the still modest depths of chess and Go.

There are two reasons for perfect or deductive rationality to break down under complication. The obvious one is that beyond a certain level of complexity human logical capacity ceases to cope—human rationality is bounded. The other is that in interactive situations of complication, agents cannot rely upon the other agents they are dealing with to behave under perfect rationality, and so they are forced to guess their behavior. This lands them in a world of subjective beliefs, and subjective beliefs about subjective beliefs. Objective, well-defined, shared assumptions then cease to apply. In turn, rational, deductive reasoning (deriving a conclusion by perfect logical processes from well-defined premises) itself cannot apply. The problem becomes ill-defined.

Economists, of course, are well aware of this. The question is not whether perfect rationality works, but rather what to put in its place. How does one model bounded rationality in economics? Many ideas have been suggested in the small but growing literature on bounded rationality; but there is not yet much convergence among them. In the behavioral sciences this is not the case. Modern psychologists are in reasonable agreement that in situations that are complicated or ill-defined, humans use characteristic and predictable methods of reasoning. These methods are not deductive, but *inductive*.

I. THINKING INDUCTIVELY

How *do* humans reason in situations that are complicated or ill-defined? Modern psychology tells us that as humans we are only moderately good at deductive logic, and we make only moderate use of it. But we *are* superb at seeing or recognizing or matching patterns—behaviors that confer obvious evolutionary benefits. In problems of complication then, we look for patterns; and we simplify the problem by using these to construct temporary internal models or hypotheses or *schemata* to work with.[1] We carry out localized deductions based on our

1. For accounts in the psychological literature, see R. Schank and R. P. Abelson (1977), David Rumelhart (1980), Gordon H. Bower and Ernest R. Hilgard (1981), and John H. Holland et al. (1986). Of course, not all decision problems work this way. Most

current hypotheses and act on them. As feedback from the environment comes in, we may strengthen or weaken our beliefs in our current hypotheses, discarding some when they cease to perform, and replacing them as needed with new ones. In other words, when we cannot fully reason or lack full definition of the problem, we use simple models to fill the gaps in our understanding. Such behavior is inductive.

One can see inductive behavior at work in chess playing. Players typically study the current configuration of the board and recall their opponent's play in past games to discern patterns (Adriann De Groot, 1965). They use these to form hypotheses or internal models about each other's intended strategies, maybe even holding several in their minds at one time: "He's using a Caro-Kann defense." "This looks a bit like the 1936 Botvinnik-Vidmar game." "He is trying to build up his mid-board pawn formation." They make local deductions based on these, analyzing the possible implications of moves several moves deep. And as play unfolds they hold onto hypotheses or mental models that prove plausible or toss them aside if not, generating new ones to put in their place. In other words, they use a sequence of pattern recognition, hypotheses formation, deduction using currently held hypotheses, and replacement of hypotheses as needed.

This type of behavior may not be familiar in economics; but one can recognize its advantages. It enables us to deal with complication: we construct plausible, simpler models that we *can* cope with. It enables us to deal with ill-definedness: where we have insufficient definition, our working models fill the gap. It is not antithetical to "reason," or to science for that matter. In fact, it is the way science itself operates and progresses.

Modeling Induction

If humans indeed reason in this way, how can one model this? In a typical problem that plays out over time, one might set up a collection of agents, probably heterogeneous, and assume they can form mental models, or hypotheses, or subjective beliefs. These beliefs might come in the form of simple mathematical expressions that can be used to describe or predict some variable or action; or of complicated expectational models of the type common in economics; or of statistical hypotheses; or of condition/prediction rules ("If situation Q is observed, predict outcome or action D"). These will normally be subjective, that is, they will differ among the agents. An agent may hold one in mind at a time, or several simultaneously.

mundane actions like walking or driving are subconsciously directed, and for these pattern-cognition maps directly into action. In this case, connectionist models work better.

Each agent will normally keep track of the performance of a private collection of such belief-models. When it comes time to make choices, he acts upon his currently most credible (or possibly most profitable) one. The others he keeps at the back of his mind, so to speak. Alternatively, he may act upon a combination of several. (However, humans tend to hold in mind many hypotheses and act on the most plausible one [Julian Feldman, 1962].) Once actions are taken, the aggregative picture is updated, and agents update the track record of all their hypotheses.

This is a system in which learning takes place. Agents "learn" which of their hypotheses work, and from time to time they may discard poorly performing hypotheses and generate new "ideas" to put in their place. Agents linger with their currently most believable hypothesis or belief model but drop it when it no longer functions well, in favor of a better one. This causes a built-in hysteresis. A belief model is clung to not because it is "correct"—there is no way to know this—but rather because it has worked in the past and must cumulate a record of failure before it is worth discarding. In general, there may be a constant slow turnover of hypotheses acted upon. One could speak of this as a system of *temporarily fulfilled expectations*—beliefs or models or hypotheses that are temporarily fulfilled (though not perfectly), which give way to different beliefs or hypotheses when they cease to be fulfilled.

If the reader finds this system unfamiliar, he or she might think of it as generalizing the standard economic learning framework which typically has agents sharing one expectational model with unknown parameters, acting upon the parameters' currently most plausible values. Here, by contrast, agents differ, and each uses several subjective models instead of a continuum of one commonly held model. This is a richer world, and one might ask whether, in a particular context, it converges to some standard equilibrium of beliefs; or whether it remains open-ended, always leading to new hypotheses, new ideas.

It is also a world that is evolutionary, or more accurately, coevolutionary. Just as species, to survive and reproduce, must prove themselves by competing and being adapted within an environment created by other species, in this world hypotheses, to be accurate and therefore acted upon, must prove themselves by competing and being adapted within an environment created by other agents' hypotheses. The set of ideas or hypotheses that are acted upon at any stage therefore coevolves.[2]

A key question remains. Where do the hypotheses or mental models come from? How are they generated? Behaviorally, this is a deep question in psychology, having to do with cognition, object representation, and pattern

2. A similar statement holds for strategies in evolutionary game theory; but there, instead of a large number of private, subjective expectational models, a small number of strategies compete.

recognition. I will not go into it here. However, there are some simple and practical options for modeling. Sometimes one might endow agents with *focal* models: patterns or hypotheses that are obvious, simple, and easily dealt with mentally. One might generate a "bank" of these and distribute them among the agents. Other times, given a suitable model-space one might allow the genetic algorithm or some similar intelligent search device to generate ever "smarter" models. One might also allow agents the possibility of "picking up" mental models from one another (in the process psychologists call *transfer*). Whatever option is taken, it is important to be clear that the framework described above is independent of the specific hypotheses or beliefs used, just as the consumer-theory framework is independent of the particular products chosen among. Of course, to use the framework in a particular problem, some system of generating beliefs must be adopted.

II. THE BAR PROBLEM

Consider now a problem I will construct to illustrate inductive reasoning and how it might be modeled. N people decide independently each week whether to go to a bar that offers entertainment on a certain night. For concreteness, let us set N at 100. Space is limited, and the evening is enjoyable if things are not too crowded—specifically, if fewer than 60% of the possible 100 are present. There is no sure way to tell the numbers coming in advance; therefore a person or agent *goes* (deems it worth going) if he expects fewer than 60 to show up or *stays home* if he expects more than 60 to go. Choices are unaffected by previous visits; there is no collusion or prior communication among the agents; and the only information available is the numbers who came in past weeks. (The problem was inspired by the bar El Farol in Santa Fe which offers Irish music on Thursday nights; but the reader may recognize it as applying to noontime lunch-room crowding, and to other commons or coordination problems with limits to desired coordination.) Of interest is the dynamics of the numbers attending from week to week.

Notice two interesting features of this problem. First, if there were an obvious model that all agents could use to forecast attendance and base their decisions on, then a deductive solution would be possible. But this is not the case here. Given the numbers attending in the recent past, a large number of expectational models might be reasonable and defensible. Thus, not knowing which model other agents might choose, a reference agent cannot choose his in a well-defined way. There is no deductively rational solution—no "correct" expectational model. From the agents' viewpoint, the problem is ill-defined, and they are propelled into a world of induction. Second, and diabolically, any commonalty of expectations gets broken up: if all believe *few* will go, *all* will go. But this would invalidate that belief. Similarly, if all believe *most* will go, *nobody* will go, invalidating that belief.[3] Expectations will be forced to differ.

At this stage, I invite the reader to pause and ponder how attendance might behave dynamically over time. Will it converge, and if so to what? Will it become chaotic? How might predictions be arrived at?

A. A Dynamic Model

To answer the above questions, I shall construct a model along the lines of the framework sketched above. Assume the 100 agents can individually form several predictors or hypotheses, in the form of functions that map the past *d* weeks' attendance figures into next week's. For example, recent attendance might be:

. . . , 44, 78, 56, 15, 23, 67, 84, 34, 45, 76, 40, 56, 22, 35.

Particular hypotheses or predictors might be: *predict next week's number to be*

- the same as last week's [35]
- a mirror image around 50 of last week's [65]
- a (rounded) average of the last four weeks [49]
- the trend in last 8 weeks, bounded by 0, 100 [29]
- the same as 2 weeks ago (2-period cycle detector) [22]
- the same as 5 weeks ago (5-period cycle detector) [76]
- etc.

Assume that each agent possesses and keeps track of an individualized set of *k* such focal predictors. He decides to go or stay according to the currently most accurate predictor in his set. (I will call this his *active* predictor.) Once decisions are made, each agent learns the new attendance figure and updates the accuracies of his monitored predictors.

Notice that in this bar problem, the set of hypotheses currently most credible and acted upon by the agents (the set of active hypotheses) determines the attendance. But the attendance history determines the set of active hypotheses. To use John Holland's term, one can think of these active hypotheses as forming an *ecology*. Of interest is how this ecology evolves over time.

3. This is reminiscent of Yogi Berra's famous comment on why he no longer went to Ruggeri's, a restaurant in St. Louis: "Nobody goes there anymore. It's too crowded."

For most sets of hypotheses, analytically this appears to be a difficult question. So in what follows I will proceed by computer experiments. In the experiments, to generate hypotheses, I first create an "alphabet soup" of predictors, in the form of several dozen focal predictors replicated many times. I then randomly ladle out k (6 or 12 or 23, say) of these to each of 100 agents. Each agent then possesses k predictors or hypotheses or "ideas" he can draw upon. We need not worry that useless predictors will muddy behavior. If predictors do not "work" they will not be used; if they do work they will come to the fore. Given starting conditions and the fixed set of predictors available to each agent, in this problem the future accuracies of all predictors are predetermined. The dynamics here are deterministic.

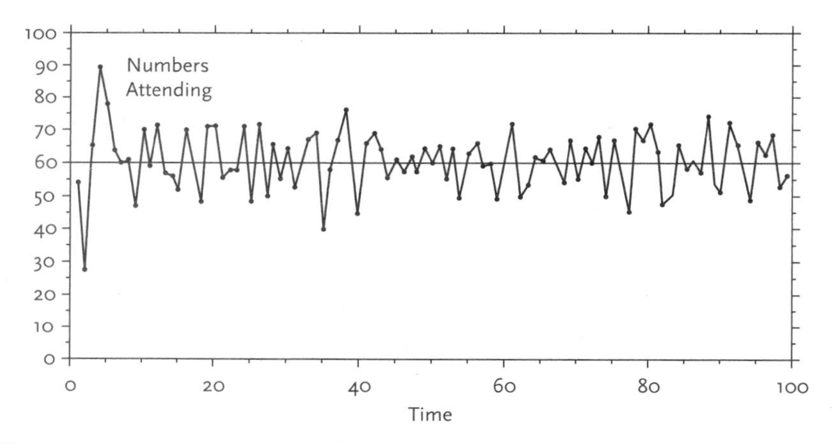

Figure 1:
Bar attendance in the first 100 weeks.

The results of the experiments are interesting (Figure 1). Where cycle-detector predictors are present, cycles are quickly "arbitraged" away so there are no persistent cycles. (If several people expect many to go because many went three weeks ago, they will stay home.) More interestingly, mean attendance converges always to 60. In fact the predictors self-organize into an equilibrium pattern or "ecology" in which, of the active predictors (those most accurate and therefore acted upon), on average 40% are forecasting above 60, 60% below 60.

This emergent ecology is almost organic in nature. For, while the population of active predictors splits into this 60/40 average ratio, it keeps changing in membership forever. This is something like a forest whose contours do not change, but whose individual trees do. These results appear throughout the experiments and are robust to changes in types of predictors created and in numbers assigned.

How do the predictors self-organize so that 60 emerges as average attendance and forecasts split into a 60/40 ratio? One explanation might be that 60 is a natural "attractor" in this bar problem; in fact, if one views it as a pure game of predicting, a mixed strategy of forecasting above 60 with probability 0.4 and below it with probability 0.6 is a Nash equilibrium. Still, this does not explain how the agents approximate any such outcome, given their realistic, subjective reasoning. To get some understanding of how this happens, suppose that 70% of their predictors forecasted above 60 for a longish time. Then on average only 30 people would show up; but this would validate predictors that forecasted close to 30 and invalidate the above-60 predictors, restoring the "ecological" balance among predictions, so to speak. Eventually the 40–60-percent combination would assert itself. (Making this argument mathematically exact appears to be nontrivial.) It is important to be clear that one does not need any 40–60 forecasting balance in the predictors that are set up. Many could have a tendency to predict high, but aggregate behavior calls the equilibrium predicting ratio to the fore. Of course, the result would fail if all predictors could only predict below 60; then all 100 agents would always show up. Predictors need to "cover" the available prediction space to some modest degree. The reader might ponder what would happen if all agents shared the same set of predictors.

It might be objected that I lumbered the agents in these experiments with fixed sets of clunky predictive models. If they could form more open-ended, intelligent predictions, different behavior might emerge. One could certainly test this using a more sophisticated procedure, say, genetic programming (John Koza, 1992). This continually generates new hypotheses, new predictive expressions, that adapt "intelligently" and often become more complicated as time progresses. However, I would be surprised if this changes the above results in any qualitative way.

The bar problem introduced here can be generalized in a number of ways (see E. R. Grannan and G. H. Swindle, 1994). I encourage the reader to experiment.

III. CONCLUSION

The inductive-reasoning system I have described above consists of a multitude of "elements" in the form of belief-models or hypotheses that adapt to the aggregate environment they jointly create. Thus it qualifies as an *adaptive complex* system. After some initial learning time, the hypotheses or mental models in use are mutually coadapted. Thus one can think of a *consistent* set of mental models as a set of hypotheses that work well with each other under some criterion—that have a high degree of mutual adaptedness. Sometimes there is a unique such set, it corresponds to a standard rational expectations equilibrium, and beliefs gravitate into it. More often there is a high, possibly very high, multiplicity of such sets. In this case one might expect inductive-reasoning systems in the economy—whether in stock-market speculating, in negotiating, in poker games, in oligopoly pricing, or in positioning products in the market—to cycle through or temporarily lock into psychological patterns that may be nonrecurrent, path-dependent, and increasingly complicated. The possibilities are rich.

Economists have long been uneasy with the assumption of perfect, deductive rationality in decision contexts that are complicated and potentially ill-defined. The level at which humans can apply perfect rationality is surprisingly modest. Yet it has not been clear how to deal with imperfect or bounded rationality. From the reasoning given above, I believe that as humans in these contexts we use *inductive* reasoning: we induce a variety of working hypotheses, act upon the most credible, and replace hypotheses with new ones if they cease to work. Such reasoning can be modeled in a variety of ways. Usually this leads to a rich psychological world in which agents' ideas or mental models compete for survival against other agents' ideas or mental models—a world that is both evolutionary and complex.

REFERENCES

Arthur, W. Brian. "On Learning and Adaptation in the Economy." Santa Fe Institute (Santa Fe, NM) Paper 92-07-038, 1992.

Bower, Gordon H., and Hilgard, Ernest R. *Theories of learning*. Englewood Cliffs, NJ: Prentice-Hall, 1981.

De Groot, Adriann. *Thought and choice in chess*, Psychological Studies, No. 4. Paris: Mouton, 1965.

Feldman, Julian. "Computer Simulation of Cognitive Processes," in Harold Borko, ed., *Computer applications in the behavioral sciences*. Englewood Cliffs, NJ: Prentice-Hall, 1962, pp. 336–359.

Grannan, E. R., and Swindle, G. H. "Contrarians and Volatility Clustering." Santa Fe Institute (Santa Fe, NM) Paper 94-03-010, 1994.

Holland, John H., Holyoak, Keith J., Nisbett, Richard E., and Thagard, Paul R. *Induction*. Cambridge, MA: MIT Press, 1986.

Koza, John. *Genetic programming*. Cambridge, MA: MIT Press, 1992.

Rumelhart, David. "Schemata: The Building Blocks of Cognition," in R. Spiro, B. Bruce, and W. Brewer, eds., *Theoretical issues in reading comprehension*. Hillside, NJ: Erlbaum, 1980, pp. 33–58.

Sargent, Thomas J. *Bounded rationality in macroeconomics*. New York: Oxford University Press, 1994.

Schank, R., and Abelson, R. P. *Scripts, plans, goals, and understanding: An inquiry into human knowledge structures*. Hillside, NJ: Erlbaum, 1977.

CHAPTER 3

Asset Pricing under Endogenous Expectations in an Artificial Stock Market

W. BRIAN ARTHUR, JOHN H. HOLLAND, BLAKE LEBARON, RICHARD PALMER, AND PAUL TAYLER*

This paper grew out of our early experiments with agent-based modeling at Santa Fe in the late 1980s. Standard neoclassical stock-market models at the time assumed identical investors who used identical forecasts (expectations) that were on average correct. But while the theory was elegant, its assumptions were not realistic. Further, it ruled out the possibility of bubbles and crashes, technical trading (using past price patterns to forecast profitably), correlated prices and volatility, and trading in significant volume—all phenomena that appeared in real markets. We created a different model that would play out within the computer, where our investors would be "artificial agents" (small computer programs) that would differ, would have to create their own forecasts, and would have to learn which worked and didn't work as they gained market experience.

Experiments with our artificial market showed that under realistic parameters it exhibited a "complex regime," where bubbles and crashes, technical trading, correlated prices and volatility, and realistic trading volume all appeared. Under a narrower—but unrealistic—set of parameters, it exhibited a "neoclassical regime," and upheld the standard theory. The paper appeared in *Economic Notes*, 26, 297–330, 1997, and in the volume *The Economy as an Evolving Complex System II*, edited by David Lane, Steven Durlauf, and myself.[1] Variations of our model, the Santa Fe Artificial Stock Market, have been widely used in economics.

* Arthur is Citibank Professor, Santa Fe Institute; Holland is Professor of Computer Science and Engineering, University of Michigan, and with the Santa Fe Institute; LeBaron is Associate Professor of Economics, University of Wisconsin, Madison; Palmer is Professor of Physics, Duke University, and with the Santa Fe Institute; Tayler is with the Department of Computer Science, Brunel University, London.

1. For an earlier version see Palmer et al., 1994.

Academic theorists and market traders tend to view financial markets in strikingly different ways. Standard (efficient-market) financial theory assumes identical investors who share rational expectations of an asset's future price, and who instantaneously and rationally discount all market information into this price.[2] It follows that no opportunities are left open for consistent speculative profit, that technical trading (using patterns in past prices to forecast future ones) cannot be profitable except by luck, that temporary price overreactions—bubbles and crashes—reflect rational changes in assets' valuations rather than sudden shifts in investor sentiment. It follows too that trading volume is low or zero, and that indices of trading volume and price volatility are not serially correlated in any way. The market, in this standard theoretical view, is rational, mechanistic, and efficient. Traders, by contrast, often see markets as offering speculative opportunities. Many believe that technical trading is profitable,[3] that something definable as a "market psychology" exists, and that herd effects unrelated to market news can cause bubbles and crashes. Some traders and financial writers even see the market itself as possessing its own moods and personality, sometimes describing the market as "nervous" or "sluggish" or "jittery." The market in this view is psychological, organic, and imperfectly efficient. From the academic viewpoint, traders with such beliefs—embarrassingly the very agents assumed rational by the theory—are irrational and superstitious. From the traders' viewpoint, the standard academic theory is unrealistic and not borne out by their own perceptions.[4]

While few academics would be willing to assert that the market has a personality or experiences moods, the standard economic view has in recent years begun to change. The crash of 1987 damaged economists' beliefs that sudden price changes reflect rational adjustments to news in the market: several studies failed to find significant correlation between the crash and market information issued at the time (e.g., Cutler et al., 1989). Trading volume and price volatility in real markets are large—not zero or small, respectively, as the standard theory would predict (see Leroy and Porter, 1981; Shiller, 1981, 1989)—and both show significant autocorrelation (see Bollerslev et al., 1990; Goodhart et al., 1995). Stock returns also contain small, but significant serial correlations (see Fama and French, 1988; Lo and MacKinlay, 1988; Poterba

2. For the classic statement see Lucas (1978) or Diba and Grossman (1988).

3. For evidence see Frankel and Froot (1990).

4. To quote one of the most successful traders, George Soros (1994): "this [efficient market theory] interpretation of the way financial markets operate is severely distorted.... It may seem strange that a patently false theory should gain such widespread acceptance."

and Summers, 1988; Summers, 1986). Certain technical-trading rules produce statistically significant, if modest, long-run profits (see Brock et al., 1991). And it has long been known that when investors apply full rationality to the market, they lack incentives both to trade and to gather information (see Grossman, 1976; Grossman and Stiglitz, 1980; Milgrom and Stokey, 1982). By now, enough statistical evidence has accumulated to question efficient-market theories and to show that the traders' viewpoint cannot be entirely dismissed. As a result, the modern finance literature has been searching for alternative theories that can explain these market realities.

One promising modern alternative, the noise-trader approach, observes that when there are "noise traders" in the market—investors who possess expectations different from those of the rational-expectations traders—technical-trading strategies such as trend chasing may become rational. For example, if noise traders believe that an upswing in a stock's price will persist, rational traders can exploit this by buying into the uptrend, thereby exacerbating the trend. In this way positive-feedback trading strategies—and other technical trading strategies—can be seen as rational, as long as there are nonrational traders in the market to prime these strategies (see De Long et al., 1990a, 1990b, 1991; Shleifer and Summers, 1990). This "behavioral" noise-trader literature moves some way toward justifying the traders' view. But it is built on two less-than-realistic assumptions: the existence of unintelligent noise traders who do not learn over time that their forecasts are erroneous; and the existence of rational players who possess, by some unspecified means, full knowledge of both the noise traders' expectations and their own class's. Neither assumption is likely to hold up in real markets. Suppose for a moment an actual market with minimally intelligent noise traders. Over time, in all likelihood, some would discover their errors and begin to formulate more intelligent (or at least different) expectations. This would change the market, which means that the perfectly intelligent players would need to readjust *their* expectations. But there is no reason these latter would know the new expectations of the noise-trader deviants; they would have to derive their expectations by some means such as guessing or observation of the market. As the rational players changed, the market would change again. And so the noise traders might again further deviate, forcing further readjustments for the rational traders. Actual noise-trader markets, assumed stationary in theory, would start to unravel; and the perfectly rational traders would be left at each turn guessing the changed expectations by observing the market.

Thus, noise-trader theories, while they explain much, are not robust. But in questioning such theories we are led to an interesting sequence of thought. Suppose we were to assume "rational," but nonidentical, agents who do not find themselves in a market with rational expectations, or with publicly known expectations. Suppose we allowed each agent continually to observe the market with an eye to discovering profitable expectations. Suppose further we allowed each agent to adopt these when discovered and to discard the less profitable as time progressed. In this situation, agents' expectations would become endogenous—individually adapted to the current state of the market—and they would cocreate the market they were designed to exploit. How would such a market work? How would it act to price assets? Would it converge to a rational-expectations equilibrium—or would it uphold the traders' viewpoint?

In this paper we propose a theory of asset pricing that assumes fully heterogeneous agents whose expectations continually adapt to the market these expectations aggregatively create. We argue that under heterogeneity, expectations have a recursive character: agents have to form their expectations from their anticipations of other agents' expectations, and this self-reference precludes expectations being formed by deductive means. So, in the absence of being able to deduce expectations, agents—no matter how rational—are forced to hypothesize them. Agents, therefore, continually form individual, hypothetical, expectational models or "theories of the market," test these, and trade on the ones that predict best. From time to time they drop hypotheses that perform badly, and introduce new ones to test. Prices are driven endogenously by these induced expectations. Individuals' expectations, therefore, evolve and "compete" in a market formed by others' expectations. In other words, agents' expectations coevolve in a world they co-create.

The natural question is whether these heterogeneous expectations coevolve into homogeneous rational-expectations beliefs, upholding the efficient-market theory, or whether richer individual and collective behavior emerges, upholding the traders' viewpoint and explaining the empirical market phenomena mentioned above. We answer this not analytically—our model, with its fully heterogeneous expectations, is too complicated to allow analytical solutions—but computationally. To investigate price dynamics, investment strategies, and market statistics in our endogenous-expectations market, we perform carefully controlled experiments within a computer-based market we have constructed, the SFI Artificial Stock Market.[5]

The picture of the market that results from our experiments, surprisingly, confirms both the efficient-market academic view and the traders' view. But each is valid under different circumstances—in different regimes. In both circumstances, we initiate our traders with heterogeneous beliefs clustered randomly in an interval near homogeneous rational expectations. We find that if our agents very slowly adapt their forecasts to new observations of the market's behavior, the market converges to a rational-expectations regime. Here "mutant" expectations cannot get a profitable footing; and technical trading,

5. For an earlier report on the SFI artificial stock market, see Palmer et al. (1994).

bubbles, crashes, and autocorrelative behavior do not emerge. Trading volume remains low. The efficient-market theory prevails.

If, on the other hand, we allow the traders to adapt to new market observations at a more realistic rate, heterogeneous beliefs persist, and the market self-organizes into a complex regime. A rich "market psychology"—a rich set of expectations—becomes observable. Technical trading emerges as a profitable activity, and temporary bubbles and crashes occur from time to time. Trading volume is high, with times of quiescence alternating with times of intense market activity. The price time series shows persistence in volatility, the characteristic GARCH signature of price series from actual financial markets. And it shows persistence in trading volume. And over the period of our experiments, at least, individual behavior evolves continually and does not settle down. In this regime, the traders' view is upheld.

In what follows, we discuss first the rationale for our endogenous-expectations approach to market behavior; and introduce the idea of collections of conditional expectational hypotheses or "predictors" to implement this. We next set up the computational model that will form the basic framework. We are then in a position to carry out and describe the computer experiments with the model. Two final sections discuss the results of the experiments, compare our findings with other modern approaches in the literature, and summarize our conclusions.

2. WHY INDUCTIVE REASONING?

Before proceeding, we show that once we introduce heterogeneity of agents, deductive reasoning on the part of agents fails. We argue that in the absence of deductive reasoning, agents must resort to *inductive* reasoning, which is both natural and realistic in financial markets.

Forming Expectations by Deductive Reasoning: An Indeterminacy

We make our point about the indeterminacy of deductive logic on the part of agents using a simple arbitrage pricing model, avoiding technical details that will be spelled out later. (This pricing model is a special case of our model in Section 3, assuming risk coefficient λ arbitrarily close to 0, and gaussian expectational distributions). Consider a market with a single security that provides a stochastic payoff or dividend sequence $\{d_t\}$, with a risk-free outside asset that pays a constant r units per period. Each agent i may form individual expectations of next period's dividend and price, $E_i\,[d_{t+1} \mid I_t]$ and $E_i\,[p_{t+1} \mid I_t]$, with conditional variance of these combined expectations, $\sigma^2_{i,t}$, given current market information I_t. Assuming perfect arbitrage, the market for the asset clears at the equilibrium price:

$$p_t = \beta \sum_j w_{j,t} \left(E_j[d_{t+1} \mid I_t] + E_j[p_{t+1} \mid I_t]\right) \tag{1}$$

In other words, the security's price p_t is bid to a value that reflects the current (weighted) average of individuals' market expectations, discounted by the factor $\beta = 1 / (1 + r)$, with weights $w_{j,t} = (1/\sigma^2_{j,t}) / \sum_k 1/\sigma^2_{k,t}$ the relative "confidence" placed in agent j's forecast.

Now, assuming intelligent investors, the key question is how the individual dividend and price expectations $E_i[d_{t+1} \mid I_t]$ and $E_i[p_{t+1} \mid I_t]$, respectively, might be formed. The standard argument that such expectations can be formed rationally (i.e., using deductive logic) goes as follows. Assume *homogeneous* investors who (i) use the available information I_t identically in forming their dividend expectations, and (ii) know that others use the same expectations. Assume further that the agents (iii) are perfectly rational (can make arbitrarily difficult logical inferences), (iv) know that price each time will be formed by arbitrage as in Eq. (1), and (v) that (iii) and (iv) are common knowledge. Then, expectations of future dividends $E_i[d_{t+k} \mid I_t]$ are by definition known, shared, and identical. And homogeneity allows us to drop the agent subscript and set the weights to $1/N$. It is then a standard exercise (see Diba and Grossman, 1988) to show that by setting up the arbitrage, Eq. (1), for future times $t + k$, taking expectations across it, and substituting backward repeatedly for $E[p_{t+k} \mid I_t]$, agents can iteratively solve for the current price as[6]

$$p_t = \sum_{k=1}^{\infty} \beta^k E[d_{t+k} \mid I_t] \tag{2}$$

If the dividend expectations are unbiased, dividend forecasts will be upheld on average by the market and, therefore, the price sequence will be in rational-expectations equilibrium. Thus, the price fluctuates as the information $\{I_t\}$ fluctuates over time, and it reflects "correct" or "fundamental" value, so that speculative profits are not consistently available. Of course, rational-expectations models in the literature are typically more elaborate than this. But the point so far is that if we are willing to adopt the above assumptions—which depend heavily on homogeneity—asset pricing becomes deductively determinate, in the sense that agents can, in principle at least, logically derive the current price.

Assume now, more realistically, that traders are intelligent but heterogeneous—each may differ from the others. Now, the available shared information

6. The second, constant-exponential-growth solution is normally ruled out by an appropriate transversality condition.

I_t consists of past prices, past dividends, trading volumes, economic indicators, rumors, news, and the like. These are merely qualitative information plus data sequences, and *there may be many different, perfectly defensible statistical ways,* based on different assumptions and different error criteria, to use them to predict future dividends (see Arthur, 1992, 1995; Kurz, 1994, 1995). Thus, there is no objectively laid down, expectational model that differing agents can coordinate upon, and so there is no objective means for one agent to know other agents' expectations of future dividends. This is sufficient to bring indeterminacy to the asset price in Eq. (1). But worse, the heterogeneous price expectations $E_i\,[p_{t+1} \mid I_t]$ are also indeterminate. For suppose agent *i* attempts rationally to deduce this expectation, he may take expectations across the market clearing Eq. (1) for time $t + 1$:

$$E_i[p_{t+1} \mid I_t] = \beta E_i\left[\sum_j \{w_{j,t+1}(E_j[d_{t+2} \mid I_t] + E_j[p_{t+2} \mid I_t])\} \mid I_t\right] \tag{3}$$

This requires that agent *i*, in forming his expectation of price, take into account his expectations of *others'* expectations of dividends and price (and relative market weights) two periods hence. To eliminate, in like manner, the price expectation $E_j\,[p_{t+2} \mid I_t]$ requires a further iteration. But this leads agents into taking into account their expectations of others' expectations of others' expectations of future dividends and prices at period $t + 3$—literally, as in Keynes' (1936) phrase, taking into account "what average opinion expects the average opinion to be."

Now, under homogeneity these expectations of others' expectations collapsed into single, shared, objectively determined expectations. Under heterogeneity, however, not only is there no objective means by which others' dividend expectations can be known, but attempts to eliminate the other unknowns, the price expectations, merely lead to the repeated iteration of subjective expectations of subjective expectations (or, equivalently, subjective priors on others' subjective priors)—an infinite regress in subjectivity. Further, this regress may lead to instability. If investor *i* believes that others believe future prices will increase, he may revise his expectations to expect upward-moving prices. If he believes that others believe a reversion to lower values is likely, he may revise his expectations to expect a reversion. We can, therefore, easily imagine swings and swift transitions in investors' beliefs, based on little more than ephemera—hints and perceived hints of others' beliefs about others' beliefs.

Under heterogeneity then, deductive logic leads to expectations that are not determinable. Notice the argument here depends in no way on agents having limits to their reasoning powers. It merely says that given differences in agent expectations, there is no logical means by which to arrive at expectations. And so, perfect rationality in the market cannot be well defined. Infinitely intelligent agents cannot form expectations in a determinate way.

Forming Expectations by Inductive Reasoning

If heterogeneous agents cannot deduce their expectations, how then do they form expectations? They may observe market data, they may contemplate the nature of the market and of their fellow investors. They may derive expectational models by sophisticated, subjective reasoning. But in the end all such models will be—can only be—hypotheses. There is no objective way to verify them, except by observing their performance in practice. Thus, agents, in facing the problem of choosing appropriate predictive models, face the same problem that statisticians face when choosing appropriate predictive models given a specific data set, but no objective means by which to choose a functional form. (Of course, the situation here is made more difficult by the fact that the expectational models investors choose affect the price sequence, so that our statisticians' very choices of model affect their data and so their choices of model).

In what follows then, we assume that each agent acts as a "market statistician."[7] Each continually creates multiple "market hypotheses"—subjective, expectational models—of what moves the market price and dividend. And each simultaneously tests several such models. Some of these will perform well in predicting market movements. These will gain the agent's confidence and be retained and acted upon in buying and selling decisions. Others will perform badly. They will be dropped. Still others will be generated from time to time and tested for accuracy in the market. As it becomes clear which expectational models predict well, and as poorly predicting ones are replaced by better ones, the agent learns and adapts. This type of behavior—coming up with appropriate hypothetical models to act upon, strengthening confidence in those that are validated, and discarding those that are not—is called *inductive* reasoning.[8] It makes excellent sense where problems are ill defined. It is, in microscale, the scientific method. Agents who act by using inductive reasoning we will call inductively rational.[9]

7. The phrase is Tom Sargent's (1993). Sargent argues similarly, within a macroeconomic context, that to form expectations agents need to act as market statisticians.

8. For earlier versions of induction applied to asset pricing and to decision problems, see Arthur (1992, 1994, 1995) (e.g., the *El Farol* problem), and Sargent (1993). For accounts of inductive reasoning in the psychological and adaptation literature, see Holland et al., 1986), Rumelhart (1977) and Schank and Abelson (1977).

9. In the sense that they use available market data to learn—and switch among—appropriate expectational models. Perfect inductive rationality, of course, is indeterminate. Learning agents can be arbitrarily intelligent, but without knowing others' learning methods cannot tell a priori that *their* learning methods are maximally efficient. They can only discover the efficacy of their methods by testing them against data.

Each inductively rational agent generates multiple expectational models that "compete" for use within his or her mind, and survive or are changed on the basis of their predictive ability. The agents' hypotheses and expectations adapt to the current pattern of prices and dividends; and the pattern of prices changes to reflect the current hypotheses and expectations of the agents. We see immediately that the market possesses a *psychology*. We define this as the collection of market hypotheses, or expectational models or mental beliefs, that are being acted upon at a given time.

If there were some attractor inherent in the price-and-expectation-formation process, this market psychology might converge to a stable unchanging set of heterogeneous (or homogeneous) beliefs. Such a set would be statistically validated, and would, therefore, constitute a rational expectations equilibrium. We investigate whether the market converges to such an equilibrium below.

3. A MARKET WITH INDUCED EXPECTATIONS

The Model

We now set up a simple model of an asset market along the lines of Bray (1982) or Grossman and Stiglitz (1980). The model will be neoclassical in structure, but will depart from standard models by assuming heterogeneous agents who form their expectations inductively by the process outlined above.

Consider a market in which N heterogeneous agents decide on their desired asset composition between a risky stock paying a stochastic dividend, and a risk-free bond. These agents formulate their expectations separately, but are identical in other respects. They possess a constant absolute risk aversion (CARA) utility function, $U(c) = -\exp(-\lambda c)$. They communicate neither their expectations nor their buying or selling intentions to each other. Time is discrete and is indexed by t; the horizon is indefinite. The risk-free bond is in infinite supply and pays a constant interest rate r. The stock is issued in N units, and pays a dividend, d_t, which follows a given exogenous stochastic process $\{d_t\}$ not known to the agents.

The dividend process, thus far, is arbitrary. In the experiments we carry out below, we specialize it to an AR (1) process

$$d_t = \bar{d} + \rho(d_{t-1} - \bar{d}) + e_t \tag{4}$$

where e_t is gaussian, i.i.d., and has zero mean, and variance σ_e^2.

Each agent attempts, at each period, to optimize his allocation between the risk-free asset and the stock. Assume for the moment that agent i's predictions at time t of the next period's price and dividend are normally distributed with (conditional) mean and variance, $E_{i,t}[p_{t+1} + d_{t+1}]$, and $\sigma^2_{t,i,p+d}$. (We say presently how such expectations are arrived at.) It is well known that under CARA utility and gaussian distributions for forecasts, agent *i*'s demand, $x_{i,t}$, for holding shares of the risky asset is given by:

$$x_{i,t} = \frac{E_{i,t}(p_{t+1} + d_{t+1} - p(1+r))}{\lambda \sigma^2_{i,t,p+d}} \tag{5}$$

where p_t is the price of the risky asset at *t*, and λ is the degree of relative risk aversion.

Total demand must equal the number of shares issued:

$$\sum_{i=1}^{N} x_{i,t} = N \tag{6}$$

which closes the model and determines the clearing price *p*—the current market price—in Eq. (5) above.

It is useful to be clear on timing in the market. At the start of time period *t*, the current dividend d_t is posted, and observed by all agents. Agents then use this information and general information on the state of the market (which includes the historical dividend sequence $\{\ldots d_{t-2}, d_{t-1}, d_t\}$ and price sequence $\{\ldots p_{t-2}, p_{t-1}\}$) to form their expectations of the next period's price and dividend $E_{i,t}(p_{t+1} + d_{t+1})$. They then calculate their desired holdings and pass their demand parameters to the specialist who declares a price p_t that clears the market. At the start of the next period the new dividend d_{t+1} is revealed, and the accuracies of the predictors active at time *t* are updated. The sequence repeats.

Modeling the Formation of Expectations

At this point we have a simple, neoclassical, two-asset market. We now break from tradition by allowing our agents to form their expectations individually and inductively. One obvious way to do this would be to posit a set of individual-agent expectational models which share the same functional form, and whose parameters are updated differently by each agent (by least squares, say) over time, starting from different priors. We reject this in favor of a different approach that better reflects the process of induction outlined in Section 2 above. We assume each agent, at any time, possesses a multiplicity of linear forecasting models—hypotheses about the direction of the market, or "theories of the market"—and uses those that are both best suited to the current state of the market and have recently proved most reliable. Agents then learn, not by updating parameters, but by discovering which of their hypotheses "prove out" best, and by developing new ones from time to time, via the genetic algorithm. This structure will offer several desirable properties: It will avoid biases introduced by a fixed, shared functional form. It will allow the individuality of expectations to emerge over time (rather than be built in only to a priori beliefs). And it will better mirror actual cognitive reasoning, in which different agents might well "cognize" different patterns and arrive at different forecasts from the same market data.

In the expectational part of the model, at each period, the time series of current and past prices and dividends are summarized by an array or information set of J market descriptors. And agents' subjective expectational models are represented by sets of *predictors*. Each predictor is a *condition/forecast* rule (similar to a Holland classifier which is a condition/action rule) that contains both a market condition that may at times be fulfilled by the current state of the market and a forecasting formula for next period's price and dividend. Each agent possesses M such individual predictors—holds M hypotheses of the market in mind simultaneously—and uses the most accurate of those that are *active* (matched by the current state of the market). In this way, each agent has the ability to "recognize" different sets of states of the market, and bring to bear appropriate forecasts, given these market patterns.

It may clarify matters to show briefly how we implement this expectational system on the computer. (Further details are in Appendix A.) Suppose we summarize the state of the market by $J = 13$ bits. The fifth bit might correspond to "the price has risen the last 3 periods," and the tenth bit to "the price is larger than 16 times dividend divided by r," with 1 signaling the occurrence of the described state, and 0 its absence or nonoccurrence. Now, the condition part of all predictors corresponds to these market descriptors, and thus, also consists of a 13-bit array, each position of which is filled with a 0, or 1, or # ("don't care"). A condition array matches or "recognizes" the current market state if all its 0's and l's match the corresponding bits for the market state with the #'s matching either a 1 or a 0. Thus, the condition (####1########) "recognizes" market states in which the price has risen in the last 3 periods. The condition (#########0###) recognizes states where the current price is not larger than 16 times dividend divided by r. The forecasting part of each predictor is an array of parameters that triggers a corresponding forecasting expression. In our experiments, all forecasts use a linear combination of price and dividend, $E(p_{t+1} + d_{t+1}) = a\,(p_t + d_t) + b$. Each predictor then stores specific values of a and b. Therefore, the full predictor (####1 ####0###) / (0.96, 0) can be interpreted as "*if* the price has risen in the last 3 periods, and if the price is not larger than 16 times dividend divided by r, *then* forecast next period's price plus dividend as 96% of this period's." This predictor would recognize—would be activated by—the market state (0110100100011) but would not respond to the state (0110111011001).

Predictors that can recognize many states of the market have few 1's and 0's. Those more particularized have more 1's and 0's. In practice, we include for each agent a default predictor consisting of all #'s. The genetic algorithm creates new predictors by "mutating" the values in the predictor array, or by "recombination"—combining part of one predictor array with the complementary part of another.

The expectational system then works at each time with each agent observing the current state of the market, and noticing which of his predictors match this state. He forecasts next period's price and dividend by combining statistically the linear forecast of the H most accurate of these active predictors, and given this expectation and its variance, uses Eq. (5) to calculate desired stock holdings and to generate an appropriate bid or offer. Once the market clears, the next period's price and dividend are revealed and the accuracies of the active predictors are updated.

As noted above, learning in this expectational system takes place in two ways. It happens rapidly as agents learn which of their predictors are accurate and worth acting upon, and which should be ignored. And it happens on a slower time scale as the genetic algorithm from time to time discards nonperforming predictors and creates new ones. Of course these new, untested predictors do not create disruptions—they will be acted upon only if they prove accurate. This avoids brittleness and provides what machine-learning theorists call "gracefulness" in the learning process.

We can now discern several advantages of this multibit, multipredictor architecture. One is that this expectational architecture allows the market to have potentially different dynamics—a different character—under different states or circumstances. Because predictors are pattern-recognizing expectational models, and so can "recognize" these different states, agents can "remember" what happened before in given states and activate appropriate forecasts. This enables agents to make swift *gestalt*-like transitions in forecasting behavior should the market change.

Second, the design avoids bias from the choice of a particular functional form for expectations. Although the forecasting part of our predictors is linear, the multiplicity of predictors conditioned upon the many combinations of market conditions yield collectively at any time and for any agent a nonlinear forecasting expression in the form of a piecewise linear, noncontinuous forecasting function whose domain is the market state space, and whose accuracy is tuned to different regions of this space. (Forecasting is, of course, limited by the choice of the binary descriptors that represent market conditions.)

Third, learning is concentrated where it is needed. For example, $J = 12$ descriptors produces predictors that can distinguish more than four thousand different states of the market. Yet, only a handful of these states might occur often. Predictor conditions that recognize states that do not occur often will be used less often, their accuracy will be updated less often and, other things being equal, their precision will be lower. They are, therefore, less likely to survive in the competition among predictors. Predictors will, therefore, cluster in the more visited parts of the market state space, which is exactly what we want.

Finally, the descriptor bits can be organized into classes or information sets which summarize fundamentals, such as price-dividend ratios or technical-trading indicators, such as price trend movements. The design allows us to track exactly which information—which descriptor bits—the agents are using or ignoring, something of crucial importance if we want to test for the "emergence" of technical trading. This organization of the information also allows the possibility of setting up different agent "types" who have access to different information sets. (In this chapter, all agents see all market information equally.)

A neural net could also supply several of these desirable qualities. However, it would be less transparent than our predictor system, which we can easily monitor to observe which information agents are individually and collectively using at each time.

4. COMPUTER EXPERIMENTS: THE EMERGENCE OF TWO MARKET REGIMES

Experimental Design

We now explore computationally the behavior of our endogenous-expectations market in a series of experiments. We retain the same model parameters throughout these experiments, so that we can make comparisons of the market outcomes using the model under identical conditions with only controlled changes. Each experiment is run for 250,000 periods to allow asymptotic behavior to emerge if it is present; and it is run 25 times under different random seeds to collect cross-sectional statistics.

We specialize the model described in the previous section by choosing parameter values, and, where necessary, functional forms. We use $N = 25$ agents, who each have $M = 100$ predictors, which are conditioned on $J = 12$ market descriptors. The dividend follows the AR (1) process in Eq. (4), with autoregressive parameter ρ set to 0.95, yielding a process close to a random walk, yet persistent.

The 12 binary descriptors that summarize the state of the market are the following:

1–6 Current price × interest rate/dividend > 0.25, 0.5, 0.75, 0.875, 1.0, 1.125
7–10 Current price > 5-period moving average of past prices (MA), 10-period MA, 100-period MA, 500-period MA
11 Always on (1)
12 Always off (0)

The first six binary descriptors—the first six bits—reflect the current price in relation to current dividend, and thus, indicate whether the stock is above or below fundamental value at the current price. We will call these "fundamental" bits. Bits 7–10 are "technical-trading" bits that indicate whether a trend in the price is under way. They will be ignored if useless, and acted upon if technical-analysis trend following emerges. The final two bits, constrained to be 0 or 1 at all times, serve as experimental controls. They convey no useful market information, but can tell us the degree to which agents act upon useless information at any time. We say a bit is "set" if it is 0 or 1, and predictors are selected randomly for recombination, other things equal, with slightly lower probabilities the higher their specificity—that is, the more set bits they contain (see Appendix A). This introduces a weak drift toward the all-# configuration, and ensures that the information represented by a particular bit is used only if agents find it genuinely useful in prediction. This market information design allows us to speak of "emergence." For example, it can be said that technical trading has emerged if bits 7–10 become set significantly more often, statistically, than the control bits.

We assume that forecasts are formed by each predictor j storing values for the parameters a_j, b_j, in the linear combination of price and dividend, $E_j[p_{t+1} + d_{t+1} \mid I_t] = a_j (p_t + d_t) + b_j$. Each predictor also stores a current estimate of its forecast variance. (See Appendix A).

Before we conduct experiments, we run two diagnostic tests on our computer-based version of the model. In the first, we test to see whether the model can replicate the rational-expectations equilibrium (r.e.e.) of standard theory. We do this by calculating analytically the homogeneous rational-expectations equilibrium (h.r.e.e.) values for the forecasting parameters a and b (see Appendix A), then running the computation with all predictors "clamped" to these calculated h.r.e.e. parameters. We find indeed that such predictions are upheld—that the model indeed reproduces the h.r.e.e.—which assures us that the computerized model, with its expectations, demand functions, aggregation, market clearing, and timing sequence, is working correctly. In the second test, we show the agents a given dividend sequence and a calculated h.r.e.e. price series that corresponds to it, and test whether they individually learn the correct forecasting parameters. They do, though with some variation due to the agents' continual exploration of expectational space, which assures us that our agents are learning properly.

The Experiments

We now run two sets of fundamental experiments with the computerized model, corresponding respectively to slow and medium rates of exploration by agents of alternative expectations. The two sets give rise to two different *regimes*—two different sets of characteristic behaviors of the market. In the slow-learning-rate experiments, the genetic algorithm is invoked every 1,000 periods on average, predictors are crossed over with probability 0.3, and the predictors' accuracy-updating parameter θ is set to 1/150. In the medium-exploration-rate experiments, the genetic algorithm is invoked every 250 periods on average, crossover occurs with probability 0.1, and the predictors' accuracy-updating parameter θ is set to 1/75.[10] Otherwise, we keep the model parameters the same in both sets of experiments, and in both we start the agents with expectational parameters selected randomly from a uniform distribution of values centered on the calculated homogeneous rational-expectations ones. (See Appendix A.) In the slow-exploration-rate experiments, no non-r.e.e. expectations can get a footing: the market enters an evolutionarily stable, rational-expectations regime. In the medium-exploration-rate experiments, we find that the market enters a complex regime in which psychological behavior emerges, there are significant deviations from the r.e.e. benchmark, and statistical "signatures" of real financial markets are observed.

We now describe these two sets of experiments and the two regimes or phases of the market they induce.

The Rational-Expectations Regime

As stated, in this set of experiments, agents continually explore in prediction space, but under low rates. The market price, in these experiments, converges rapidly to the homogeneous rational-expectations value adjusted for risk, even though the agents start with nonrational expectations. In other words, homogeneous rational expectations are an attractor for a market with endogenous, inductive expectations.[11] This is not surprising. If some agents forecast differently than the h.r.e.e. value, then the fact that most other agents are using something close to the h.r.e.e. value will return a market-clearing price that corrects these deviant expectations: There is a natural, if weak, attraction to h.r.e.e. The equilibrium within this regime differs in two ways from the standard, theoretical, rational-expectations equilibrium. First, the equilibrium is neither assumed nor arrived at by deductive means. Our agents instead arrive inductively at a homogeneity that overlaps that of the homogeneous,

10. At the time of writing, we have discovered that the two regimes emerge, and the results are materially the same, if we vary *only* the rate of invocation of the genetic algorithm.

11. Within a simpler model, Blume and Easley (1982) prove analytically the evolutionary stability of r.e.e.

theoretical rational expectations. Second, the equilibrium is a stochastic one. Agents continually explore alternatives, albeit at low rates. This testing of alternative explorations, small as it is, induces some "thermal noise" into the system. As we would expect, in this regime, agents' holdings remain highly homogeneous, trading volume remains low (reflecting only variations in forecasts due to mutation and recombination), and bubbles, crashes, and technical trading do not emerge. We can say that in this regime the efficient-market theory and its implications are upheld.

The Complex or Rich Psychological Regime

We now allow a more realistic level of exploration in belief space. In these experiments, as we see in Figure 1, the price series still appears to be nearly identical to the price in the rational—expectations regime. (It is lower because of risk attributable to the higher variance caused by increased exploration.)

On closer inspection of the results, however, we find that complex patterns have formed in the collection of beliefs, and that the market displays characteristics that differ materially from those in the rational-expectations regime. For example, when we magnify the difference between the two price series, we see systematic evidence of temporary price bubbles and crashes (Figure 2). We call this new set of market behaviors the rich psychological, or complex, regime.

This appearance of bubbles and crashes suggests that technical trading, in the form of buying or selling into trends, has emerged in the market. We can check this rigorously by examining the information the agents condition their forecasts upon. Figure 3 shows the number of technical-trading bits that are used (are 1's or 0's) in the population of predictors as it evolves over time. In both sets of experiments, technical-trading bits are initially seeded randomly in the predictor population. In the rational-expectations regime, however, technical-trading bits provide no useful information and fall off as useless predictors are discarded. But in the complex regime, they bootstrap in the population, reaching a steady-state value by 150,000 periods. Technical trading, once it emerges, remains[12].

Price statistics in the complex regime differ from those in the rational-expectations regime, mainly in that kurtosis is evident in the complex case (Table 1) and that volume of shares traded (per 10,000 periods) is about 300% larger in the complex case, reflecting the degree to which the agents remain heterogeneous in their expectations as the market evolves. We

12. When we run these experiments informally to 1,000,000 periods, we see no signs that technical-trading bits disappear.

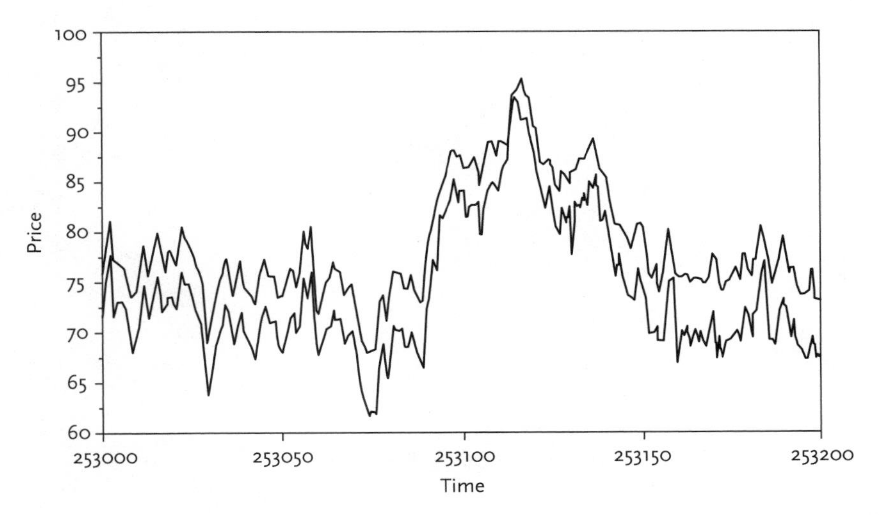

Figure 1:
Rational-expectations price vs. price in the rich psychological regime. The two price series are generated on the same random dividend series. The upper is the homogeneous r.e.e. price, the lower is the price in the complex regime. The higher variance in the latter case causes the lower price through risk aversion.

note that fat tails and high volume are also characteristic of price data from actual financial markets.

How does technical trading emerge in psychologically rich or complex regime? In this regime the "temperature" of exploration is high enough to

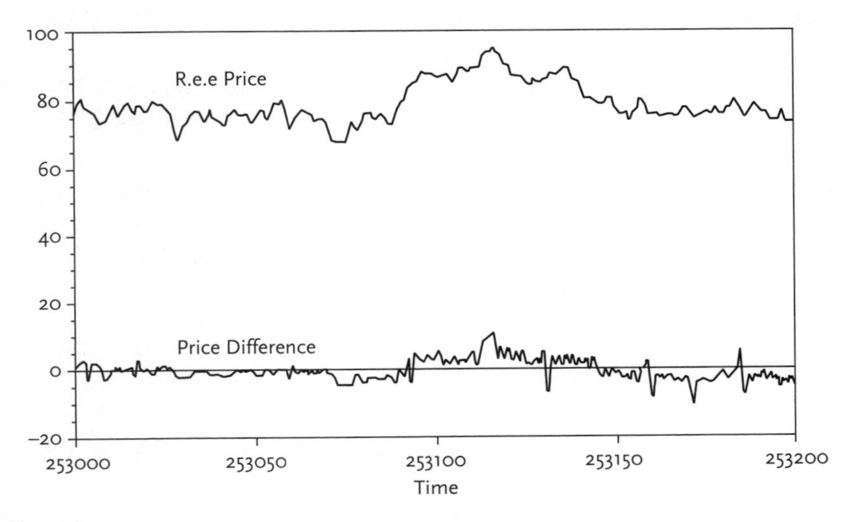

Figure 2:
Deviations of the price series in the complex regime from fundamental value. The bottom graph shows the difference between the two price series in Figure 1 (with the complex series rescaled to match the r.e.e. one and the difference between the two doubled for ease of observation). The upper series is the h.r.e.e. price.

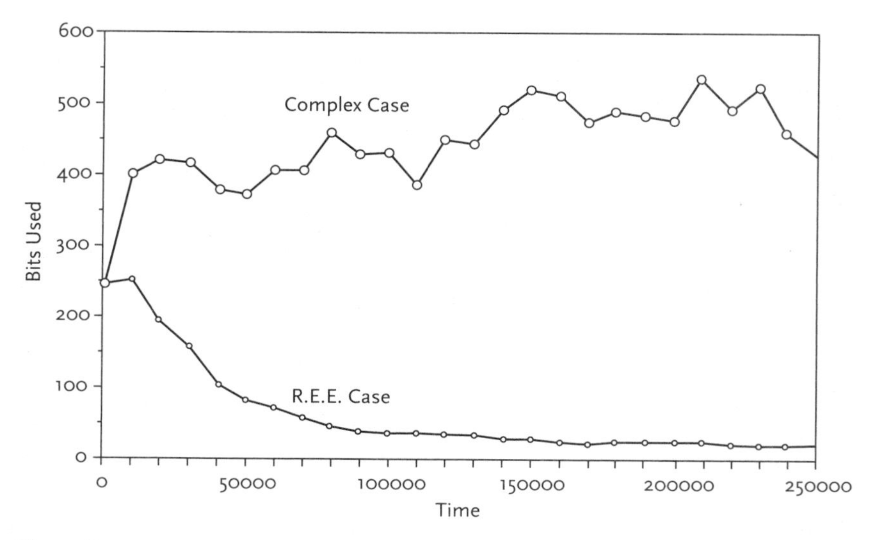

Figure 3:
Number of technical-trading bits that become set as the market evolves (median over 25 experiments in the two regimes).

offset, to some degree, expectations' natural attraction to the r.e.e. And so, subsets of non-r.e.e. beliefs need not disappear rapidly. Instead they can become mutually reinforcing. Suppose, for example, predictors appear early on that, by chance, condition an upward price forecast upon the markets showing a current rising trend. Then, agents who hold such predictors are more likely to buy into the market on an uptrend, raising the price over what it might otherwise be, causing a slight upward bias that might be sufficient to lend validation to such rules and retain them in the market. A similar story holds for predictors that forecast reversion to fundamental value. Such predictors need to appear in sufficient density to validate each other and remain in the population of predictors. The situation here is analogous to that in theories of the origin of life, where there needs to be a certain density of mutually reinforcing RNA units in the "soup" of monomers and polymers for such replicating units to gain a footing (see Eigen and Schuster, 1979; Kauffman, 1993). Thus,

Table 1. RETURNS AND VOLUME STATISTICS (MEDIANS) IN THE TWO REGIMES COLLECTED FOR 25 EXPERIMENTS AFTER 250,000 PERIODS

	Mean	Std. Dev.	Skewness	Kurtosis[13]	Vol. traded
R.e.e. Regime	0.000	2.1002	0.0131	0.0497	2,460.9
Complex Regime	0.000	2.1007	0.0204	0.3429	7,783.8

13. Kurtosis numbers are excess kurtosis (i.e., kurtosis-3).

technical analysis can emerge if trend-following (or mean-reversion) beliefs are, by chance, generated in the population, and if random perturbations in the dividend sequence activate them and subsequently validate them. From then on, they may take their place in the population of patterns recognized by the agents and become mutually sustainable. This emergence of structure from the mutual interaction of system subcomponents justifies our use of the label "complex" for this regime.

What is critical to the appearance of subpopulations of mutually reinforcing forecasts, in fact, is the presence of market information to condition upon. Market states act as "sunspot-like" signals that allow predictors to coordinate upon a direction they associate with that signal. (Of course, these are not classic sunspots that convey no real information.) Such coordination or mutuality can remain in the market once it establishes itself by chance. We can say the ability of market states to act as signals primes the mutuality that causes complex behavior. There is no need to assume a separate class of noise traders for this purpose. We can test this signaling conjecture in further experiments where we "turn off" the condition part of all predictors (by filling them with nonreplaceable #'s). Now forecasts cannot differentiate among states of the market, and market states cannot act as signals. We find, consistent with our conjecture that signaling drives the observed patterns, that the complex regime does not emerge. As a further test of the significance of technical-trading signals, we regress the current price on the previous periods plus the technical indicator (price > 500-period moving average). In the rational-expectations regime, the technical indicator is of course not significant. In the complex regime, the trend indicator *is* significant (with t-value of 5.1 for the mean of the sample of 25 experiments), showing that the indicator does indeed carry useful market information. The corresponding test on actual financial data shows a similar result (see Brock et al., 1991).

One of the striking characteristics of actual financial markets is that both their price volatility and trading volume show persistence or autocorrelation. And volatility and volume show significant cross-correlation. In other words, both volume and volatility remain high or low for periods of random length, and they are interrelated. Our inductive market also shows persistence in volatility or GARCH behavior in the complex regime (see Figure 4), with the Chi-square statistic in the Engle GARCH Test significant at the 95% level.[14] It also shows persistence in trading volume (see Figure 5), as well as significant cross-correlation between trading volume and volatility (see Figure 6). The figures include corresponding correlations for the often-used market standard, IBM stock. Note that because our time period and actual market days do not necessarily match, we should expect no exact overlap. But qualitatively,

14. Autocorrelated volatility is often fitted with a Generalized Autoregressive Conditional Heteroscedastic time series. Hence, the GARCH label. See Bollerslev et al. (1990); and Goodhart and O'Hara (1995).

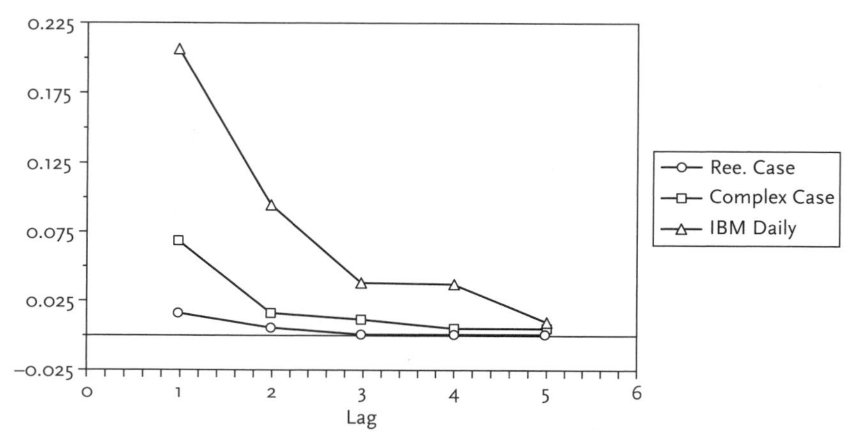

Figure 4:
Autocorrelation of volatility in rational-expectations and complex regimes, and in IBM daily returns.

persistence in our market and IBM's is similar.) These correlations are not explained by the standard model, where theoretically they are zero.

Why financial markets—and our inductive market—show these empirical "signatures" remains an open question. We conjecture a simple evolutionary explanation. Both in real markets and in our artificial market, agents are constantly exploring and testing new expectations. Once in a while, randomly, more successful expectations will be discovered. Such expectations will change the market, and trigger further changes in expectations, so that small and large "avalanches" of change will cascade through the system. (Of course, on this very short time-lag scale, these avalanches occur not through the

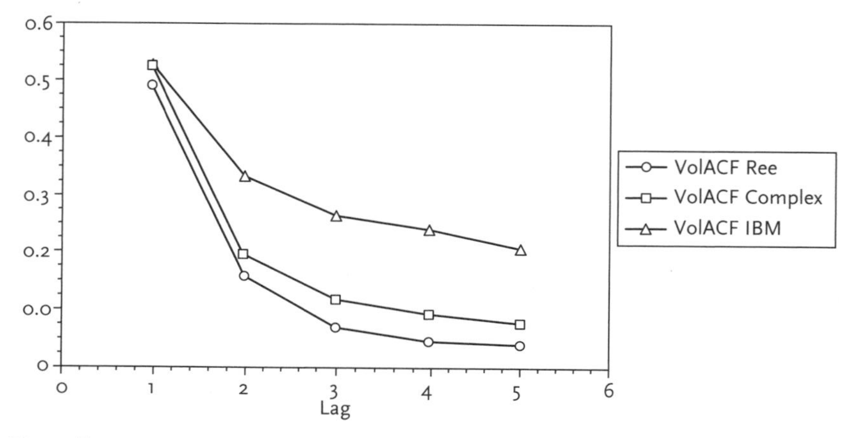

Figure 5:
Autocorrelation of trading volume in the rational-expectations and complex regimes, and in IBM daily returns.

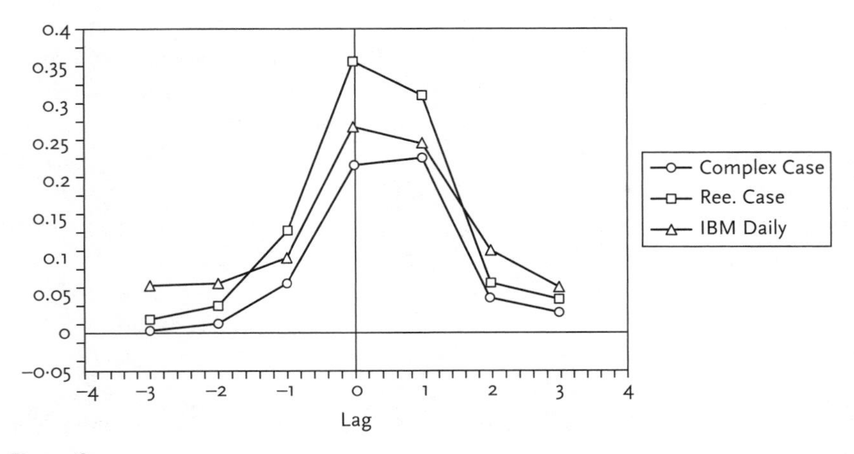

Figure 6:
Cross-correlation of trading volume with volatility, in the rational-expectations and complex regimes, and in IBM daily returns.

genetic algorithm, but by agents changing their active predictors.) Changes then manifest in the form of increased volatility and increased volume. One way to test this conjecture is to see whether autocorrelations increase as the predictor accuracy-updating parameter θ in Eq. (A.1) in Appendix A is increased. The larger θ is, the faster individual agents "switch" among their predictors. Thus, the more such switches should cascade. Experiments confirm that autocorrelations indeed increase with θ. Such cascades of switching in time are absorbed by the market, and die away. Hence, our evolutionary market exhibits periods of turbulence followed by periods of quiescence, as do actual markets.[15]

5. DISCUSSION

To what extent is the existence of the complex regime an artifact of design assumptions in our model? We find experimentally, by varying both the model's parameters and the expectational-learning mechanism, that the complex regime and the qualitative phenomena associated with it are robust. These are not an artifact of some deficiency in the model.[16]

15. For a discussion of volatility clustering in a different model, see Youssefmir and Huberman (1995); and also Grannan and Swindle (1994).

16. One design choice might make a difference. We have evaluated the usefulness of expectational beliefs by their accuracy rather than by the profit they produce. In practice, these alternatives may produce different outcomes. For example, buying into a price rise on the basis of expectations may yield a different result if validated by profit instead of by accuracy of forecast when "slippage" is present, that is, when traders on the other side of the market are hard to find. We believe, but have not proved, that the two criteria lead to the same qualitative results.

It might be objected that if some agents could discover a superior means of forecasting to exploit the market, this might arbitrage complex patterns away, causing the market again to converge to rational expectations. We believe not. If a clever metaexpectational model was "out there" that might exploit others' expectations, such a model would, by aggregation of others' expectations, be a complicated nonlinear function of current market information. To the degree that the piecewise linear form we have assumed covers the space of nonlinear expectational models conditioned on current market information, agents would indeed, via the genetic algorithm, pick up on an approximate form of this superior metamodel. The complex regime owes its existence then not to limitations of forecasting, but rather to the fact that in our endogenous-expectations model market information can be used as signals, so that a much wider space of possibilities is open—in particular, the market can self-organize into mutually supporting subpopulations of predictors. (In fact, in a simpler, analytical model, with a small number of classes of trader whose beliefs adapt endogenously, Brock and Hommes (1996) find similar, rich, asset-price dynamics.) There is no reason these emergent subpopulations should be in stochastic equilibrium. Indeed, agents may mutually adapt their expectations forever, so that the market explores its way through this large space, and is nonstationary. In some early exploratory experiments, we "froze" successful agents' expectations, then reinjected these agents with their previously successful expectations much later. The reintroduced agents proved less successful than average, indicating that the market had evolved and was nonstationary.

It might be also objected that by our use of condition bits in the predictors, we have built technical trading into our model. And so it is no surprise that it appears in the complex regime. But actually, only the possibility of technical trading is built in, not its use. The use of market descriptors is selected against in the model. Thus, market signals must be of value to be used, and technical trading emerges only because such market signals induce mutually supporting expectations that condition themselves on these market signals.

If the market has a well-defined psychology in our model, does it also experience "moods?" Obviously not. But, notice we assume that agents entertain more than one market hypothesis. Thus, we can imagine circumstances of a prolonged "bull-market" uptrend to a level well above fundamental value in which the market state activates predictors that indicate the uptrend will continue, and simultaneously other predictors that predict a rapid downward correction. Such combinations, which occur easily in both our market and actual markets, could well be described as "nervous."

What about trade, and the motivation to trade in our market? In the rational-expectations literature, the deductively rational agents have no motivation to trade, even where they differ in beliefs. Assuming other agents have access to different information sets, each agent in a prebidding arrangement arrives at identical beliefs. Our inductively rational agents (who do not communicate directly), by contrast, do not necessarily converge in beliefs. They thus retain a motivation to trade, betting ultimately on their powers as market statisticians. It might appear that, because our agents have equal abilities as statisticians, they are irrational to trade at all. But although their *abilities* are the same, their luck in finding good predictors diverges over time. And at each period, the accuracy of their predictors is fully accounted for in their allocations between the risk-free and risky asset. Given that agents can only act as market statisticians, their trading behavior is rational.

Our endogenous-expectation theory fits with two other modern approaches. Our model generalizes the learning models of Bray and others (Bossaerts, 1995; Sargent, 1993), which also assume endogenous updating of expectations. But while the Bray models assume homogeneous updating from a shared nonrational forecast, our approach assumes heterogeneous agents who can discover expectations that might exploit any patterns present. Our evolutionary approach also has strong affinities with the evolutionary models of Blume and Easley (1982, 1990). These assume populations of expectational (or more correctly, investment) rules that compete for survival in the market in a given population of rules, and that sometimes adapt. But the concern in this literature is the selective survival of different, competing, rule types, not the emergence of mutually supportive subpopulations that give rise to complex phenomena, nor the role of market signals in this emergence.

Our inductively rational market, of course, leaves out many details of realism. In actual financial markets, investors do not perfectly optimize portfolios, nor is full market clearing achieved each period. Indeed, except for the formation of expectations, our market is simple and neoclassical. Our object, however, is not market realism. Rather it is to show that given the inevitable inductive nature of expectations when heterogeneity is present, rich psychological behavior emerges—even under neoclassical conditions. We need not, as in other studies (see Kirman, 1991; Friedman and Aoki, 1992; Sargent, 1993), assume sharing of information nor sharing of expectations nor herd effects to elicit these phenomena. Nor do we need to invoke "behaviorism" or other forms of irrationality (see Thaler, 1993). Herding tendencies and quasi-rational behavior may be present in actual markets, but they are not necessary to our findings.

6. CONCLUDING REMARKS

In asset markets, agents' forecasts create the world that agents are trying to forecast. Thus, asset markets have a reflexive nature in that prices are generated by traders' expectations, but these expectations are formed on the basis of anticipations of *others'* expectations.[17] This reflexivity, or self-referential character of expectations, precludes expectations being formed by deductive means, so that perfect rationality ceases to be well defined. Thus, agents can only treat their expectations as hypotheses: they act inductively, generating individual expectational models that they constantly introduce, test, act upon, discard. The market becomes driven by expectations that adapt endogenously to the ecology these expectations cocreate.

Experiments with a computerized version of this endogenous-expectations market explain one of the more striking puzzles in finance: Standard theory tends to see markets as efficient, with no rationale for herd effects, and no possibility of systematic speculative profit, whereas traders tend to view the market as exhibiting a "psychology," bandwagon effects, and opportunities for speculative profit. Recently the traders' view has been justified by invoking behavioral assumptions, such as the existence of noise traders. We show, without behavioral assumptions, that both views can be correct. A market of inductively rational traders can exist in two different regimes: Under a low enough rate of exploration of alternative forecasts, the market settles into a simple regime which corresponds to the rational-expectations equilibrium of the efficient-market literature. Under a more realistic rate of exploration of alternative forecasts, the market self-organizes into a complex regime in which rich psychological behavior emerges. Technical trading appears, as do temporary bubbles and crashes. And prices show statistical features—in particular, GARCH behavior—characteristic of actual market data. These phenomena arise when individual expectations that involve trend following or mean reversion become mutually reinforcing in the population of expectations, and when market indicators become used as signaling devices that coordinate these sets of mutually reinforcing beliefs.

Our endogenous-expectations market shows that heterogeneity of beliefs, deviations from fundamental trading, and persistence in time series can be maintained indefinitely in actual markets with inductively rational traders. We conjecture that actual financial markets lie within the complex regime.

17. This point was also made by Soros (1994) whose term *reflexivity* we adopt.

APPENDIX A
Details of the Market's Architecture

Model Parameters. Throughout the experiments we set the interest rate r to 0.1, and agents' risk-aversion parameter λ to 0.5. The parameters of the dividend process in Eq. (4) are $\rho = 0.95$, $\bar{d} = 10$, $r = 0.1$, $\sigma_\varepsilon^2 = 0.0743$. (This error variance value is selected to yield a combined price-plus-dividend variance of 4.0 in the h.r.e.e.)

Predictor Accuracy. The accuracy, or precision, of agent i's jth predictor is updated each time the predictor is active, and is recorded as the inverse of the moving average of squared forecast error:

$$e_{t,i,j}^2 = (1-\theta)\, e_{t-1,i,j}^2 + \theta[(p_{t+1} + d_{t+1}) - E_{t,i,j}(p_{t+1} + d_{t+1})]^2 \qquad \text{(A.1)}$$

with $\theta = 1/75$ in the complex regime, and 1/150 in the rational-expectations regime.

This accuracy is used in three places. First, if multiple predictors are active, only the most accurate is used. Second, it is part of the fitness measure for selecting predictors for recombination in the genetic algorithm. This fitness measure is defined as

$$f_{t,i,j} = M - e_{t,i,j}^2 - Cs \qquad \text{(A.2)}$$

where M is a constant; s is specificity, the number of bits that are set (not #) in the predictor's condition array; and $C = 0.005$ is a cost levied for specificity. The value of M is irrelevant, given tournament rankings.

Third, agents use the error variance of their current predictor for the forecast variance in the demand Eq. (5). (We keep this latter variance fixed between genetic algorithm implementations, updating it to its current value in Eq. (A.1) at each invocation.)

Initial Expectations. We initialize agents' expectations in both regimes by drawing the forecasting parameters from a uniform distribution of values centered upon the h.r.e.e. ones. We select a to be uniform (0.7, 1.2) and b to be uniform (–10, 19.002). The variance of all new predictors is initialized in all cases to the h.r.e.e. value of 4.0.

The genetic algorithm. New predictors are generated by updating each agent's predictor set at random intervals, on average every 250 periods or 1,000 periods, depending on the regime, asynchronously across agents. The worst performing (least accurate) 20% of the agent's 100 predictors are dropped, and are replaced by new ones, using uniform crossover and mutation. The agents are initialized by seeding them with random predictors: condition bits are set to 0 or 1 with probability 0.1, otherwise to #. This avoids bias in choosing predictors at the outset, and allows intelligent behavior to bootstrap itself up as the artificial agents generate predictive models that perform better. For the bitstrings, these procedures are standard genetic algorithm procedures for mutation and crossover (uniform crossover is used, which chooses a bit at random from each of the two parents). The forecasting parameter vectors are mutated by adding random variables to each individual component. And they are crossed over component-wise, or by taking linear combinations of the two vectors, or by selecting one or the other complete vector. Each of these procedures is performed with equal probability. Crossover on a predictor is performed with probability 0.3 or 0.1 in the rational-expectations and complex regimes, respectively. Individual bits are mutated with probability 0.03. New predictors are brought into the predictor set with variance set to the average of their parents. If a bit has been changed, the new predictor's variance is set to the average of that of all predictors. If this new variance is lower than the variance of the current default predictor less an absolute deviation, its variance is set to the median of the predictors' variance. This procedure gives new predictors a reasonable chance of becoming used.

Market Clearing. The price is adjusted each period by directly solving Eqs. (5) and (6) for p, which entails passing agents' forecasting parameters to the clearing equation. In actual markets, of course, the price is adjusted by a specialist who may not have access to agents' demand functions. But we note that actual specialists, either from experience or from their "books," have a keen feel for the demand function in their markets, and use little inventory to balance day-to-day demand. Alternatively, our market-clearing mechanism simulates an auction in which the specialist declares different prices and agents continually resubmit bids until a price is reached that clears the market.

Calculation of the Homogeneous Rational-Expectations Equilibrium. We calculate the homogeneous r.e.e. for the case where the market price is a linear function of the dividend $p_t = f d_t + g$ which corresponds to the structure of our forecasts. We can then calculate f and g from the market conditions at equilibrium. A homogenous equilibrium demands that all agents hold 1 share, so that, from Eq. (5)

$$E_t(p_{t+1} + d_{t+1}) - (1+r)p_t = \lambda\sigma^2_{p+d} \tag{A.3}$$

From the dividend process Eq. (4) and the linear form for the price, we can calculate $\sigma^2_{p+d} = (1+f)\,\sigma^2_e$ and $E_t\,(p_{t+1} + d_{t+1})$ as

$$E_t(p_{t+1} + d_{t+1}) = (1+f)\,[(1-\rho)\,\bar{d} + \rho d_t] + g$$

Noting that the right side of Eq. (A.3) is constant, we can then solve for f and g as

$$f = \frac{\rho}{1+r-\rho}$$

$$g = \frac{(1+f)[(1-\rho)\,\bar{d} - \lambda\sigma_e^2]}{r}$$

Therefore, the expression:

$$E_t(p_{t+1} + d_{t+1}) = (1+r)p_t + \frac{\lambda(2+r)\sigma_e^2}{1+r-\rho} \tag{A.4}$$

is the h.r.e.e. forecast we seek.

APPENDIX B
The Santa Fe Artificial Stock Market

The Santa Fe Artificial Stock Market has existed since 1989 in various designs (see Palmer et al. (1994) for a description of an earlier version). Since then a number of other artificial markets have appeared: e.g., Beltratti and Margarita (1992), Marengo and Tordjman (1995), and Rieck (1994). The Santa Fe Market is a computer-based model that can be altered, experimented with, and studied in a rigorously controlled way. Most of the artificial market's features are malleable and can be changed to carry out different experiments. Thus, the artificial market is a framework or template that can be specialized to focus on particular questions of interest in finance: for example, the effects of different agents having access to different information sets or predictive behaviors; or of a transaction tax on trading volume; or of different market-making mechanisms.

The framework allows other classes of utility functions, such as constant relative risk aversion. It allows a specialist or market maker, with temporary imbalances in fulfilled bids and offers, made up by changes in an inventory held by the specialist. It allows a number of alternative random processes for $\{d_t\}$. And it allows for the evolutionary selection of agents via wealth.

The market runs on a NeXTStep computational platform, but is currently being ported to the Swarm platform. For availability of code, and for further information, readers should contact Blake LeBaron or Richard Palmer.

REFERENCES

W. B. Arthur (1992), "On Learning and Adaptation in the Economy," Working Paper 92-07-038, Santa Fe Institute, Santa Fe, NM.

W. B. Arthur (1994), "Inductive Behavior and Bounded Rationality," *Amer. Econ. Rev.*, 84, pp. 406–411.

W. B. Arthur (1995), "Complexity in Economic and Financial Markets," *Complexity*, 1, pp. 20–25.

A. Beltratti - S. Margarita (1992), "Simulating an Artificial Adaptive Stock Market," mimeo, Turin University.

L. Blume - D. Easley (1982), "Learning to Be Rational," *J. Econ. Theory*, 26, pp. 340–351.

L. Blume - D. Easley (1990), "Evolution and Market Behavior," *J. Econ. Theory*, 58, pp. 9–40.

T. Bollerslev - R. Y. Chou - N. Jayaraman - K. F. Kroner (1990), "ARCH Modeling in Finance: A Review of the Theory and Empirical Evidence," *J. Econometrics*, 52, pp. 5–60.

P. Bossaerts (1995), "The Econometrics of Learning in Financial Markets," *Econometric Theory*, 11, pp. 151–189.

M. Bray (1982), "Learning, Estimation, and Stability of Rational Expectations," *J. Econ. Theory*, 26, pp. 318–339.

W. Brock - J. Lakonishok - B. LeBaron (1991), "Simple Technical Trading Rules and the Stochastic Properties of Stock Returns," Working Paper 91-01-006, Santa Fe Institute, Santa Fe, NM.

W. Brock - C. H. Hommes (1996), "Models of Complexity in Economics and Finance," mimeo, Department of Economics, University of Wisconsin, Madison.

D. M. Cutler - J. M. Poterba - L. H. Summers (1989), "What Moves Stock Prices?," *J. Portfolio Mgmt.*, 15, pp. 4–12.

J. B. De Long - A. Shleifer - L. H. Summers - R. J. Waldmann (1990a), "Noise Trader Risk in Financial Markets," *J. Pol. Econ.*, 98, pp. 703–738.

J. B. De Long - A. Shleifer - L. H. Summers - R. J. Waldmann (1990b), "Positive Feedback Strategies and Destabilizing Rational Speculation," *J. Fin.*, 45, pp. 379–395.

J. B. De Long - A. Shleifer - L. H. Summers - R. J. Waldmann (1991), "The Survival of Noise Traders in Financial Markets," *J. Bus.*, 64, pp. 1–18.

B. T. Diba - H. I. Grossman (1988), "The Theory of Rational Bubbles in Stock Prices," *Econ. Jour.*, 98, pp. 746–754.

M. Eigen - P. Schuster (1979), *The Hypercycle: A Principle of Natural Self-Organization*, Springer, New York.

E. F. Fama - K. R. French (1988), "Permanent and Temporary Components of Stock Market Prices," *J. Pol. Econ.*, 96, pp. 246–273.

J. A. Frankel - K. A. Froot (1990), "Chartists, Fundamentalists, and Trading in the Foreign Exchange Market," *AEA Papers & Proc.*, 80, pp. 181–185.

D. Friedman - M. Aoki (1992), "Inefficient Information Aggregation as a Source of Asset Price Bubbles," *Bull. Econ. Res.*, 44, pp. 251–279.

C. A. E. Goodhart - M. O'Hara (1995), "High Frequency Data in Financial Markets: Issues and Applications," Unpublished manuscript, London School of Economics.

E. R. Grannan - G. H. Swindle (1994), "Contrarians and Volatility Clustering," Working Paper 94-03-010, Santa Fe Institute, Santa Fe, NM.

S. J. Grossman (1976), "On the Efficiency of Competitive Stock Markets Where Traders Have Diverse Information," *J. Fin.*, 31 pp. 573–585.

S. J. Grossman - J. Stiglitz (1980), "On the Impossibility of Informationally Efficient Markets," *Amer. Econ. Rev.*, 70, pp. 393–408.

J. H. Holland - K. J. Holyoak - R. E. Nisbett - P. R. Thagard (1986), *Induction,* MIT Press, Cambridge, MA.
S. Kauffman (1993), *The Origin of Order: Self-Organization and Selection in Evolution,* Oxford University Press, New York.
J. M. Keynes (1936), *General Theory of Employment, Interest, and Money*, Macmillan, London.
A. Kirman (1991), "Epidemics of Opinion and Speculative Bubbles in Financial Markets," in *Money and Financial Markets,* M. Taylor (ed.), Macmillan, London.
A. W. Kleidon (1986), "Anomalies in Financial Economics: Blueprint for Change?," *J. Bus.*, 59, pp. 285–316 (supplement).
M. Kurz (1994), "On the Structure and Diversity of Rational Beliefs," *Econ. Theory*, 4, pp. 877–900.
M. Kurz (1995), "Asset Prices with Rational Beliefs," Working Paper 96-003, Economics Department, Stanford University.
S. F. Leroy - R. D. Porter (1981), "Stock Price Volatility: Tests Based on Implied Variance Bounds," *Econometrica*, 49, pp. 97–113.
A. W. Lo - C. Mackinlay (1988), "Stock Prices Do Not Follow Random Walks: Evidence from a Simple Specification Test," *Rev. Fin. Stud.*, 1, pp. 41–66.
R. E. Lucas (1978), "Asset Prices in an Exchange Economy," *Econometrica*, 46, pp. 1429–1445.
L. Marengo - H. Tordjman (1995), "Speculation, Heterogeneity, and Learning: A Model of Exchange Rate Dynamics," Working Paper WP-95-17, IIASA.
P. Milgrom - N. Stokey (1982), "Information, Trade, and Common Knowledge," *J. Econ. Theory*, 26, pp. 17–27.
R. Nelson - S. Winter (1982), *An Evolutionary Theory of Economic Change,* Harvard University, Press/Bellknap, Cambridge, MA.
R. G. Palmer - W. B. Arthur - J. H. Holland - B. Lebaron - P. Tayler (1994), "Artificial Economic Life: A Simple Model of a Stockmarket," *Physica D*, 75, pp. 264–274.
J. M. Poterba - L. H. Summers (1988), "Mean Reversion in Stock Prices: Evidence and Implications," *J. Fin. Econ.*, 22, pp. 27–59.
C. Rieck (1994), "Evolutionary Simulation of Asset Trading Strategies," in *Many-Agent Simulation and Artificial Life,* E. Hillenbrand and J. Stender (eds.), IOS Press, Washington, DC.
D. E. Rumelhart (1977), *Human Information Processing,* Wiley, New York.
T. J. Sargent (1993), *Bounded Rationality in Macroeconomics,* Oxford University Press, New York.
R. Schank - R. P. Abelson (1977), *Scripts, Plans, Goals, and Understanding,* Erlbaum, Hillsdale, NJ.
R. J. Shiller (1981), "Do Stock Prices Move Too Much to Be Justified by Subsequent Changes in Dividends?," *Amer. Econ. Rev.*, 71, pp. 421–436.
R. J. Shiller (1989), *Market Volatility,* MIT Press, Cambridge, MA.
A. Shleifer - L. H. Summers (1990), "The Noise Trader Approach to Finance," *J. Econ. Perspectives*, 4, pp. 19–33.
G. Soros (1994), *The Theory of Reflexivity,* Soros Fund Management, New York.
L. H. Summers (1986), "Does the Stock Market Rationally Reflect Fundamental Values?," *J. Fin.*, 46, pp. 591–601.
R. H. Thaler (1993), *Advances in Behavioral Finance,* Russell Sage Foundation, New York.
M. Youssefmir - B. Huberman (1995), "Clustered Volatility in Multiagent Dynamics," Working Paper 95-05- 051, Santa Fe Institute, Santa Fe, NM.

CHAPTER 4

Competing Technologies, Increasing Returns, and Lock-In by Historical Events

W. BRIAN ARTHUR*

This paper introduced many of the concepts of increasing returns economics: competing technologies, lock-in by small historical events, and the possibility of non-predictable, path-dependent outcomes. It was known beforehand that increasing returns could lead to multiple equilibria, not all of which could be optimal. What wasn't known was how one particular outcome out of the many possible would be selected; from a static viewpoint, which outcome would be "chosen" was indeterminate. This paper put forward a solution to the selection problem by redefining increasing returns problems as dynamic problems subject to random events. In a given realization under a particular set of small random events one outcome would be selected, in another realization under a different set of small random events a different outcome would be selected. Increasing returns problems should therefore be studied as probabilistic systems that unfold over time, an approach that has since become the accepted one.

The paper first appeared in September 1983 as Working Paper WP-83-90 at the International Institute for Applied Systems Analysis. But with its emphasis on possible lock-in to non-predicable, inferior outcomes, it proved difficult to publish. The paper underwent six years of submissions before this version finally appeared in the *Economic Journal*, 99, 116–131, 1989. Since then it has become one of the most heavily cited papers in economics.[1] I included it in my previous collected papers volume, *Increasing*

* I thank Robin Cowan, Paul David, Joseph Farrell, Ward Hanson, Charles Kindleberger, Richard Nelson, Nathan Rosenberg, Paul Samuelson, Martin Shubik, and Gavin Wright for useful suggestions and criticisms. An earlier version of part of this paper appeared in 1983 as Working Paper 83-90 at the International Institute for Applied Systems Analysis, Laxenburg, Austria. Support from the Centre for Economic Policy Research, Stanford, and from the Guggenheim Foundation is acknowledged.

1. See H. Kim, A. Morse, and L. Zingales. "What Has Mattered to Economics since 1970." *J. Econ. Perspectives* 20, 4, 2006.

Returns and Path Dependence in the Economy, University of Michigan Press, 1994, but because it is considered a foundational paper in complexity economics, I've included it here too.

This paper explores the dynamics of allocation under increasing returns in a context where increasing returns arise naturally: agents choosing between technologies competing for adoption.

Modern, complex technologies often display increasing returns to adoption in that the more they are adopted, the more experience is gained with them, and the more they are improved.[2] When two or more increasing-return technologies "compete" then, for a "market" of potential adopters, insignificant events may by chance give one of them an initial advantage in adoptions. This technology may then improve more than the others, so it may appeal to a wider proportion of potential adopters. It may therefore become further adopted and further improved. Thus a technology that by chance gains an early lead in adoption may eventually "corner the market" of potential adopters, with the other technologies becoming locked out. Of course, under different "insignificant events"—unexpected successes in the performance of prototypes, whims of early developers, political circumstances—a different technology might achieve sufficient adoption and improvement to come to dominate. Competitions between technologies may have multiple potential outcomes.

It is well known that allocation problems with increasing returns tend to exhibit multiple equilibria, and so it is not surprising that multiple outcomes should appear here. Static analysis can typically locate these multiple equilibria, but usually it cannot tell us *which* one will be "selected." A dynamic approach might be able to say more. By allowing the possibility of "random events" occurring during adoption, it might examine how these influence "selection" of the outcome—how some sets of random "historical events" might cumulate to drive the process towards one market-share outcome, others to drive it towards another. It might also reveal how the two familiar increasing-returns properties of *non-predictability* and *potential inefficiency* come about: how increasing returns act to magnify chance events as adoptions take place, so that *ex ante* knowledge of adopters' preferences and the technologies' possibilities may not suffice to predict the "market outcome;"

2. Rosenberg (1982) calls this "Learning by Using" (see also Atkinson and Stiglitz, 1969). Jet aircraft designs like the Boeing 727, for example, undergo constant modification and they improve significantly in structural soundness, wing design, payload capacity, and engine efficiency as they accumulate actual airline adoption and use.

and how increasing returns might drive the adoption process into developing a technology that has inferior long-run potential. A dynamic approach might also point up two new properties: *inflexibility* in that once an outcome (a dominant technology) begins to emerge it becomes progressively more "locked in"; and *non-ergodicity* (or path-dependence) in that historical "small events" are not averaged away and "forgotten" by the dynamics—they may decide the outcome.

This paper contrasts the dynamics of technologies' "market shares" under conditions of increasing, diminishing, and constant returns. It pays special attention to how returns affect predictability, efficiency, flexibility, and ergodicity; and to the circumstances under which the economy might become locked-in by "historical events" to the monopoly of an inferior technology.

I. A SIMPLE MODEL

Nuclear power can be generated by light-water, or gas-cooled, or heavy-water, or sodium-cooled reactors. Solar energy can be generated by crystalline-silicon or amorphous-silicon technologies. I abstract from cases like this and assume in an initial, simple model that two new technologies, A and B, "compete" for adoption by a large number of economic agents. The technologies are not *sponsored*[3] or strategically manipulated by any firm; they are open to all. Agents are simple consumers of the technologies who act directly or indirectly as developers of them.

Agent i comes into the market at time t_i; at this time he chooses the latest version of either technology A or technology B; and he uses this version thereafter.[4] Agents are of two types, R and S, with equal numbers in each, the two types independent of the times of choice but differing in their preferences, perhaps because of the use to which they will put their choice. The version of A or B each agent chooses is fixed or frozen in design at his time of choice, so that his payoff is affected only by past adoptions of his chosen technology. (Later I examine the expectations case where payoffs are also affected by future adoptions.)

Not all technologies enjoy increasing returns with adoption. Sometimes factor inputs are bid upward in price so that diminishing returns accompany

3. Following terminology introduced in Arthur (1983), *sponsored* technologies are proprietary and capable of being priced and strategically manipulated; *unsponsored* technologies are generic and not open to manipulation or pricing.

4. Where technologies are improving, it may pay adopters under certain conditions to wait; so that no adoptions take place (Balcer and Lippman, 1984; Mamer and McCardle, 1987). We can avoid this problem by assuming adopters need to replace an obsolete technology that breaks down at times $\{t_i\}$.

Table 1. RETURNS TO CHOOSING A OR B GIVEN PREVIOUS ADOPTIONS

	Technology A	*Technology B*
R-agent	a_R+rn_A	b_R+rn_B
S-agent	a_S+sn_A	b_S+sn_B

adoption. Hydro-electric power, for example, becomes more costly as dam sites become scarcer and less suitable. And some technologies are unaffected by adoption—their returns are constant. I include these cases by assuming that the returns to choosing *A* or *B* realised by any agent (the net present value of the version of the technology available to him) depend upon the number of previous adopters, n_A and n_B, at the time of his choice (as in Table 1)[5] with increasing, diminishing, or constant returns to adoption given by *r* and *s* simultaneously positive, negative, or zero. I also assume $a_R > b_R$ and $a_S < b_S$ so that *R*-agents have a natural preference for *A*, and *S*-agents have a natural preference for *B*.

To complete this model, I want to define carefully what I mean by "chance" or "historical events." Were we to have infinitely detailed prior knowledge of events and circumstances that might affect technology choices—political interests, the prior experience of developers, timing of contracts, decisions at key meetings—the outcome or adoption market-share gained by each technology would presumably be determinable in advance. We can conclude that our limited discerning power, or more precisely the limited discerning power of an implicit *observer,* may cause indeterminacy of outcome. I therefore define "historical small events" to be those events or conditions that are outside the *ex-ante* knowledge of the observer—beyond the resolving power of his "model" or abstraction of the situation.

To return to *our* model, let us assume an observer who has full knowledge of all the conditions and returns functions, except the set of events that determines the times of entry and choice $\{t_i\}$ of the agents. The observer thus "sees" the choice order as a binary sequence of *R* and *S* types with the property that an *R* or an *S* comes *n*th in the adoption line with equal likelihood, that is, with probability one half.

We now have a simple neoclassical allocation model where two types of agents choose between *A* and *B,* each agent choosing his preferred alternative when his time comes. The supply (or returns) functions are known, as is the demand (each agent demands one unit inelastically). Only one small element

5. More realistically, where the technologies have uncertain monetary returns we can assume von Neumann-Morgenstern agents, with Table 1 interpreted as the resulting determinate expected-utility payoffs.

is left open, and that is the set of historical events that determine the sequence in which the agents make their choice. Of interest is the adoption-share outcome in the different cases of constant, diminishing, and increasing returns, and whether the fluctuations in the order of choices these small events introduce make a difference to adoption shares.

We will need some properties. I will say that the process is: *predictable* if the small degree of uncertainty built in "averages away" so that the observer has enough information to pre-determine market shares accurately in the long-run; *flexible* (not locked-in) if a subsidy or tax adjustment to one of the technologies' returns can always influence future market choices; *ergodic* (not path-dependent) if different sequences of historical events lead to the same market outcome with probability one. In this allocation problem choices define a "path" or sequence of *A*—and *B*-technology versions that become adopted or "developed," with early adopters possibly steering the process onto a development path that is right for them, but one that may be regretted by later adopters. Accordingly, and in line with other sequential-choice problems, I will adopt a "no-regret" criterion and say that the process is *path-efficient* if at all times equal development (equal adoption) of the technology that is behind in adoption would not have paid off better.[6] (These informal definitions are made precise in the Appendix.)

Allocation in the Three Regimes

Before examining the outcome of choices in our *R* and *S* agent model, it is instructive to look at how the dynamics would run in a trivial example with increasing-returns where agents are of one type only (Table 2). Here choice order does not matter; agents are all the same; and unknown events can make no difference so that ergodicity is not an issue. The first agent chooses the more favourable technology, *A* say. This enhances the returns to adopting *A*. The next agent *a-fortiori* chooses *A* too. This continues, with *A* chosen each time, and *B* incapable of "getting started." The end result is that *A* "corners the market" and *B* is excluded. This outcome is trivially predictable, and path-efficient if returns rise at the same rate. Notice though that if returns increase at different rates, the adoption process may easily become path-inefficient, as Table 2 shows.

6. An alternative efficiency criterion might be total or aggregate payoff (after n choices). But in this problem we have two agent types with different preferences operating under the "greedy algorithm" of each agent taking the best choice at hand for himself; it is easy to show that under any returns regime maximisation of total payoffs is never guaranteed.

Table 2. AN EXAMPLE: ADOPTION PAYOFFS FOR HOMOGENEOUS AGENTS

Number of previous adoptions	0	10	20	30	40	50	60	70	80	90	100
Technology *A*	10	11	12	13	14	15	16	17	18	19	20
Technology *B*	4	7	10	13	16	19	22	25	28	31	34

In this case after thirty choices in the adoption process, all of which are *A*, equivalent adoption of *B* would have delivered higher returns. But if the process has gone far enough, a given subsidy-adjustment *g* to *B* can no longer close the gap between the returns to *A* and the returns to *B* at the starting point. Flexibility is not present here; the market becomes increasingly "locked-in" to an inferior choice.

Now let us return to the case of interest, where the unknown choice-sequence of two types of agents allows us to include some notion of historical "small events." Begin with the constant-returns case, and let $n_A(n)$ and $n_B(n)$ be the number of choices of *A* and *B* respectively, when *n* choices in total have been made. We can describe the process by x_n, the market share of *A* at stage *n*, when *n* choices in total have been made. We will write the difference in adoption, $n_A(n) - n_B(n)$ as d_n. The market share of *A* is then expressible as

$$x_n = 0{\cdot}5 + d_n / 2n. \qquad (1)$$

Note that through the variables d_n and *n*—the difference and total—we can fully describe the dynamics of adoption of *A* versus *B*. In this constant-returns situation *R*-agents always choose *A* and *S*-agents always choose *B*, regardless of the number of adopters of either technology. Thus the way in which adoption of *A* and *B* cumulates is determined simply by the sequence in which *R*- and *S*-agents "line up" to make their choice, $n_A(n)$ increasing by one unit if the next agent in line is an *R*, with $n_B(n)$ increasing by one unit if the next agent in line is an *S*, and with the difference in adoption, d_n, moving upward by one unit or downward one unit accordingly. To our observer, the choice-order is random, with agent types equally likely. Hence to him, the state d_n appears to perform a simple coin-toss gambler's random walk with each "move" having equal probability 0·5.

In the increasing-returns case, these simple dynamics are modified. New *R*-agents, who have a natural preference for *A*, will switch allegiance if by chance adoption pushes *B* far enough *ahead* of *A* in numbers and in payoff. That is, new *R*-agents will "switch" if

$$d_n = n_A(n) - n_B(n) < \Delta_R = \frac{(b_R - a_R)}{r}. \qquad (2)$$

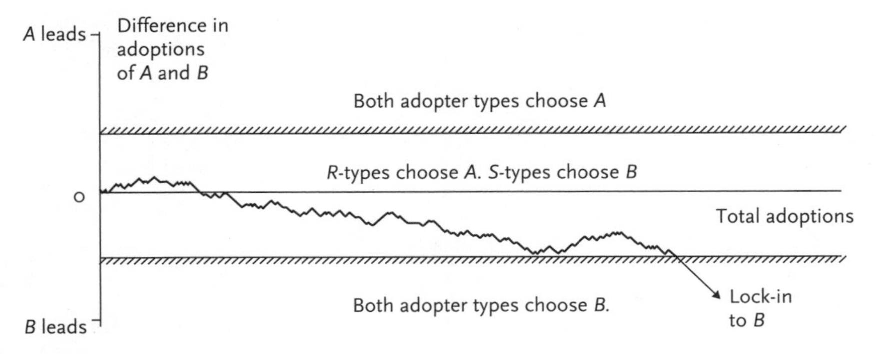

Figure 1:
Increasing returns adoption: a random walk with absorbing barriers.

Similarly new *S*-agents will switch preference to *A* if numbers adopting *A* become sufficiently ahead of the numbers adopting *B*, that is, if

$$d_n = n_A(n) - n_B(n) > \Delta_S = \frac{(b_S - a_S)}{s}. \tag{3}$$

Regions of choice now appear in the d_n, n plane (see Figure 1), with boundaries between them given by (2) and (3). Once one of the outer regions is entered, both agent types choose the same technology, with the result that this technology further increases its lead. Thus in the d_n, n plane (2) and (3) describe barriers that "absorb" the process. Once either is reached by random movement of d_n, the process ceases to involve both technologies—it is "locked-in" to one technology only. Under increasing returns then, the adoption process becomes a random walk with absorbing barriers. I leave it to the reader to show that the allocation process with diminishing returns appears to our observer as a random walk with *reflecting* barriers given by expressions similar to (2) and (3).

Properties of the Three Regimes

We can now use the elementary theory of random walks to derive the properties of this choice process under the different linear returns regimes. For convenient reference the results are summarized in Table 3.

To prove these properties, we need first to examine long-term adoption shares. Under constant returns, the market is shared. In this case the random walk ranges free, but we know from random walk theory that the standard deviation of d_n increases with $\sqrt{n}$. It follows that the $d_n/2n$ term in equation (1) disappears and that x_n tends to 0·5 (with probability one), so that the market is split 50-50. In the diminishing returns case, again the adoption market

Table 3. PROPERTIES OF THE THREE REGIMES

	Predictable	Flexible	Ergodic	Necessarily path-efficient
Constant returns	Yes	No	Yes	Yes
Diminishing returns	Yes	Yes	Yes	Yes
Increasing returns	No	No	No	No

is shared. The difference-in-adoption, d_n, is trapped between finite constants; hence $d_n/2n$ tends to zero as n goes to infinity, and x_n must approach 0·5. (Here the 50-50 market split results from the returns falling at the same rate.) In the increasing-returns-absorbing-barrier case, by contrast, the adoption share of A *must* eventually become zero or one. This is because in an absorbing random walk d_n eventually crosses a barrier with probability one. Therefore the two technologies cannot coexist indefinitely: one *must* exclude the other.

Predictability is therefore guaranteed where the returns are constant, or diminishing: in both cases a forecast that the market will settle to 50-50 will be correct, with probability one. In the increasing returns case, however, for accuracy the observer must predict A's eventual share either as 0 or 100%. But either choice will be wrong with probability one-half. Predictability is lost. Notice though that the observer *can* predict that one technology will take the market; theoretically he can also predict that it will be A with probability $s(a_R - b_R)/[s(a_R - b_R)+r(b_S - a_S)]$; but he cannot predict the actual market-share outcome with any accuracy—in spite of his knowledge of supply and demand conditions.

Flexibility in the constant-returns case is at best partial. Policy adjustments to the returns can affect choices at all times, but only if they are large enough to bridge the gap in preferences between technologies. In the two other regimes adjustments correspond to a shift of one or both of the barriers. In the diminishing-returns case, an adjustment g can always affect future choices (in absolute numbers, if not in market shares), because reflecting barriers continue to influence the process (with probability one) at times in the future. Therefore diminishing returns are flexible. Under increasing returns, however, once the process is absorbed into A and B, the subsidy or tax adjustment necessary to shift the barriers enough to influence choices (a precise index of the degree to which the system is "locked-in") increases without bound. Flexibility does not hold.

Ergodicity can be shown easily in the constant and diminishing returns cases. With constant returns only extraordinary line-ups (for example, twice as many R-agents as S-agents appearing indefinitely) with associated probability zero can cause deviation from 50-50. With diminishing returns, any sequence of historical events—any line-up of the agents—must still cause the process to remain between the reflecting barriers and drive the market to 50-50. Both cases forget their small-event history. In the increasing returns case the situation is quite different. Some proportion of agent sequences causes the market outcome to "tip" towards *A*, the remaining proportion causes it to "tip" towards *B*. (Extraordinary line-ups—say *S* followed by *R* followed by *S* followed by *R* and so on indefinitely—that could cause market sharing, have probability or measure zero.) Thus, the small events that determine $\{t_i\}$ *decide* the path of market shares; the process is non-ergodic or path-dependent—it is determined by its small-event history.

Path-efficiency is easy to prove in the constant—and diminishing-returns cases. Under constant-returns, previous adoptions do not affect pay-off. Each agent-type chooses its preferred technology and there is no gain foregone by the failure of the lagging technology to receive further development (further adoption). Under diminishing returns, if an agent chooses the technology that is ahead, he must prefer it to the available version of the lagging one. But further adoption of the lagging technology by definition lowers its payoff. Therefore there is no possibility of choices leading the adoption process down an inferior development path. Under increasing returns, by contrast, development of an inferior option can result. Suppose the market locks in to technology *A*. *R*-agents do not lose; but *S*-agents would each gain $(b_S - a_S)$ if their favoured technology *B* had been equally developed and available for choice. There is regret, at least for one agent type. Inefficiency can be exacerbated if the technologies improve at different rates. An early run of agent-types who prefer an initially attractive but slow-to-improve technology can lock the market in to this inferior option; equal development of the excluded technology in the long run would pay off better to both types.

Extensions, and the Rational Expectations Case

It is not difficult to extend this basic model in various directions. The same qualitative results hold for *M* technologies in competition, and for agent types in unequal proportions (here the random walk "drifts"). And if the technologies arrive in the market at different times, once again the dynamics go through as before, with the process now starting with initial n_A or n_B not at zero. Thus in practice an early-start technology may already be locked in, so that a new potentially-superior arrival cannot gain a footing.

Where agent numbers are finite, and not expanding indefinitely, absorption or reflection and the properties that depend on them still assert themselves providing agent numbers are large relative to the numerical width of the gap between switching barriers.

For technologies *sponsored* by firms, would the possibility of strategic action alter the outcomes just described? A complete answer is not yet known.

Hanson (1985) shows in a model based on the one above that again market exclusion goes through: firms engage in penetration pricing, taking losses early on in exchange for potential monopoly profits later, and all but one firm exit with probability one. Under strong discounting, however, firms may be more interested in immediate sales than in shutting rivals out, and market sharing can reappear.[7]

Perhaps the most interesting extension is the expectations case where agents' returns are affected by the choices of future agents. This happens for example with *standards,* where it is matters greatly whether later users fall in with one's own choice. Katz and Shapiro (1985, 1986) have shown, in a two-period case with strategic interaction, that agents' expectations about these future choices act to destabilise the market. We can extend their findings to our stochastic-dynamic model. Assume agents form expectations in the shape of beliefs about the type of stochastic process they find themselves in. When the *actual* stochastic process that results from these beliefs is identical with the *believed* stochastic process, we have a rational-expectations fulfilled-equilibrium process. In the Appendix, I show that under increasing returns, rational expectations also yield an absorbing random walk, but one where expectations of lock-in hasten lock-in, narrowing the absorption barriers and worsening the fundamental market instability.

II. A GENERAL FRAMEWORK

It would be useful to have an analytical framework that could accommodate sequential-choice problems with more general assumptions and returns mechanisms than the basic model above. In particular it would be useful to know under what circumstances a competing-technologies adoption market must end up dominated by a single technology.

In designing a general framework it seems important to preserve two properties: (*i*) That choices between alternative technologies may be affected by the numbers of each adopted at the time of choice; (*ii*) That small events "outside the model" may influence adoptions, so that randomness must be allowed for. Thus adoption market shares may determine not the next technology chosen directly but rather the *probability* of each technology's being chosen.

Consider then a dynamical system where one of K technologies is adopted each time an adoption choice is made, with probabilities $p_1(\mathbf{x}), p_2(\mathbf{x}), \ldots, p_K(\mathbf{x})$, respectively. This vector of probabilities $\mathbf{p}$ is a function of the vector $\mathbf{x},$ the adoption-shares of technologies 1 to $K,$ out of the total number n of adoptions

7. For similar findings see the literature on the dynamics of commodity competition under increasing returns (e.g. Spence, 1981; Fudenberg and Tirole, 1983).

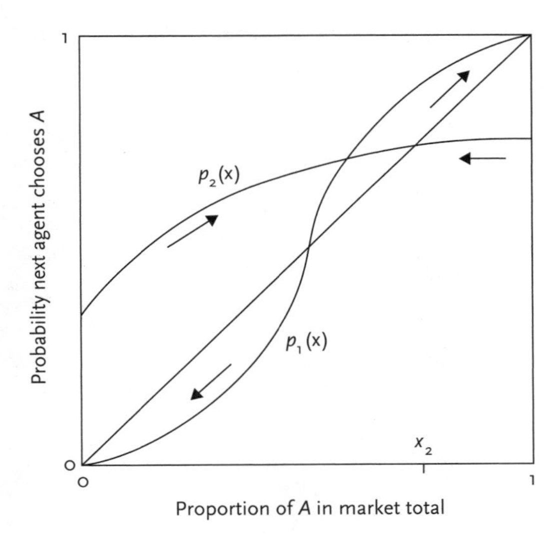

Figure 2:
Two illustrative adoption functions.

so far. The initial vector of proportions is given as $\mathbf{x}_0$. I will call $\mathbf{p(x)}$ the *adoption function.*

We may now ask what happens to the long run proportions or adoption shares in such a dynamical system. Consider the two different adoption functions in Figure 2, where $K = 2$. Now, where the probability of adoption of A is higher than its market share, in the adoption process A tends to increase in proportion; and where it is lower, A tends to decrease. If the proportions or adoption-shares settle down as total adoptions increase, we would conjecture that they settle down at a fixed point of the adoption function.

In 1983 Arthur, Ermoliev, and Kaniovski proved that under certain technical conditions (see the Appendix) this conjecture is true.[8] A stochastic process of this type converges with probability one to one of the fixed points of the mapping from proportions (adoption shares) to the probability of adoption. Not all fixed points are eligible. Only "attracting" or stable fixed points (ones that expected motions of the process lead towards) can emerge as the long run outcomes. And where the adoption function varies with time n, but tends to a limiting function $\mathbf{p}$, the process converges to an attracting fixed point of $\mathbf{p}$.

Thus in Figure 2 the possible long-run shares are 0 and 1 for the function p_1 and x_2 for the function p_2). Of course, where there are multiple fixed points, *which* one is chosen depends on the path taken by the process: it depends on the cumulation of random events that occur as the process unfolds.

8. See Arthur, Ermoliev, and Kaniovski (1987a) for a readable account of this work.

We now have a general framework that immediately yields two useful theorems on path-dependence and single-technology dominance.

THEOREM I. *An adoption process is non-ergodic and non-predictable if and only if its adoption function* $\mathbf{p}$ *possesses multiple stable fixed points.*

THEOREM II. *An adoption process converges with probability one to the dominance of a single technology if and only if its adoption function* $\mathbf{p}$ *possesses stable fixed points only where* $\mathbf{x}$ *is a unit vector.*

These theorems follow as simple corollaries of the basic theorem above. Thus where two technologies compete, the adoption process will be path-dependent (multiple fixed points must exist) as long as there exists at least one unstable "watershed" point in adoption shares, above which adoption of the technology with this share becomes self-reinforcing in that it tends to increase its share, below which it is self-negating in that it tends to lose its share. It is therefore not sufficient that a technology gain advantage with adoption; the advantage must (at some market share) be self-reinforcing (see Arthur, 1988).

Non-Linear Increasing Returns with a Continuum of Adopter Types

Consider, as an example, a more general version of the basic model above, with a continuum of adopter types rather than just two, choosing between K technologies, with possibly non-linear improvements in payoffs. Assume that if n_j previous adopters have chosen technology j previously, the next agent's payoff to adopting j is $\Pi_j(n_j) = a_j + r(n_j)$ where a_j represents the agent's "natural preference" for technology j and the monotonically increasing function r represents the technological improvement that comes with previous adoptions. Each adopter has a vector of natural preferences $\mathbf{a} = (a_1, a_2, \ldots, a_K)$ for the K alternatives, and we can think of the continuum of agents as a distribution of points $\mathbf{a}$ (with bounded support) on the positive orthant. We assume an adopter is drawn at random from this probability distribution each time a choice occurs. Dominance of a single technology j corresponds to positive probability of the distribution of payoffs Π being driven by adoptions to a point where Π_j exceeds Π_i for all $i \neq j$.

The Arthur-Ermoliev-Kaniovski theorem above allows us to derive:

THEOREM III. *If the improvement function r increases at least at rate* ε *as* n_j *increases, the adoption process converges to the dominance of a single technology, with probability one.*

Proof. In this case, the adoption function varies with total adoptions n. (We do not need to derive it explicitly, however.) It is not difficult to establish that as n

becomes large: (i) At any point in the neighbourhood of any unit vector of adoption shares, unbounded increasing returns cause the corresponding technology to dominate *all* choices; therefore the unit-vector shares are stable fixed points. (ii) The equal-share point is also a fixed point, but unstable. (iii) No other point is a fixed point. Therefore, by the general theorem, since the limiting adoption function has stable fixed points only at unit vectors the process converges to one of these with probability one. Long-run dominance by a single technology is assured. ■

Dominance by a single technology is no longer inevitable, however, if the improvement function r is bounded, as when learning effects become exhausted. This is because certain sequences of adopter types could bid improvements for two or more technologies upward more or less in concert. These technologies could then reach the upper bound of r together, so that none of these would dominate and the market would remain shared from then on. Under other adopter sequences, by contrast, one of the technologies may reach the upper bound sufficiently fast to shut the others out. Thus, in the bounded case, some event histories dynamically lead to a shared market; other event histories lead to dominance. Increasing returns, if they are bounded, are in general *not* sufficient to guarantee eventual monopoly by a single technology.

III. REMARKS

(1) To what degree might the actual economy be locked-in to inferior technology paths? As yet we do not know. Certainly it is easy to find cases where an early-established technology becomes dominant, so that later, superior alternatives cannot gain a footing.[9] Two important studies of historical events leading to lock-ins have now been carried out: on the QWERTY typewriter keyboard (David, 1985); and on alternating current (David and Bunn, 1987). (In both cases increasing returns arise mainly from coordination externalities.)

Promising empirical cases that may reflect lock-in through learning are the nuclear-reactor technology competition of the 1950s and 1960s and the US steam-versus-petrol car competition in the 1890s. The US nuclear industry is practically 100% dominated by light-water reactors. These reactors were originally adapted from a highly compact unit designed to propel the first nuclear

9. Examples might be the narrow gauge of British railways (Kindleberger, 1983); the US colour television system; the 1950s programming language FORTRAN; and of course the QWERTY keyboard (Arthur, 1984; David, 1985; Hartwick, 1985). In these particular cases the source of increasing returns is network externalities, however, rather than learning effects. Breaking out of locked-in technological standards has been investigated by Farrell and Saloner (1985, 1986).

submarine, the U.S.S. *Nautilus,* launched in 1954. A series of circumstances—among them the Navy's role in early construction contracts, political expediency, the Euratom programme, and the behaviour of key personages—acted to favour light water. Learning and construction experience gained early on appear to have locked the industry in to dominance of light water and shut other reactor types out (Bupp and Darian, 1978; Cowan, 1987). Yet much of the engineering literature contends that, given equal development, the gas-cooled reactor would have been superior (see Agnew, 1981). In the petrol-versus-steam car case, two different developer types with predilections toward steam or petrol depending on their previous mechanical experience, entered the industry at varying times and built upon on the best available versions of each technology. Initially petrol was held to be the less promising option: it was explosive, noisy, hard to obtain in the right grade, and it required complicated new parts.[10] But in the United States a series of trivial circumstances (McLaughlin, 1954; Arthur, 1984) pushed several key developers into petrol just before the turn of the century and by 1920 had acted to shut steam out. Whether steam might have been superior given equal development is still in dispute among engineers (see Burton, 1976; Strack, 1970).

(2) The argument of this paper suggests that the interpretation of economic history should be different in different returns regimes. Under constant and diminishing returns, the evolution of the market reflects only a-priori endowments, preferences, and transformation possibilities; small events cannot sway the outcome. But while this is comforting, it reduces history to the status of mere carrier—the deliverer of the inevitable. Under increasing returns, by contrast many outcomes are possible. Insignificant circumstances become magnified by positive feedbacks to "tip" the system into the actual outcome "selected." The small events of history become important[11] Where we observe the predominance of one technology or one economic outcome over its competitors we should thus be cautious of any exercise that seeks the means by which the winner's innate "superiority" came to be translated into adoption.

(3) The usual policy of letting the superior technology reveal itself in the outcome that dominates is appropriate in the constant- and diminishing-returns cases. But in the increasing-returns case laissez-faire gives no guarantee that the "superior" technology (in the long-run sense) will be the one that survives. Effective policy in the (unsponsored) increasing-returns case would be predicated on the nature of the market breakdown: in our model early adopters impose externalities on later ones by rationally choosing technologies to suit

10. Amusingly, Fletcher (1904) writes: "...unless the objectionable features of the petrol carriage can be removed, it is bound to be driven from the road by its less objectionable rival, the steam-driven vehicle of the day."

11. For earlier recognition of the significance of both non-convexity and path-dependence for economic history see David (1975).

only themselves; missing is an inter-agent market to induce them to explore promising but costly infant technologies that might pay off handsomely to later adopters.[12] The standard remedy of assigning to early developers (patent) rights of compensation by later users would be effective here only to the degree that early developers can appropriate later payoffs. As an alternative, a central authority could underwrite adoption and exploration along promising but less popular technological paths. But where eventual returns to a technology are hard to ascertain—as in the U.S. Strategic Defence Initiative case for example—the authority then faces a classic multi-arm bandit problem of choosing which technologies to bet on. An early run of disappointing results (low "jackpots") from a potentially superior technology may cause it perfectly rationally to abandon this technology in favour of other possibilities. The fundamental problem of possibly locking-in a regrettable course of development remains (Cowan, 1987).

IV. CONCLUSION

This paper has attempted to go beyond the usual static analysis of increasing-returns problems by examining the dynamical process that "selects" an equilibrium from multiple candidates, by the interaction of economic forces and random "historical events." It shows how dynamically, increasing returns can cause the economy gradually to lock itself in to an outcome not necessarily superior to alternatives, not easily altered, and not entirely predictable in advance.

Under increasing returns, competition between economic objects—in this case technologies—takes on an evolutionary character, with a "founder effect" mechanism akin to that in genetics.[13] "History" becomes important. To the degree that the technological development of the economy depends upon small events beneath the resolution of an observer's model, it may become impossible to predict market shares with any degree of certainty. This suggests that there may be theoretical limits, as well as practical ones, to the predictability of the economic future.

Stanford University

Date of receipt of final typescript: May 1988

12. Competition between *sponsored* technologies suffers less from this missing market. Sponsoring firms can more easily appropriate later payoffs, so they have an incentive to develop initially costly, but promising technologies. And financial markets for sponsoring investors together with insurance markets for adopters who may make the "wrong" choice, mitigate losses for the risk-averse. Of course, if a product succeeds and locks-in the market, monopoly-pricing problems may arise. For further remarks on policy see David (1987).
13. For other selection mechanisms affecting technologies see Dosi (1988), Dosi et al. (1988), and Metcalfe (1985).

APPENDIX A

A. DEFINITIONS OF THE PROPERTIES

Here I define precisely the properties used above. Denote the market share of A after n choices as x_n. The allocation process is:

(i) *predictable* if the observer can *ex-ante* construct a forecasting sequence $\{x_n^*\}$ with the property that $|x_n - x_n^*| \to 0$, with probability one, as $n \to \infty$;

(ii) *flexible* if a given marginal adjustment g to the technologies' returns can alter future choices;

(iii) *ergodic* if, given two samples from the observer's set of possible historical events, $\{t_i\}$ and $\{t'_i\}$, with corresponding time-paths $\{x_n\}$ and $\{x'_n\}$, then $|x'_n - x_n| \to 0$, with probability one, as $n \to \infty$;

(iv) *path-efficient* if, whenever an agent chooses the more-adopted technology α, versions of the lagging technology β would not have delivered more had they been developed and available for adoption. That is, path-efficiency holds if returns Π remain such that $\Pi_\alpha(m) \geq \mathrm{Max}_j\{\Pi_\beta(j)\}$ for $k \leq j \leq m$, where there have been m previous choices of the leading technology and k of the lagging one.

B. THE EXPECTATIONS CASE

Consider here the competing standards case where adopters are affected by *future* choices as well as past choices. Assume in our earlier model that R-agents receive additional net benefits of Π_A^R, Π_B^R, if the process locks-in to their choice, A or B respectively; similarly S-agents receive Π_A^S, Π_B^S. (Technologies improve with adoption as before.) Assume that agents know the state of the market (n_A, n_B) when choosing and that they have expectations or beliefs that adoptions follow a stochastic process Ω. They choose rationally under these expectations, so that actual adoptions follow the process $\Gamma(\Omega)$. This actual process is a *rational expectations equilibrium process* when it bears out the expected process, that is, when $\Gamma(\Omega) \equiv \Omega$.

We can distinguish two cases, corresponding to the degree of heterogeneity of preferences in the market.

Case (i). Suppose initially that $a_R - b_R > \Pi_B^R$ and $b_S - a_S > \Pi_A^S$ and that R and S-types have beliefs that the adoption process is a random walk Ω with absorption barriers at Δ'_R, Δ'_S, with associated probabilities of lock-in to

A, $P(n_A, n_B)$ and lock-in to B, $1 - P(n_A, n_B)$. Under these beliefs, R-type expected payoffs for choosing A or B are, respectively:

$$a_R + rn_A + P(n_A, n_B)\Pi_A^R \tag{4}$$

$$b_R + rn_B + [1 - P(n_A, n_B)]\Pi_B^R. \tag{5}$$

S-type payoffs may be written similarly. In the actual process R-types will switch to B when n_A and n_B are such that these two expressions become equal. Both types choose B from then on. The actual probability of lock-in to A is zero here; so that if the expected process is fulfilled, P is also zero here and we have n_A and n_B such that

$$a_R + rn_A = b_R + rn_B + \Pi_B^R$$

with associated barrier given by

$$\Delta_R = n_A - n_B = -(a_R - b_R - \Pi_B^R)/r. \tag{6}$$

Similarly S-types switch to A at boundary position given by

$$\Delta_S = n_A - n_B = (b_S - a_S - \Pi_A^S)/s. \tag{7}$$

It is easy to confirm that beyond these barriers the actual process is indeed locked in to A or to B and that within them R-agents prefer A, and S-agents prefer B. Thus if agents believe the adoption process is a random walk with absorbing barriers Δ'_R, Δ'_S given by (6) and (7), these beliefs will be fulfilled, and this random walk will be a rational expectations equilibrium.

Case (ii). Suppose now that $a_R - b_R < \Pi_B^R$ and $b_S - a_S < \Pi_A^S$. Then (4) and (5) show that switching will occur immediately if agents hold expectations that the system will definitely lock-in to A or to B. These expectations become self-fulfilling and the absorbing barriers narrow to zero. Similarly, when non-improving standards compete, so that r and s are zero, in this case again beliefs that A or B will definitely lock-in become self-fulfilling.

Taking cases (i) and (ii) together, expectations either narrow or collapse the switching boundaries. They exacerbate the fundamental market instability.

C. THE PATH-DEPENDENT STRONG-LAW THEOREM

Consider a dependent-increment stochastic process that starts with an initial vector of units $\mathbf{b}_0$, in the K categories, 1 through K. At each event-time a unit is added to one of the categories 1 through K, with probabilities $\mathbf{p} = [p_1(x), p_2(x), \ldots, p_K(x)]$, respectively. (The Borel function $\mathbf{p}$ maps the unit simplex of proportions S^K into the unit simplex of probabilities S^K.) The process is iterated to yield the vectors of proportions $\mathbf{X}_1, \mathbf{X}_2, \mathbf{X}_3, \ldots$.

THEOREM. Arthur, Ermoliev, and Kaniovski (1983, 1986)

(i) Suppose $p: S^K \rightarrow S^K$ is continuous, and suppose the function $p(x) - x$ possesses a Lyapunov function (that is, a positive, twice-differentiable function V with inner product $\langle [p(x) - x], V_x \rangle$ negative). Suppose also that the set of fixed points of p, $B = \{x: p(x) = x\}$ has a finite number of connected components. Then the vector of proportions $\{X_n\}$ converges, with probability one, to a point z in the set of fixed points B, or to the border of a connected component.
(ii) Suppose p maps the interior of the unit simplex into itself, and that z is a stable point (as defined in the conventional way). Then the process has limit point z with positive probability.
(iii) Suppose z is a non-vertex unstable point of p. Then the process cannot converge to z with positive probability.
(iv) Suppose probabilities of addition vary with time n, and the sequence $\{p_n\}$ converges to a limiting function p faster than $1/n$ converges to zero. Then the above statements hold for the limiting function p. That is, if the above conditions are fulfilled, the process converges with probability one to one of the stable fixed points of the limiting function p.

The theorem is extended to non-continuous functions p and to non-unit and random increments in Arthur, Ermoliev and Kaniovski (1987*b*). For the case $K = 2$ with p stationary see the elegant analysis of Hill et al. (1980).

REFERENCES

Agnew, H. (1981). "Gas-cooled nuclear power reactors." *Scientific American*, vol. 244, pp. 55–63.

Arthur, W. B. (1983). "Competing technologies and lock-in by historical small events: the dynamics of allocation under increasing returns." International Institute for Applied Systems Analysis Paper WP-83-92, Laxenburg, Austria. (Center for Economic Policy Research, Paper 43, Stanford).

Arthur, W. B. (1984). "Competing technologies and economic prediction." *Options*, International Institute for Applied Systems Analysis, Laxenburg, Austria. No. 1984/2, pp. 10–13.

Arthur, W. B., Ermoliev, Yu, and Kaniovski, Yu. (1983). "On generalized urn schemes of the polya kind." *Kibernetika*, vol. 19, pp. 49–56. English translation in *Cybernetics*, vol. 19, pp. 61–71.

Arthur, W. B., Ermoliev, Yu, and Kaniovski, Yu. (1986). "Strong laws for a class of path-dependent urn processes." In *Proceedings of the International Conference on Stochastic Optimization, Kiev 1984*, Springer Lecture Notes Control and Information Sciences, vol. 81, pp. 187–300.

Arthur, W. B., Ermoliev, Yu, and Kaniovski, Yu. (1987*a*). "Path-dependent processes and the emergence of macro-structure." *European Journal of Operational Research*, vol. 30, pp. 294–303.

Arthur, W. B., Ermoliev, Yu, and Kaniovski, Yu. (1987*b*). "Non-linear urn processes: asymptotic behavior and applications." International Institute for Applied Systems Analysis. Paper WP-87-85, Laxenburg, Austria.

Arthur, W. B., Ermoliev, Yu, and Kaniovski, Yu. (1988). "Self-reinforcing mechanisms in economics." In *The Economy as an Evolving Complex System* (P. Anderson, K. Arrow, and D. Pines (eds)). Reading, Massachusetts: Addison–Wesley.

Atkinson, A. and Stiglitz, J. (1969). "A new view of technical change." Economic Journal, vol. 79, pp. 573–580.

Balcer, Y., and Lippman, S. (1984). "Technological expectations and the adoption of improved technology," *Journal of Economic Theory*, vol. 34, pp. 292–318.

Bupp, I., and Derian, J. (1978). *Light Water: How The Nuclear Dream Dissolved.* New York: Basic.

Burton, R. (1976). "Recent advances in vehicular steam engine efficiency." Society of Automotive Engineers, Preprint 760340.

Cowan, R. (1987). "Backing the wrong horse: sequential choice among technologies of unknown merit." Ph.D. Dissertation, Stanford.

David, P. (1975). *Technical Choice, Innovation, and Economic Growth.* Cambridge: Cambridge University Press.

David, P. (1985). "Clio and the economics of QWERTY." *American Economic Review Proceedings*, vol. 75, pp. 332–337.

David, P. (1987). "Some new standards for the economics of standardization in the information age." In *Economic Policy and Technological Performance,* (P. Dasgupta and P. Stoneman, eds.) Cambridge: Cambridge University Press.

David, P., and Bunn, J. (1987). "The economics of gateway technologies and network evolution: lessons from electricity supply history." Centre for Economic Policy Research, Paper 119, Stanford.

Dosi, G. (1988). "Sources, procedures and microeconomic effects of innovation." *Journal of Economic Literature*, vol. 26, pp. 1120–1171.

Dosi, G., Freeman, C., Nelson, R., Silverberg, G. and Soete, L. (eds.) (1988). *Technical Change and Economic Theory,* London: Pinter.
Farrell, J., and Saloner, G. (1985). "Standardization, compatibility, and innovation." *Rand Journal of Economics*, vol. 16, pp. 70–83.
Farrell, J., and Saloner, G. (1986). "Installed base and compatibility: innovation, product preannouncements and predation." *American Economic Review*, vol. 76. pp. 940–955.
Fletcher, W. (1904). *English and American Steam Carriages and Traction Engines* (reprinted 1973). Newton Abbot: David and Charles.
Fudenberg, D., and Tirole, J. (1983). "Learning by doing and market performance." *Bell Journal of Economics*, vol. 14, pp. 522–530.
Hanson, W. (1985). "Bandwagons and orphans: dynamic pricing of competing systems subject to decreasing costs." Ph.D. Dissertation, Stanford.
Hartwick, J. (1985). "The persistence of QWERTY and analogous suboptimal standards." Mimeo, Queen's University, Kingston, Ontario.
Hill, B., Lane, D. and Sudderth, W. (1980). "A strong law for some generalized urn processes." *Annals of Probability*, vol. 8, pp. 214–226.
Katz, M., and Shapiro, C. (1985). "Network externalities, competition, and compatibility." *American Economic Review*, vol. 75, pp. 424–440.
Katz, M., and Shapiro, C. (1986). "Technology adoption in the presence of network externalities." *Journal of Political Economy*, vol. 94, pp. 822–841.
Kindleberger, C. (1983). "Standards as public, collective and private goods." *Kyklos*, vol. 36, pp. 377–396.
Mamer, J., and McCardle, K. (1987). "Uncertainty, competition and the adoption of new technology." *Management Science*, vol. 33, pp. 161–177.
McLaughlin, C. (1954). "The Stanley Steamer: a study in unsuccessful innovation." *Explorations in Entrepreneurial History*, vol. 7, pp. 37–47.
Metcalfe, J. S. (1985). "On technological competition." Mimeo, University of Manchester.
Rosenberg, N. (1982). *Inside the Black Box: Technology and Economics.* Cambridge: Cambridge University Press.
Strack, W. (1970). *"Condensers and Boilers for Steam-powered Cars."* NASA Technical Note, TN D-5813, Washington, D.C.
Spence, A. M. (1981). "The learning curve and competition." *Bell Journal of Economics*, vol. 12, pp. 49–70.

CHAPTER 5
Process and Emergence in the Economy

W. BRIAN ARTHUR, STEVEN N. DURLAUF,
AND DAVID A. LANE*

This paper written in 1997 is as close as our Economics Program at the Santa Fe Institute came to a manifesto. It bears the unmistakable stamp of my two co-authors, Steven Durlauf and David Lane, both of whom have given considerable thought over the years to complexity and economics.

We argue that the economy consists of heterogeneous agents acting in parallel and responding to the aggregate states they together co-create. In doing so they continually adapt to a perpetually changing world in which there is no global controller, a world in which human cognition, hierarchy, and interaction are important. The economy, we argue, shows all the hallmarks of complexity. The paper was an introduction to the volume *The Economy as an Evolving Complex System II*, W. B. Arthur, S. Durlauf, D. Lane (Eds.), SFI Studies in the Sciences of Complexity, Vol. XXVII, Addison-Wesley, 1–14, 1997. The papers in this 1997 volume give a good idea of the state of the complexity approach at that time.

In September 1987, twenty people came together at the Santa Fe Institute to talk about "the economy as an evolving, complex system." Ten were theoretical economists, invited by Kenneth J. Arrow, and ten were physicists, biologists, and computer scientists, invited by Philip W. Anderson. The meeting was motivated by the hope that new ideas bubbling in the natural sciences, loosely tied together under the rubric of "the sciences of complexity," might stimulate new ways of thinking about economic problems. For ten days, economists

* Arthur is Citibank Professor, Santa Fe Institute; Durlauf is with the Department of Economics, University of Wisconsin at Madison, and the Santa Fe Institute; and Lane is with the Department of Political Economy, University of Modena.

and natural scientists took turns talking about their respective worlds and methodologies. While physicists grappled with general equilibrium analysis and noncooperative game theory, economists tried to make sense of spin glass models, Boolean networks, and genetic algorithms.

The meeting left two legacies. The first was a volume of essays, *The Economy as an Evolving Complex System,* edited by Arrow, Anderson, and David Pines. The other was the founding, in 1988, of the Economics Program at the Santa Fe Institute, the Institute's first resident research program. The Program's mission was to encourage the understanding of economic phenomena from a complexity perspective, which involved the development of theory as well as tools for modeling and for empirical analysis. To this end, since 1988, the Program has brought researchers to Santa Fe, sponsored research projects, held several workshops each year, and published several dozen working papers. And, since 1994, it has held an annual summer school for economics graduate students.

This volume, *The Economy as an Evolving Complex System II,* represents the proceedings of an August 1996 workshop sponsored by the SFI Economics Program. The intention of this workshop was to take stock, to ask: What has the complexity perspective contributed to economics in the past decade? In contrast to the 1987 workshop, almost all of the presentations addressed economic problems, and most participants were economists by training. In addition, while some of the work presented was conceived or carried out at the Institute, some of the participants had no previous relation with SFI—research related to the complexity perspective is under active development now in a number of different institutes and university departments.

But just what *is* the complexity perspective in economics? That is not an easy question to answer. Its meaning is still very much under construction, and, in fact, the present volume is intended to contribute to that construction process. Indeed, the authors of the essays in this volume by no means share a single, coherent vision of the meaning and significance of complexity in economics. What we will find instead is a family resemblance, based upon a set of interrelated themes that together constitute the current meaning of the complexity perspective in economics.

Several of these themes, already active subjects of research by economists in the mid-1980s, are well described in the earlier *The Economy as an Evolving Complex System*: In particular, applications of nonlinear dynamics to economic theory and data analysis, surveyed in the 1987 meeting by Michele Boldrin and William Brock; and the theory of positive feedback and its associated phenomenology of path dependence and lock-in, discussed by W. Brian Arthur. Research related to both these themes has flourished since 1987, both in and outside the SFI Economics Program. While chaos has been displaced from its place in 1987 at center stage of the interest in nonlinear dynamics, in the last decade economists have made substantial progress in identifying patterns of nonlinearity in financial time series and in proposing models that both offer explanations for these patterns and help to analyze and, to some extent, predict the series in which they are displayed. Brock surveys both these developments in his chapter in this volume, while positive feedback plays a central role in the models analyzed by Lane (on information contagion), Durlauf (on inequality) and Krugman (on economic geography), and lurk just under the surface of the phenomena described by North (development) and Leijonhufvud (high inflation).

Looking back over the developments in the past decade and the papers produced by the program, we believe that a coherent perspective—sometimes called the "Santa Fe approach"—has emerged within economics. We will call this the complexity perspective, or Santa Fe perspective, or occasionally the process-and-emergence perspective. Before we describe this, we first sketch the two conceptions of the economy that underlie standard, neoclassical economics (and indeed most of the presentations by economic theorists at the earlier 1987 meeting). We can call these conceptions the "equilibrium" and "dynamical systems" approaches. In the equilibrium approach, the problem of interest is to derive, from the rational choices of individual optimizers, aggregate-level "states of the economy" (prices in general equilibrium analysis, a set of strategy assignments in game theory with associated payoffs) that satisfy some aggregate-level consistency condition (market-clearing, Nash equilibrium), and to examine the properties of these aggregate-level states. In the dynamical systems approach, the state of the economy is represented by a set of variables, and a system of difference equations or differential equations describes how these variables change over time. The problem is to examine the resulting trajectories, mapped over the state space. However, the equilibrium approach does not describe the *mechanism* whereby the state of the economy changes over time—nor indeed how an equilibrium comes into being.[1] And the dynamical system approach generally fails to accommodate the distinction between *agent*- and *aggregate*-levels (except by obscuring it through the device of "representative agents"). Neither accounts for the emergence of new kinds of relevant state variables, much less new entities, new patterns, new structures.[2]

1. Since an a priori intertemporal equilibrium hardly counts as a mechanism.

2. Norman Packard's contribution to the 1987 meeting addresses just this problem with respect to the dynamical systems approach. As he points out, "if the set of relevant variables changes with time, then the state space is itself changing with time, which is not commensurate with a conventional dynamical systems model."

To describe the complexity approach, we begin by pointing out six features of the economy that together present difficulties for the traditional mathematics used in economics:[3]

DISPERSED INTERACTION. What happens in the economy is determined by the interaction of many dispersed, possibly heterogeneous, agents acting in parallel. The action of any given agent depends upon the anticipated actions of a limited number of other agents and on the aggregate state these agents cocreate.

NO GLOBAL CONTROLLER. No global entity controls interactions. Instead, controls are provided by mechanisms of competition and coordination among agents. Economic actions are mediated by legal institutions, assigned roles, and shifting associations. Nor is there a universal competitor—a single agent that can exploit all opportunities in the economy.

CROSS-CUTTING HIERARCHICAL ORGANIZATION. The economy has many levels of organization and interaction. Units at any given level—behaviors, actions, strategies, products—typically serve as "building blocks" for constructing units at the next higher level. The overall organization is more than hierarchical, with many sorts of tangled interactions (associations, channels of communication) across levels.

CONTINUAL ADAPTATION. Behaviors, actions, strategies, and products are revised continually as the individual agents accumulate experience—the system constantly adapts.

PERPETUAL NOVELTY. Niches are continually created by new markets, new technologies, new behaviors, new institutions. The very act of filling a niche may provide new niches. The result is ongoing, perpetual novelty.

OUT-OF-EQUILIBRIUM DYNAMICS. Because new niches, new potentials, new possibilities, are continually created, the economy operates far from any optimum or global equilibrium. Improvements are always possible and indeed occur regularly.

Systems with these properties have come to be called *adaptive nonlinear networks* (the term is John Holland's[5]). There are many such in nature and society: nervous systems, immune systems, ecologies, as well as economies. An essential element of adaptive nonlinear networks is that they do not act simply in terms of stimulus and response. Instead they anticipate. In

3. John Holland's paper at the 1987 meeting beautifully—and presciently—frames these features. For an early description of the Santa Fe approach, see also the program's March 1989 newsletter, "Emergent Structures."

particular, economic agents form expectations—they build up models of the economy and act on the basis of predictions generated by these models. These anticipative models need neither be explicit, nor coherent, nor even mutually consistent.

Because of the difficulties outlined above, the mathematical tools economists customarily use, which exploit linearity, fixed points, and systems of differential equations, cannot provide a deep understanding of adaptive nonlinear networks. Instead, what is needed are new classes of combinatorial mathematics and population-level stochastic processes, in conjunction with computer modeling. These mathematical and computational techniques are in their infancy. But they emphasize the *discovery* of structure and the *processes* through which structure *emerges* across different levels of organization.

This conception of the economy as an adaptive nonlinear network—as an evolving, complex system—has profound implications for the foundations of economic theory and for the way in which theoretical problems are cast and solved. We interpret these implications as follows:

COGNITIVE FOUNDATIONS. Neoclassical economic theory has a unitary cognitive foundation: economic agents are rational optimizers. This means that (in the usual interpretation) agents evaluate uncertainty probabilistically, revise their evaluations in the light of new information via Bayesian updating, and choose the course of action that maximizes their expected utility. As glosses on this unitary foundation, agents are generally assumed to have common knowledge about each other and rational expectations about the world they inhabit (and of course cocreate). In contrast, the Santa Fe viewpoint is pluralistic. Following modern cognitive theory, we posit no single, dominant mode of cognitive processing. Rather, we see agents as having to cognitively structure the problems they face—as having to "make sense" of their problems—as much as solve them. And they have to do this with cognitive resources that are limited. To "make sense," to learn, and to adapt, agents use variety of distributed cognitive processes. The very categories agents use to convert information about the world into action emerge from experience, and these categories or cognitive props need not fit together coherently in order to generate effective actions. Agents therefore inhabit a world that they must cognitively interpret—one that is complicated by the presence and actions of other agents and that is ever changing. It follows that agents generally do not optimize in the standard sense, not because they are constrained by finite memory or processing capability, but because the very concept of an optimal course of action often cannot be defined. It further follows that the deductive rationality of neoclassical economic agents occupies at best a marginal position in guiding effective action in the world. And it follows that any "common knowledge" agents might have about one another must be attained from concrete, specified cognitive processes operating on experiences obtained through concrete interactions. Common knowledge cannot simply be assumed into existence.

STRUCTURAL FOUNDATIONS. In general equilibrium analysis, agents do not interact with one another directly, but only through impersonal markets. By contrast, in game theory all players interact with all other players, with outcomes specified by the game's payoff matrix. So interaction structures are simple and often extreme—one-with-all or all-with-all. Moreover, the internal structure of the agents themselves is abstracted away.[4] In contrast, from a complexity perspective, structure matters. First, network-based structures become important. All economic action involves interactions among agents, so economic functionality is both constrained and carried by networks defined by recurring patterns of interaction among agents. These network structures are characterized by relatively sparse ties. Second, economic action is structured by emergent social roles and by socially supported procedures—that is, by institutions. Third, economic entities have a recursive structure: they are themselves comprised of entities. The resulting "level" structure of entities and their associated action processes is not strictly hierarchical, in that component entities may be part of more than one higher-level entity, and entities at multiple levels of organization may interact. Thus, reciprocal causation operates between different levels of organization—while action processes at a given level of organization may sometimes by viewed as autonomous, they are nonetheless constrained by action patterns and entity structures at other levels. And they may even give rise to new patterns and entities at both higher and lower levels. From the Santa Fe perspective, the fundamental principle of organization is the idea that units at one level combine to produce units at the next higher level.[5]

PROCESS AND EMERGENCE. It should be clear by now that exclusively posing economic problems as multiagent optimization exercises makes little sense from the viewpoint we are outlining—a viewpoint that puts emphasis on process, not just outcome. In particular, it asks how new "things" arise in the world—cognitive things, like "internal models;" physical things, like "new technologies;" social things, like new kinds of economic "units." And it is clear that if we posit a world of perpetual novelty, then outcomes cannot correspond to steady-state equilibria, whether Walrasian, Nash, or dynamic-systems-theoretical. The only descriptions that can matter in such a world are about transient phenomena—about process and about emergent structures. What then can we know about the economy from a

4. Except in principal-agent theory or transaction-costs economics, where a simple hierarchical structure is supposed to obtain.

5. We need not commit ourselves to what constitutes economic "units" and "levels." This will vary from problem context to problem context.

process-and-emergence viewpoint, and how can we come to know it? Studying process and emergence in the economy has spawned a growth industry in the production of what are now generally called "agent-based models." And what counts as a solution in an agent-based model is currently under negotiation. Many of the papers in this volume—including those by Arthur et al., Darley and Kauffman, Shubik, Lindgren, Kollman et al., Kirman, and Tesfatsion—address this issue, explicitly or implicitly. We can characterize these as seeking emergent structures arising in interaction processes, in which the interacting entities anticipate the future through cognitive procedures that themselves involve interactions taking place in multilevel structures.

A description of an approach to economics, however, is not a research program. To build a research program around a process-and-emergence perspective, two things have to happen. First, concrete economic problems have to be identified for which the approach may provide new insights. A number of candidates are offered in this volume: artifact innovation (Lane and Maxfield), the evolution of trading networks (Ioannides, Kirman, and Tesfatsion), money (Shubik), the origin and spatial distribution of cities (Krugman), asset pricing (Arthur et al. and Brock), high inflation (Leijonhufvud), and persistent differences in income between different neighborhoods or countries (Durlauf). Second, cognitive and structural foundations for modeling these problems have to be constructed and methods developed for relating theories based on these foundations to observable phenomena (Manski). Here, while substantial progress has been made since 1987, the program is far from complete.

The essays in this volume describe a series of parallel explorations of the central themes of process and emergence in an interactive world—of how to study systems capable of generating perpetual novelty. These explorations do not form a coherent whole. They are sometimes complementary, sometimes even partially contradictory. But what could be more appropriate to the Santa Fe perspective, with its emphasis on distributed processes, emergence, and self-organization? Here are our interpretations of the research directions that seem to be emerging from this process:

COGNITION. The central cognitive issues raised in this volume are ones of interpretation. As Shubik puts it, "the interpretation of data is critical. It is not what the numbers are, but what they mean." How do agents render their world comprehensible enough so that "information" has meaning? The two papers by Arthur, Holland, LeBaron, Palmer, and Tayler and by Darley and Kauffman consider this. They explore problems in which a group of agents take actions whose effects depend on what the other agents do. The agents base their actions on expectations they generate about how other agents will behave. Where do these expectations come from? Both papers reject common knowledge or common expectations as a starting point. Indeed, Arthur et al.

argue that common beliefs cannot be deduced. Because agents must derive their expectations from an imagined future that is the aggregate result of other agents' expectations, there is a self-reference of expectations that leads to deductive indeterminacy. Rather, both papers suppose that each agent has access to a variety of "interpretative devices" that single out particular elements in the world as meaningful and suggest useful actions on the basis of the "information" these elements convey. Agents keep track of how useful these devices turn out to be, discarding ones that produce bad advice and tinkering to improve those that work. In this view, economic action arises from an evolving ecology of interpretive devices that interact with one another through the medium of the agents that use them to generate their expectations.

Arthur et al. build a theory of asset pricing upon such a view. Agents—investors—act as market statisticians. They continually generate expectational models—interpretations of what moves prices in the market—and test these by trading. They discard and replace models if not successful. Expectations in the market therefore become endogenous—they continually change and adapt to a market that they create together. The Arthur et al. market settles into a rich psychology, in which speculative bubbles, technical trading, and persistence of volatility emerge. The homogeneous rational expectations of the standard literature become a special case—possible in theory but unlikely to emerge in practice. Brock presents a variant of this approach, allowing agents to switch between a limited number of expectational models. His model is simpler than that of Arthur et al., but he achieves analytical results, which he relates to a variety of stylized facts about financial times series, many of which have been uncovered through the application of nonlinear analysis over the past decade.

In the world of Darley and Kauffman, agents are arrayed on a lattice, and they try to predict the behavior of their lattice neighbors. They generate their predictions via an autoregressive model, and they can individually tune the number of parameters in the model and the length of the time series they use to estimate model parameters. Agents can change parameter number or history length by steps of length 1 each period, if by doing so they would have generated better predictions in the previous period. This induces a coevolutionary "interpretative dynamics," which does not settle down to a stable regime of precise, coordinated mutual expectations. In particular, when the system approaches a "stable rational-expectations state," it tends to break down into a disordered state. They use their results to argue against conventional notions of rationality, with infinite foresight horizons and unlimited deductive capability.

In his paper on high inflation, Leijonhufvud poses the same problem as Darley and Kauffman: Where should we locate agent cognition, between the extremes of "infinite-horizon optimization" and "myopic adaptation?"

Leijonhufvud argues that the answer to this question is context dependent. He claims that in situations of institutional break-down like high inflation, agent cognition shifts toward the "short memory/short foresight adaptive mode." The causative relation between institutional and cognitive shifts becomes reciprocal. With the shrinking of foresight horizons, markets for long-term loans (where long-term can mean over 15 days) disappear. And as inflation accelerates, units of accounting lose meaning. Budgets cannot be drawn in meaningful ways, the executive arm of government becomes no longer fiscally accountable to parliament, and local governments become unaccountable to national governments. Mechanisms of social and economic control erode. Ministers lose control over their bureaucracies, shareholders over corporate management.

The idea that "interpretative devices" such as explicit forecasting models and technical-trading rules play a central role in agent cognition fits with a more general set of ideas in cognitive science, summarized in Clark.[2] This work rejects the notion that cognition is all "in the head." Rather, interpretive aids such as autoregressive models, computers, languages, or even navigational tools (as in Hutchins[6]) and institutions provide a "scaffolding," an external structure on which much of the task of interpreting the world is off-loaded. Clark[2] argues that the distinctive hallmark of in-the-head cognition is "fast pattern completion," which bears little relation to the neoclassical economist's deductive rationality. In this volume, North takes up this theme, describing some of the ways in which institutions scaffold interpretations of what constitutes possible and appropriate action for economic agents.

Lane and Maxfield consider the problem of interpretation from a different perspective. They are particularly interested in what they call attributions of functionality: interpretations about what an artifact does. They argue that new attributions of functionality arise in the context of particular kinds of agent relationships, where agents can differ in their interpretations. As a consequence, cognition has an unavoidable social dimension. What interpretations are possible depend on who interacts with whom, about what. They also argue that new functionality attributions cannot be foreseen outside the particular generative relationships in which they arise. This unforeseeability has profound consequences for what constitutes "rational" action in situations of rapid change in the structure of agent-artifact space.

All the papers mentioned so far take as fundamental the importance of cognition for economic theory. But the opposite point of view can also be legitimately defended from a process-and-emergence perspective. According to this argument, overrating cognition is just another error deriving from methodological individualism, the very bedrock of standard economic theory. How individual agents decide what to do may not matter very much. What happens as a result of their actions may depend much more on the interaction structure through which they act—who interacts with whom, according to which rules. Blume makes this point in the introduction to his paper on population games, which, as he puts it, provide a class of models that shift attention "from the fine points of individual-level decision theory to dynamics of agent interaction." Padgett makes a similar claim, though for a different reason. He is interested in formulating a theory of the firm as a locus of transformative "work," and he argues that "work" may be represented by "an orchestrated sequence of actions and reactions, the sequence of which produces some collective result (intended or not)." Hence, studying the structure of coordinated action-reaction sequences may provide insight into the organization of economic activity, without bringing "cognition" into the story at all. Padgett's paper is inspired by recent work in chemistry and biology (by Eigen and Schuster[3] and by Fontana and Buss,[4] among others) that are considered exemplars of the complexity perspective in these fields.

STRUCTURE. Most human interactions, even those taking place in "economic" contexts, have a primarily social character: talking with friends, asking advice from knowledgeable acquaintances, working together with colleagues, living next to neighbors. Recurring patterns of such social interactions bind agents together into networks.[6] According to standard economic theory, what agents do depends on their values and available information. But standard theory typically ignores where values and information come from. It treats agents' values and information as exogenous and autonomous. In reality, agents learn from each other, and their values may be influenced by others' values and actions. These processes of learning and influencing happen through the social interaction networks in which agents are embedded, and they may have important economic consequences. For example, one of the models presented in Durlauf's paper implies that value relationships among neighbors can induce persistent income inequalities between neighborhoods. Lane examines a model in which information flowing between agents in a network determines the market shares of two competing products. Kirman's paper reviews a number of models that derive economic consequences from interaction networks.

Ioannides, Kirman, and Tesfatsion consider the problems of how networks emerge from initially random patterns of dyadic interaction and what kinds of structure the resulting networks exhibit. Ioannides studies mathematical models based on controlled random fields, while Tesfatsion works in the context of a particular agent-based model, in which the "agents" are strategies that play Prisoner's Dilemma with one another. Ioannides and Tesfatsion are

6. There is a voluminous sociological literature on interaction networks. Recent entry points include Noria and Eccles,[7] particularly the essay by Granovetter entitled "Problems of Explanation in Economic Sociology," and the methodological survey of Wasserman and Faust.[8]

both primarily interested in networks involving explicitly economic interactions, in particular trade. Their motivating idea, long recognized among sociologists (for example, Baker[1]), is that markets actually function by means of networks of traders, and what happens in markets may reflect the structure of these networks, which in turn may depend on how the networks emerge.

Local interactions can give rise to large-scale spatial structures. This phenomenon is investigated by several of the papers in this volume. Lindgren's contribution is particularly interesting in this regard. Like Tesfatsion, he works with an agent-based model in which the agents code strategies for playing two-person games. In both Lindgren's and Tesfatsion's models, agents adapt their strategies over time in response to their past success in playing against other agents. Unlike Tesfatsion's agents, who meet randomly and decide whether or not to interact, Lindgren's agents only interact with neighbors in a prespecified interaction network. Lindgren studies the emergence of spatiotemporal structure in agent space—metastable ecologies of strategies that maintain themselves for many agent-generations against "invasion" by new strategy types or "competing" ecologies at their spatial borders. In particular, he compares the structures that arise in a lattice network, in which each agent interacts with only a few other agents, with those that arise in a fully connected network, in which each agent interacts with all other agents. He finds that the former "give rise to a stable coexistence between strategies that would otherwise be outcompeted. These spatiotemporal structures may take the form of spiral waves, irregular waves, spatiotemporal chaos, frozen patchy patterns, and various geometrical configurations." Though Lindgren's model is not explicitly economic, the contrast he draws between an agent space in which interactions are structured by (relatively sparse) social networks and an agent space in which all interactions are possible (as is the case, at least in principle, with the impersonal markets featured in general equilibrium analysis) is suggestive. Padgett's paper offers a similar contrast, in a quite different context.

Both Durlauf and Krugman explore the emergence of geographical segregation. In their models, agents may change location—that is, change their position in a social structure defined by neighbor ties. In these models (especially Durlauf's), there are many types of agents, and the question is under what circumstances, and through what mechanisms, do aggregate-level "neighborhoods" arise, each consisting predominantly (or even exclusively) of one agent type. Thus, agents' choices, conditioned by current network structure (the agent's neighbors and the neighbors at the sites to which the agent can move), change that structure; over time, from the changing local network structure, an aggregate-level pattern of segregated neighborhoods emerges.

Kollman, Miller, and Page explore a related theme in their work on political platforms and institutions in multiple jurisdictions. In their agent-based model, agents may relocate between jurisdictions. They show that when there are more than three jurisdictions, two-party competition outperforms democratic referenda. The opposite is the case when there is only one jurisdiction and, hence, no agent mobility. They also find that two-party competition results in more agent moves than does democratic referenda.

Manski reminds us that while theory is all very well, understanding of real phenomena is just as important. He distinguishes between three kinds of causal explanation for the often observed empirical fact that "persons belonging to the same group tend to behave similarly." One is the one we have been describing above: the behavioral similarities may arise through network interaction effects. But there are two other possible explanations: *contextual,* in which the behavior may depend on exogenous characteristics of the group (like socioeconomic composition); or *correlated effects,* in which the behavior may be due to similar *individual* characteristics of members of the group. Manski shows, among other results, that a researcher who uses the popular linear-in-means model to analyze his data and "observes equilibrium outcomes and the composition of reference groups cannot empirically distinguish" endogenous interactions from these alternative explanations. One moral is that nonlinear effects require nonlinear inferential techniques.

In the essays of North, Shubik, and Leijonhufvud, the focus shifts to another kind of social structure, the institution. North's essay focuses on institutions and economic growth, Shubik's on financial institutions, and Leijonhufvud's on high-inflation phenomenology. All three authors agree in defining institutions as "the rules of the game," without which economic action is unthinkable. They use the word "institution" in at least three senses: as the "rules" themselves (for example, bankruptcy laws); as the entities endowed with the social and political power to promulgate rules (for example, governments and courts); and as the socially legitimized constructions that instantiate rules and through which economic agents act (for example, fiat money and markets). In whichever sense institutions are construed, the three authors agree that they cannot be adequately understood from a purely economic, purely political, or purely social point of view. Economics, politics, and society are inextricably mixed in the processes whereby institutions come into being. And they change and determine economic, political, and social action. North also insists that institutions have a cognitive dimension through the aggregate-level "belief systems" that sustain them and determine the directions in which they change.

North takes up the question of the emergence of institutions from a functionalist perspective: institutions are brought into being "in order to reduce uncertainty," that is, to make agents' worlds predictable enough to afford recognizable opportunities for effective action. In particular, modern economies depend upon institutions that provide low transaction costs in impersonal markets.

Shubik takes a different approach. His analysis starts from his notion of strategic market games. These are "fully defined process models" that specify actions "for all points in the set of feasible outcomes." He shows how, in the context of constructing a strategic market game for an exchange economy using fiat money, the full specification requirement leads to the logical necessity of certain kinds of rules that Shubik identifies with financial institutions. Geanakoplos' paper makes a similar point to Shubik's. Financial instruments represent promises, he argues. What happens if someone cannot or will not honor a promise? Shubik already introduced the logical necessity of one institution, bankruptcy law, to deal with defaults. Geanakoplos introduces another, collateral. He shows that, in equilibrium, collateral as an institution has institutional implications—missing markets.

Finally, in his note concluding the volume, Philip Anderson provides a physicist's perspective on a point that Fernand Braudel argues is a central lesson from the history of long-term socioeconomic change. Averages and assumptions of agent homogeneity can be very deceptive in complex systems. And processes of change are generally driven by the inhabitants of the extreme tails of some relevant distribution. Hence, an interesting theoretical question from the Santa Fe perspective is: How do distributions with extreme tails arise, and why are they so ubiquitous and so important?

WHAT COUNTS AS A PROBLEM AND AS A SOLUTION. While the papers here have much to say on cognition and structure, they contain much less discussion on what constitutes a problem and solution from this new viewpoint. Perhaps this is because it is premature to talk about methods for generating and assessing understanding when what is to be understood is still under discussion. While a few of the papers completely avoid mathematics, most of the papers do present mathematical models—whether based on statistical mechanics, strategic market games, random graphs, population games, stochastic dynamics, or agent-based computations. Yet sometimes the mathematical models the authors use leave important questions unanswered. For example, in what way do equilibrium calculations provide insight into emergence? This troublesome question is not addressed in any of the papers, even those in which models are presented from which equilibria are calculated—and insight into emergence is claimed to result. Blume raises two related issues in his discussion of population games: whether the asymptotic equilibrium selection theorems featured in the theory happen "soon enough" to be economically interesting; and whether the invariance of the "global environment" determined by the game and interaction model is compatible with an underlying economic reality in which rules of the game undergo endogenous change. It will not be easy to resolve the inherent tension between traditional mathematical tools and phenomena that may exhibit perpetual novelty.

As we mentioned previously, several of the papers introduce less traditional, agent-based models. Kollman, Miller, and Page discuss both advantages and difficulties associated with this set of techniques. They end up expressing cautious optimism about their future usefulness. Tesfatsion casts her own paper as an illustration of what she calls "the alife approach for economics, as well as the hurdles that remain to be cleared." Perhaps the best recommendation we can make to the reader with respect to the epistemological problems associated with the process-and-emergence perspective is simple. Read the papers, and see what you find convincing.

REFERENCES

1. Baker, W. "The Social Structure of a National Securities Market." *Amer. J. Sociol.* 89, (1984): 775–811.
2. Clark, A. *Being There: Putting Brain, Body, and World Together Again*. Cambridge, MA: MIT Press, 1997.
3. Eigen, M., and P. Schuster. *The Hypercycle*. Berlin: Springer Verlag, 1979.
4. Fontana, W., and L. Buss. "The Arrival of the Fittest: Toward a Theory of Biological Organization." *Bull. Math. Biol.* 56 (1994): 1–64.
5. Holland, J. H. "The Global Economy as an Adaptive Process." In *The Economy as an Evolving Complex System*, edited by P. W. Anderson, K. J. Arrow, and D. Pines, 117–124. Santa Fe Institute Studies in the Sciences of Complexity, Proc. Vol. V. Redwood City, CA: Addison-Wesley, 1988.
6. Hutchins, E. *Cognition in the Wild*. Cambridge, MA: MIT Press, 1995.
7. Noria, N., and R. Eccles (Eds.) *Networks and Organizations: Structure, Form, and Action*. Cambridge, MA: Harvard Business School Press, 1992.
8. Wasserman, W., and K. Faust. *Social Network Analysis: Methods and Applications*. Cambridge, UK: Cambridge University Press, 1994.

CHAPTER 6

All Systems Will Be Gamed

Exploitive Behavior in Economic and Social Systems

W. BRIAN ARTHUR[1]

After the 2008 Wall Street crash, it became clear to many economists that financial systems, along with other social and economic systems, were not immune to being manipulated by small groups of players to their own advantage. And so, two natural questions arose. For a given policy design or proposed economic system, could such manipulation be foreseen in advance and possibly prevented? And could we design methods—possibly automatic ones—that would test proposed policy systems for possible failure modes and for their vulnerability to possible manipulation, and thereby prevent such behavior in the future?

The paper argues that exploitive behavior within the economy is not rare and falls into specific classes; that policy studies can be readily extended to investigate the possibility of the policy's being "gamed;" and that economics needs a strong sub-discipline of failure-mode analysis, parallel to the successful failure-mode-analysis disciplines within structural engineering and aircraft design. The paper was written in 2010 when I was with IBM Almaden's Smarter Planet Platform for Analysis and Simulation of Health (SPLASH) group. It is published here for the first time.[1]

There is a general rule in social and economic life: given any system, people will find a way to exploit it. Or to say this more succinctly: All systems will be gamed. I do not mean to be cynical here. Rather, I am making the general observation that given any governmental system, any legal system,

1. I thank my fellow IBM team members, Paul Maglio, Peter Haas, and Pat Selinger for useful comments; and also Sai Hung Cheung and Daria Rothmaier.

regulatory system, corporate system, election system, set of policies, set of organizational rules, set of international agreements, people can—and will—find unexpected ways to exploit it to their advantage. "Show me a 50-foot wall," said Arizona's governor Janet Napolitano, speaking in 2005 of illegal immigration at the US-Mexico border, "and I'll show you a 51-foot ladder."

Foreseeing 51-foot ladders may not be particularly challenging—Napolitano is merely making a wry political point. But anticipating more generally how exploitive behavior can arise in a given policy system *is* challenging; there are many ways in which systems can be exploited and some are by no means obvious. Yet we do need to foresee possible manipulations, not least because they can sometimes have disastrous consequences. Consider the aftermath of Russia's 1990 transition from planned socialism to capitalism, in which a small number of well-positioned players seized control of the state's newly freed assets. Or consider California's 2000 freeing of its energy market, in which a small number of suppliers were able to manipulate the market to the detriment of the state. Or consider Iceland's banking system in 2008, where a few financial players who had taken control of the state's banks used depositors' assets to speculate in overseas property markets and ran the banks into insolvency. Or consider Wall Street's loosely regulated mortgage-backed securities market in 2008, in which easy credit and complicated derivative products built a highly unstable structure that spectacularly collapsed. All these systems were manipulated—some were "gamed," to use a stronger term. All, in retrospect, posed incentives that rendered them open to manipulation—and all careened into eventual system breakdowns.

This raises an obvious question. Given that economics is sophisticated and that economists study proposed policy systems in advance, how could these various economic disasters have happened? In the cases I mentioned, some economists did indeed foresee possibilities for future exploitation and warn of these. But such warnings normally have little effect. The reason is that economics, in the way it is practiced, contains a bias that inhibits economists from seeing future potential exploitation. Economic analysis assumes equilibrium of the system in question, and by definition equilibrium is a condition where no agent has any incentive to diverge from its present behavior. It follows that for any system being studied invasive or exploitive behavior cannot happen: If a system could be invaded, some agents would be initiating new behavior, and the system could not have been in equilibrium. Equilibrium economics then, by its base assumptions, is not primed to look for the exploitation of systems, and as a result systematic studies of how systems might fail or be exploited are not central to how the discipline thinks.[2]

2. For critiques of economics in the face of the 2008 financial crisis and other crises, see Colander et al., 2008; and Koppl and Luther, 2010.

In this paper I want to get away from the equilibrium assumption and take as our basis a different, nonequilibrium assumption: that any policy system at any time presents incentives to the parties engaged in it, and these incentives may in turn induce parties to discover ways in which they might privately benefit that policy designers had not thought of. Given this, we would want to know how exploitive behavior for policy systems might typically arise, and how we can use formal modeling and analysis to allow for such behavior, and to foresee or even warn of it in advance.

I will pose our problem of foreseeing possible exploitation as four questions I will look at in sequence. First, what are the causes of exploitive behavior and how does it typically arise? Second, given a particular economic system or proposed policy, how might we anticipate where it might fail, and what can we learn from disciplines such as structural engineering that try to foresee potential failure modes, and could help us in this? Third, how can we construct models of systems being gamed or exploited, and of agents in these models "discovering" ways to exploit such systems? And fourth, what are the future prospects for constructing artificially intelligent methods that could automatically anticipate how economic and social systems might be exploited? Fully definitive answers to these questions are of course not possible, but I hope the discussion here will at least open the subject for debate.

Before we go on, a word about some of the terms I will use. *Exploitation* has two meanings: "to use something in order to gain a benefit," and to take "selfish or unfair advantage of a person or situation, usually for personal gain."[3] The first meaning suits us well (note it is not necessarily pejorative), but the second also covers many of the cases I will talk about. *Gaming* itself has a more pernicious meaning: it denotes people using a system cynically to their own ends, often in a way that betrays trust placed in them and harms other people.[4] I will also talk of *policy systems*, meaning economic or social or military or business or governmental systems that play out over time, given a set of policies that define them. The 2010 Obama Affordable Health Care system is a policy system.

3. Microsoft Word Dictionary (1991) uses "exploitation" in its first sense, as the use and refinement of existing opportunities, and contrasts this with "exploration," the ongoing search for new opportunities. See March (1991) on this. "Exploitation" in this paper contains elements of both of these: we are talking of agents exploring for opportunities to exploit.

4. Wikipedia (October 9, 2010) defines gaming as "[using] the rules and procedures meant to protect a system in order, instead, to manipulate the system for a desired outcome."

CAUSES OF EXPLOITIVE BEHAVIOR

Before we talk about modeling exploitive behavior, it will be useful to build up some knowledge about its causes and mechanisms.

Our first observation is that exploitive behavior is not rare. This is not because of some inherent human tendency toward selfish behavior; it is because all policy systems—all social policies—pose incentives that are reacted to by groups of agents acting in their own interest, and often these reactions are unexpected and act counter to the policy's intentions. Examples are legion. The 2003 US invasion of Iraq—a military policy system—was well planned and well executed, but it generated insurgency, a less than fully expected reaction to the presence of American soldiers that went on to obstruct US goals in Iraq. The 1965 Medicare system, launched under Lyndon Johnson with the purpose of providing health care for the elderly, paid fee-for-service, compensating hospitals and physicians for their incurred costs of treatment. Hospitals and physicians in the program responded by purchasing expensive equipment and providing services that were unnecessary. As a result, within five years of its inception, the program's costs nearly tripled (Mahar, 2006). A decade or two later, the United States opened health care to market forces. The freeing of the market was intended to produce competition and to lower costs. Instead it produced a system where each of the key players found specific ways to work the system to their own advantage, to the detriment of the system as a whole. Maher (2006) describes the outcome as "a Hobbesian marketplace" that pitted "the health care industry's players against one another: hospital vs. hospital, doctor vs. hospital, doctor vs. doctor, hospital vs. insurer, insurer vs. hospital, insurer vs. insurer, insurer vs. drugmaker, drugmaker vs. drugmaker."

These examples are large-scale ones, but exploitation happens on every scale. Apartment building managers have been known to visit their competitors' buildings and post negative ratings online to enhance their own competitive standing. Whatever the scale at which exploitation takes place, its frequency of occurrence should give us pause about implementing any social policy without thinking through how it could potentially be used to players' advantage, and it should also caution us about accepting the results of economic models designed to demonstrate a policy system's outcome. In fact, it should caution us about accepting the results of *all* policy models without questioning their built-in assumptions.

But just how should we question the outcome of policy systems? The examples I have given seem scattered and unique, so it doesn't seem easy to build general insights from them. It would be better if we could find generic categories of exploitation, standard hacks, or patterns of behavior or incentives that we see repeated from one circumstance to another. Or to put this another way, it would be useful if we had a "failure mode analysis" tradition in economics for assessing policy systems. Such a tradition exists in other disciplines where life or safety or well-being are at stake: Failure mode analysis in engineering investigates the ways in which structures have failed in the past and might fail or not function as intended; preventive medicine and disease control investigates the causes of diseases, death, and epidemics and looks to their future prevention. These modalities seek not just to study past failures but to construct an organized body of knowledge that might help prevent failure or breakdown in the future.

It would be a large undertaking to construct a policy-system failure mode sub-discipline of economics, worthwhile of course, but beyond the scope of this paper. What we *can* do is think about how such a discipline would work. One good place to start is to look at how systems have been exploited or gamed in the past and point to general categories or motifs by which this happens. I will talk about four motifs and label these by their causes:

1. **Use of asymmetric information.** In many social systems, different parties have access to different information, and often one party offers a service or puts forward an opportunity based upon its understanding of the available information. Another party then responds with behavior based on its more detailed understanding and uses the system to profit from its privileged information. The financial and the marketing industries are particularly prone to such behavior; in each of these some parties are well informed about the product they are promoting, while others—the potential investors or customers—are not. In 2007 Goldman Sachs created a package of mortgage-linked bonds it sold to its clients. But it allowed a prominent hedge fund manager, John A. Paulson, to select bonds for this that privately he thought would lose value, then to bet against the package. Paulson profited, and so allegedly did Goldman by buying insurance against loss of value of the instrument; but investors lost more than $1 billion (Appleton, 2010). The package (a synthetic collateralized debt obligation tied to the performance of subprime residential mortgage-backed securities) was complicated, and its designers, Goldman and Paulson, were well informed on its prospects. Their clients were not.

The health care industry is also prone to information asymmetries; both physicians and patients are better informed on ailments and their appropriate treatments than are the insurance companies or governmental bodies paying for them (Arrow, 1963). In 2006 the state of Massachusetts mandated individual health care insurance, and the program appeared to work initially, but after some few months insurers discovered they were losing money. The reason was, as Suderman (2010) reports, "[t]housands of consumers are gaming Massachusetts' 2006 health insurance law by buying insurance when they need to cover pricey medical care, such as fertility treatments and knee surgery, and then swiftly dropping coverage." This behavior is not illegal, nor is it quite immoral, but it is certainly exploitive.

2. **Tailoring behavior to conform to performance criteria.** A second type of exploitation—better to call it manipulation here—occurs when agent behavior is judged, monitored, or measured by strict criteria of evaluation and agents optimize their behavior to conform to these narrow criteria, rather than to what was more widely intended. Agents, in other words, game the criteria. Before the 2008 financial crisis, financial ratings agencies such as Moody's or Standard & Poor's for years performed evaluations of the risk inherent in financial instruments proposed by investment and banking houses. A few years before the financial crash, in an act of transparency and implicit trust, they made their ratings models available to the Wall Street investment firms. Says Morgenson (2010): "The Wall Street firms learned how to massage these models, change one or two little inputs and then get a better rating as a result. They learned how to game the rating agency's models so that they could put lesser quality bonds in these portfolios, still get a high rating, and then sell the junk that they might not otherwise have been able to sell."[5]

Gaming performance criteria is not confined to Wall Street. It occurs within all systems where judgment of performance is important: conformance to the law; educational testing;[6] adherence to standards of human rights; adherence to environmental standards; adherence to criteria for receiving funding; the production of output within factories; financial accounting; tax reporting; the performance of bureaucrats; the performance of governments. In all these cases, the parties under surveillance adjust their behavior to appear virtuous under the stated performance measures, while their actual behavior may be anywhere from satisfactory to reprehensible. In fact, in the case of government performance, two particular expressions of this form of exploitation already exist. One is Campbell's law (1976): "the more any quantitative social indicator is used for social decision-making, the more subject it will be to corruption pressures and the more apt it will be to distort and corrupt the social processes it is intend to monitor." The other is Goodhart's law (1975): "Any observed statistical regularity will tend to collapse once pressure is placed upon it for control purposes."[7] Both of these apply to governmental behavior. I prefer a broader truism: Any performance criterion will be optimized against, and will thereby lose its value.

3. **Taking partial control of a system.** A third type of exploitation occurs when a small group of agents manages to take control of some significant portion of the resources of a system and use this for its own purposes. This is the economic equivalent of the way viruses operate. The group in effect takes over part of the machinery of the system and uses that to its own advantage.

5. See White (2009).
6. See Nichols and Berliner (2007).
7. Chrystal and Mizen (2001).

The financial sector has seen a great deal of this type of exploitation. Within the insurance giant AIG, some years before the 2008 crash, a small group of people (the Financial Products Unit) managed to take effective control of much of the company's assets and risk bearing, and began to invest heavily in credit default swaps. The group profited greatly through their own personal compensation—they were paid a third of the profits they generated—but the investments collapsed, and that in turn sank AIG (Zuill, 2009). A similar set of events unfolded in Iceland, where a small group of entrepreneurs took out loans, used these to buy control of the assets of the country's banks, and invested these in international properties and derivatives (Boyes, 2009; Jonsson, 2009). The international investments collapsed, and so did Iceland's banks, along with their customers' deposits.

4. **Using system elements in a way not intended by policy designers.** Still another type of exploitation happens when agents use the behavior of the system itself to manipulate the system. An example would be using a website's rating possibilities to manipulate others' ratings. Often too, players find a rule they can use as a loophole to justify behavior the designers of the system did not intend. Usually this forces a flow of money or energy through the rule, to the detriment of the system at large. Following the Arab Oil Embargo in the early 1970s, the US Congress set up fuel economy standards for motor vehicles. Understandably, the requirements for commercial light trucks were more lenient than those for passenger vehicles. But in due course and with a little congressional manipulation, Detroit found it could declare its sports utility vehicles to be light trucks. These then passed through the light-truck loophole, the highways in due course filled with SUVs, and between 1988 and 2005 average fuel economy actually fell in the United States (Pew, 2010). This was not what the energy policy's designers intended.

The four motifs I have described are by no means exhaustive; there are no doubt other ways in which systems might be gamed. But these give us a feel for the types of exploitation we might expect to see, and they show us that exploitive behavior is not rare in systems. It is rife.

ANTICIPATING FAILURE MODES

For some policy systems, it is obvious that their possible exploitation falls into one of the four motifs just given. For others, no particular mode of exploitive behavior might be obvious. In general we have a given policy system and a mental model or analytical studies of how it is expected to work, and we would like to anticipate where the system might in real life be exploited. So how do we proceed in general? How would we go about failure mode analysis in a particular economic situation? There is no prescribed answer to these questions, but we can usefully borrow some directives from engineering failure analysis.

An obvious first step is to have at hand knowledge of how similar systems have failed in the past. We have at least the beginnings of such knowledge with the motifs I described earlier. Aircraft designers know from forensic studies the causes by which failures (they call these "anomalies") typically occur: fatigue failure, explosive decompression, fire and explosions, burst engines (Bibel, 2008). By analogy, as I said, we need a failure mode analysis of how policy systems have been exploited in the past.

Second, we can observe that in general the breakdown of a structure starts at a more micro level than that of its overall design. Breakdown in engineering designs happens not because the overall structure gives way, but because stresses cause hairline cracks in some part of an assembly, or some component assembly fails, and these malfunctions propagate to higher levels, possibly to cause eventual whole-system degradation. This suggests in our case that for any system we are studying, exploitive behavior will typically take place at a smaller scale than the overall system. Exploitive behavior after all is created—is "invented"—by individual people, individual human agents, or small groups of these, and we will have to have detailed knowledge of the options and possibilities agents possess if we want to understand how manipulation may happen.

Third, and again by analogy, we can look for places of high "stress" in the proposed system and concentrate our attentions there. In social systems these places tend to be the points that present strong incentives for agents to do something different from their prescribed behavior. Typically, in an analytical model, points of behavioral action are represented as rates (the rate, say, at which individuals buy health insurance), or as simple rules (if income exceeds $X, and age exceeds Y, buy health insurance). The modeler needs to query whether simple rates or rules are warranted, given the pattern of incentives agents faces. Very often they are not.

All this would suggest that if we have a design for social system and an analytical model of it, we can "stress test" it by first identifying where actual incentives would yield strong inducements for agents to engage in behavior different from the assumed behavior. These might, to give some examples, be places where agents have power to affect other players' well-being (they can issue building permits, say, to wealthy property developers), yet we assume they make impartial decisions; or places where agents can profit by compromising on performance or safety of some activity (say, they decide on aircraft maintenance), yet we assume they conform to given standards; or places where agents have inside information (say, they have knowledge of a company's future plans), yet we assume they do not trade on this information.

Next we construct the agents' possibilities from our sense of the detailed incentives and information the agents have at this location. That is, we construct detailed strategic options for the agents. The key word here is "detailed": the options or opportunities possible here are driven by the imagination and experience of the analyst looking at the system, they are drawn from the real world, and they require careful, detailed description. This is why we will need to have knowledge of the fine-grained information and opportunities the agents will draw from to create their actions.

Once we have identified where and how exploitation might take place, we can break open the overall economic model of the policy system at this location, and insert a module that "injects" the behavior we have in mind. We now have a particular type of exploitation in mind, and a working model of it that we can use to study what difference the strategic agents make in the behavior of the overall system. Sometimes they will make little difference; the strategic behavior may not affect much outside its sphere. Sometimes they will have a major effect; they may even in certain cases cause the collapse of the structure they were inserted into. What is important here is that we are looking for weak points in a policy system and the consequences that might follow from particular behaviors that system might be prone to. It is important that this testing not be rushed. In engineering it often takes months or years to painstakingly test, debug, and rework a novel design of importance, especially where public safety is at stake. There is no reason we should place less emphasis on the safety of economic and social policy outcomes.

This method I have just outlined presumes one system designer, or a team, working to discover flaws in a given set of policies or given simulated economic system. Things can be speeded up if multiple designers work in parallel and are invited to probe a model to find its weak points. Where we have a working model of a proposed policy system—think of a new health care policy, or an altered set of financial regulations—we can solicit "strategy" modules that exploit it. Here the overall simulation model or overall policy situation would be given, and we would be inviting outside participants to submit strategies to exploit it. This was first carried out in the famous prisoner's dilemma tournament several decades ago, where Robert Axelrod (1984) solicited strategies that would compete in a repeated prisoner's dilemma game. To do this in the more general systems context, participants would need to study the system thoroughly, identify its myriad incentives, home in on the places were it leaves open opportunities for exploitation, and model these.

Something similar to this is carried out routinely in the beta testing of encryption systems. When, say, the US Navy develops a novel encryption scheme, it invites a group of selected people to see if they can crack the scheme. If they cannot, the scheme can proceed. It is important that testers come from the outside. Says Schneier (1999): "Consider the Internet IP security protocol. It was designed in the open by committee and was the subject of considerable public scrutiny from the start.... Cryptographers at the Naval Research Laboratory recently discovered a minor implementation flaw. The work continues, in public, by anyone and everyone who is interested. On the other hand, Microsoft developed its own Point-to-Point Tunneling Protocol (PPTP) to do much the same thing. They invented their own authentication protocol, their own hash functions, and their own key-generation algorithm. Every one of these items was badly flawed.... But since they did all this work internally, no one knew that their PPTP was weak."

MODELING EXPLOITATION WITHIN COMPUTER MODELS

In the previous section I talked in general about probing policy systems for possible failure. Now I want to narrow this and talk more about probing computer-based models of policy systems—usually simulation models—for possible failure. One difficulty we immediately face is that most computer-based models are closed to novel behavior: they use equations or Markov states or other architectures that assume fixed categories of behavior laid down in advance or embedded within them, so they can't easily be modified to conjure up the unforeseen—the 51-foot ladders that might appear.

But we *can* proceed. Certainly, as I said before, we can "inject" foreseen exploitive behavior into the computer model; that's a matter of breaking open the model and adding more detail. More generally, though, we would like to be able to have our simulation model allow for the spontaneous arising or "discovery" of unforeseen novel behaviors, and this seems more challenging. Notice we are really asking how new behaviors might emerge from agents' discovering or learning within a system, and emergence is something that modeling, especially agent-based modeling, has experience with. So we might expect that we can indeed modify a simulation model to allow agents to "discover" manipulative behavior.

Let me illustrate with a real-world example. Consider the health insurance case I mentioned from Massachusetts. We don't have a simulation model of this policy system at hand, so for our purposes we will construct one. And because we are interested not in social details but in issues of how we can simulate exploitation, we can keep this simple and stylized. We will proceed in steps by constructing versions that progressively capture the behavior that interests us.

First we construct a basic model of health insurance. (I used NetLogo for this simulation, a convenient platform for agent-based modeling.) The model has N (typically from 100 to 1,000) people who individually and randomly incur health care costs, perhaps from diseases, hospital care, surgical procedures, or accidents, and initially they cover these costs themselves. In this model, the distribution of health costs is uniform, stationary, and identical for all (we can assume people are all of the same age). People receive a fixed income, common to all, and their consumption c equals this less their health costs. I assume a concave utility function over consumption, $U(c) = c^{1/2}$: people are risk averse. There is one insurance company. At first it offers no policies, but instead for a fixed period collects actuarial data: It has access to the population's health costs and uses these to figure average health costs per person per period. Once it has a sufficiently accurate estimate it issues a voluntary health insurance policy. The policy's cost is set to be "fair" (equal to its estimate of the expected cost per person per period) plus a markup of $m\%$ to cover administrative costs. When we run the model we find that when insurance markup values are sufficiently low ($m < 23.3\%$) people find that their utility is higher with the policy and they buy it. Otherwise they do not. We now have a simple working agent-based model of insurance.

As a second step, let us build in the Massachusetts edict and its consequences. Central to what happened was a class of people who believed or found out they could do without coverage; instead they could pay the fine for non-participation in the scheme. There are several ways we could modify our model to allow for such a class. We could assume, for example, people who have small risk of incurring health costs. But the simplest way is to assume that a proportion of the population (let us say 50%) is not risk-averse. It has a linear utility function, $U(c) = c$, and thus finds it profitable to pay the government fine, assuming (as is true in Massachusetts) this is less than the insurance markup. When we run this model we find not surprisingly that one-half of the population insures, the other half does not.

As a third step we build in the exploitive behavior. We now allow that all people can see costs in advance for some types of health care (shoulder operations, say, or physical therapy). So we build into the model—"inject" the behavior—that these can be foreseen at the start of the period, giving people the option of taking out coverage for that period and possibly canceling it the next. The 50% already insured will not be affected; they are paying insurance regardless. But the uninsured will be affected, and we find when we run this model that they opt in and out of coverage according to whether this suits their pockets. In the sense that they are taking out insurance on an outcome they know in advance, but the insurance company does not, they are "gaming" the system. Figure 1 shows the consequences for the insurance company's profits when it switches in. They plummet.

As a last stage in our modeling, realistically, we can assume that the system responds. The state may raise its non-participation fine. Once it does this sufficiently we find that everyone participates and normality resumes. Or the insurance company can react by increasing the mandatory policy-holding period. Once it does this to a sufficient point, we find again that normality resumes.

I have constructed this model in stages because it is convenient to break out the base model, demarcate the agents that will strategize, allow them to do so, and build in natural responses of the other agents. When finished, the model runs through all these dynamics in sequence, of course.

So far this demonstrates that we can take a given simulation model of a policy system (we constructed this one) and modify it by injecting foreseen "exploitive" behavior and response into it. But, as I mentioned earlier, in real

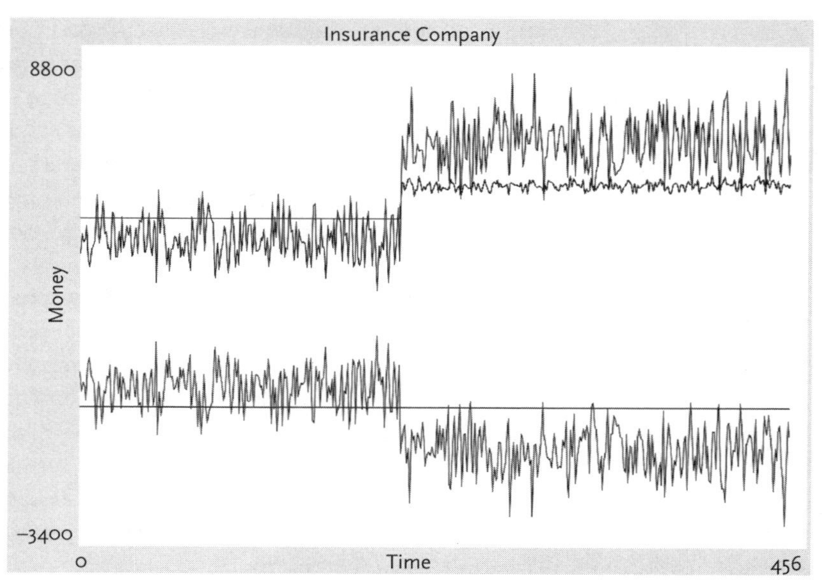

Figure 1:
Agents are allowed to see some upcoming health expenses starting around time 300. The upper plots show the effect on the insurance company's income from policy payments (smoother line) which rises because it acquires additional policy-holders, and expenses (upper jagged line). The lower plot shows the company's profits (lower jagged line), which now fall below the flat zero line.

life, exploitation *emerges*: it arises—seemingly appears—in the course of a policy system's existence. In fact, if we look at what happens in real life more closely, we see that players *notice* that certain options are available to them, and they learn from this—or sometimes *discover* quite abruptly—that certain actions can be profitably taken. So let us see how we can build "noticing" and "discovery" into our example. To keep things short I will only briefly indicate how to do this.[8]

First, "noticing" is fairly straightforward. We can allow our agents to "notice" certain things—what happened say in the recent past, what options are possible—simply by making these part of the information set they are aware of as they become available (cf. Lindgren, 1992).

We still need to include "discovery." To do this we allow agents to generate and try out a variety of potential actions or strategies based on their information. There are many ways to do this (Holland, 1975; Holland et al., 1986). Agents can randomly generate contingent actions or rules of the type: *If* the system fulfills a certain condition *K then* execute strategy *G*. Or they can construct novel actions randomly from time to time by forming combinations of ones that have worked before: *If* conditions *K* and *P* are true, then execute

8. See Arthur et al. (1997) for a study that implements the procedure I describe.

strategy *F*. Or they can generate families of possible actions: Buy in if this period's pre-known health costs exceed *k* dollars (where *k* can be pegged at different levels). We further allow agents to keep these potential strategies in mind (there may be many) and monitor each one's putative performance, thus learning over time which ones are effective in what circumstances. They can then use or execute the strategy they deem most effective at any time; and drop strategies that prove ineffective.

This sort of design will bring in the effect we seek. (For detailed illustrations of it in action, see Arthur, 1994, and Arthur et al., 1997.) If some randomly generated strategy is monitored and proves particularly effective, certain agents will quickly "discover" it. To an outsider it will look as if the strategy has suddenly been switched on—it will suddenly emerge and have an effect. In reality, the agents are merely inductively probing the system to find out what works, thereby at random times "discovering" effective strategies that take advantage of the system. Exploitation thus "appears."

I have described a rather simple model in our example and sketched a way to build the emergence of possible exploitations into it. Obviously we could elaborate this in several directions.[9]

But I want to emphasize my main point. Nothing special needs to be added by way of "scheming" or "exploitive thinking" to agent-based simulation models when we want to model system manipulation. Agents are faced with particular information about the system and the options available to them when it becomes available, and from these they generate putative actions. From time to time they discover particularly effective ones and "exploitation"—if we want to call it that—emerges. Modeling this calls only for standard procedures already available in agent-based modeling.

AUTOMATIC PRE-DISCOVERY OF EXPLOITIVE BEHAVIOR

But this is still not the last word. In the previous section, if we wanted computation to "discover" exploitive behaviors as in the previous section, we needed to specify a given class of behaviors within which they could explore. Ideally, in the future, we would want computation to automatically "discover" a wide range of gaming possibilities that we hadn't thought of, and to test these out, and thereby anticipate possible manipulation.

What are the prospects for this? What would it take for a simulation model of US-Mexico border crossings to foresee—to be able to "imagine"—the use of 51-foot ladders? Of course, it would be trivially easy to prompt the computer

9. For example, realistically we could allow information on what works to be shared among agents and spread through their population, and we could assume that if a strategy works, people would focus attention on it and construct variants on it—they would "explore" around it.

to see such solutions. We could easily feed the simulation the option of ladders of varying length, 40-foot, 64-foot, 25-foot, and allow it to learn that 51-foot ladders would do the job just right. But that would be cheating.

What we really want, in this case, is to have the computer proceed completely without human prompting, to "ponder" the problem of border crossing in the face of a wall, and "discover" the category of ladders or invent some other plausible way to defeat obstacles, without these being built in. To do this the computer would need to have knowledge of the world, and this would have to be a deep knowledge. It would have to be a general intelligence that would know the world's possibilities, know what is available, what is "out there" in general outside itself. It would need in other words something like our human general intelligence. There is more than a whiff of artificial intelligence here. We are really asking for an "invention machine": a machine that is aware of its world and can together put available components conceptually to solve general problems. Seen this way, the problem joins the category of computational problems that humans find doable but machines find difficult, the so-called "AI-complete" problems, such as reading and understanding text, interpreting speech, translating languages, recognizing visual objects, playing chess, judging legal cases. To this we can add: imagining solutions.

It is good to recognize that the problem here is not so much a conceptual one as a practical one. We can teach computers to recognize contexts, and to build up a huge store of general worldly knowledge. In fact, as is well known, in 2010 IBM taught a computer to successfully answer questions in the quiz show *Jeopardy*, precisely through building a huge store of general worldly knowledge. So it is not a far cry from this to foresee computers that have semantic knowledge of a gigantic library of past situations and how they have been exploited in the past, so that it can "recognize" analogies and use them for the purpose at hand. In the case of the 2003 US invasion of Iraq, such computation or simulation would have run through previous invasions in history, and would have encountered previous insurgencies that followed from them, and would have warned of such a possibility in the future of Iraq, and built the possibility into the simulation. It would have anticipated the "emergent" behavior. Future simulations may well be able to dip into history, find analogies there—find the overall category of ladders as responses to walls—and display them. But even if it is conceptually feasible, I believe full use of this type of worldly machine intelligence still lies decades in the future.

CONCLUSION

Over the last hundred years or more, economics has improved greatly in its ability to stabilize macro-economic outcomes, design international trade policies, regulate currency systems, implement central banking, and execute antitrust policy. What it hasn't been able to do is prevent financial and economic crises, most of which are caused by exploitive behavior. This seems an anomaly given our times. Airline safety, building safety, seismic safety, food and drug safety, disease safety, surgical safety—all these have improved steadily decade by decade in the last fifty years. "Economic safety" by contrast has not improved in the last five decades; if anything it has gotten worse.

Many economists—myself included—would say that unwarranted faith in the ability of free markets to regulate themselves bears much of the blame (e.g. Cassidy, 2009; Tabb, 2012). But so too does the absence of a systematic methodology in economics of looking for possible failure modes in advance of policy implementation. Failure-mode studies are not at the center of our discipline for the simple reason that economics' adherence to equilibrium analysis *assumes* that the system quickly settles to a place where no agent has an incentive to diverge from its present behavior, and so exploitive behavior cannot happen. We therefore tend to design policies and construct simulations of their outcomes without sufficiently probing the robustness of their behavioral assumptions, and without identifying where they might fail because of systemic exploitation.

I suggest that it is time to revise our thinking on this. It is no longer enough to design a policy system and analyze it and even carefully simulate its outcome. We need to see social and economic systems not as a set of behaviors that have no motivation to change, but as a web of incentives that always induce further behavior, always invite further strategies, always cause the system to change. We need to emulate what is routine in structural engineering, or in epidemiology, or in encryption, and anticipate where the systems we study might be exploited. We need to stress test our policy designs, to find their weak points and see if we can "break" them. Such failure-mode analysis in engineering, carried out over decades, has given us aircraft that fly millions of passenger-miles without mishap and high-rise buildings that do not collapse in earthquakes. Such exploitation-mode analysis, applied to the world of policy, would give us economic and social outcomes that perform as hoped for, something that would avert much misery in the world.

REFERENCES

Appleton, Michael, "SEC Sues Goldman over Housing Market Deal." *New York Times*, Apr. 16, 2010.

Arrow, Kenneth, "Uncertainty and the Welfare Economics of Medical Care," *American Economic Review*, 53: 91–96, 1963.

Arthur, W. Brian. "Bounded Rationality and Inductive Behavior (the El Farol problem)," *American Economic Review Papers and Proceedings*, 84, 406–411, 1994.

Arthur, W. Brian, J. H. Holland, B. LeBaron, R. Palmer, and P. Tayler, "Asset Pricing under Endogenous Expectations in an Artificial Stock Market," in *The Economy as an Evolving Complex System II*, Arthur, W. B., Durlauf, S., Lane, D., eds. Addison-Wesley, Redwood City, CA, 1997.

Axelrod, Robert. *The Evolution of Cooperation*. Basic Books, New York, 1984.
Bibel, George. *Beyond the Black Box: The Forensics of Airplane Crashes*. Johns Hopkins University Press, Baltimore, MD, 2008.
Boyes, Roger. *Meltdown Iceland: How the Global Financial Crisis Bankrupted an Entire Country*. Bloomsbury Publishing, London, 2009.
Campbell, Donald, "Assessing the Impact of Planned Social Change," Public Affairs Center, Dartmouth, NH, Dec. 1976.
Cassidy, J., *How Markets Fail: the Logic of Economic Calamities*. Farrar, Straus and Giroux, New York, 2009.
Chrystal, K. Alec, and Paul Mizen, "Goodhart's Law: Its Origins, Meaning and Implications for Monetary Policy," (http://cyberlibris.typepad.com/blog/files/Goodharts_Law.pdf), 2001.
Colander, David, A. Haas, K. Juselius, T. Lux, H. Föllmer, M. Goldberg, A. Kirman, B. Sloth, "The Financial Crisis and the Systemic Failure of Academic Economics," mimeo, 98th Dahlem Workshop, 2008.
Holland, John. *Adaptation in Natural and Artificial Systems*. MIT Press, Cambridge, MA, 1992. (Originally published 1975.)
Holland, John H., K. J. Holyoak, R. E. Nisbett and P. R. Thagard, *Induction*. Cambridge, MA, MIT Press, 1986.
Jonsson, Asgeir. *Why Iceland? How One of the World's Smallest Countries Became the Meltdown's Biggest Casualty*, Mc-Graw-Hill, New York, 2009.
Koppl, Roger, and W. J. Luther, "BRACE for a new Interventionist Economics," mimeo, Fairleigh Dickinson University, 2010.
Lindgren, Kristian. "Evolutionary Phenomena in Simple Dynamics," in C. Langton, C. Taylor, D. Farmer, S. Rasmussen, (eds.), *Artificial Life II*. Addison-Wesley, Reading, MA, 1992.
Mahar, Maggie. *Money-driven Medicine*. HarperCollins, New York, 2006.
March, James, "Exploration and Exploitation in Organizational Learning," *Organization Science*, 2, 1, 71–87, 1991.
Morgenson, Gretchen (*New York Times* reporter), "Examining Goldman Sachs," NPR interview in *Fresh Air*, May 4, 2010.
Nichols, S. L., and D. Berlner, *Collateral Damage: How High-stakes Testing Corrupts America's Schools.* Harvard Education Press, Cambridge, MA, 2007.
Pew Charitable Trusts, "History of Fuel Economy: One Decade of Innovation, Two Decades of Inaction" (www.pewtrusts.org), 2010.
Schneier, Bruce, "Cryptography: The Importance of Not Being Different," *IEEE Computer*, 32, 3, 108–109, 1999.
Suderman, Peter, "Quit Playing Games with my Health Care System," *Reason*, April 5, 2010.
Tabb, William, *The Restructuring of Capitalism in our Time*. Columbia University Press, New York, 2012.
White, Lawrence J. "The Credit Rating Agencies and the Subprime Debacle." *Critical Review*, 21 (2–3): 389–399, 2009.
Zuill, Lilla, "AIG's Meltdown Has Roots in Greenberg Era." *Insurance Journal*, 87, March 3, 2009.

CHAPTER 7

The Evolution of Technology within a Simple Computer Model

W. BRIAN ARTHUR*, AND WOLFGANG POLAK**

New technologies are constructed—put together—from technologies that already exist; these in turn offer themselves as building-block components for the creation of yet further new technologies. In this way technology (the collection of devices and methods available to society) builds itself out of itself. I call this mechanism of evolution by the creation of novel combinations and selection of those that work well *combinatorial evolution*, and describe it in detail in my 2009 book, *The Nature of Technology: What It Is and How It Evolves*. It differs from Darwin's mechanism, which relies on the gradual accumulation of incremental changes due to variation and selection.

Can combinatorial evolution be demonstrated "in the lab?" In 2005 Wolfgang Polak and I decided to test combinatorial evolution by designing a computer algorithm that starts from a set of primitive logic circuits (Nand gates) and combines these randomly. If the resulting circuit does something logically useful it is retained and encapsulated, then thrown in the mix as a building block for further random combination. We found that over time increasingly sophisticated circuits came into being by this process of successive integration, and we ended up with a plethora of sophisticated adders, comparators, and exclusive-ors. Combinatorial evolution could indeed create sophisticated technologies, but it does this by first creating simpler ones as building blocks. Our results mirror biology's finding [2] that complex features can be created only if simpler ones are first favored and act as stepping stones. We also found evidence that the resulting collection of technologies exists at self-organized criticality. The results show the power of this form of evolution. The paper appeared in *Complexity*, 11, 5, 23–31, 2006.

* Santa Fe Institute, Santa Fe, New Mexico.
** Fuji Xerox Palo Alto Laboratory, Palo Alto, California.

New technologies are never created from nothing. They are constructed—put together—from components that previously exist; and in turn these new technologies offer themselves as possible components—building blocks—for the construction of further new technologies.[1] In this sense, technology (the collection of mechanical devices and methods available to a culture) builds itself out of itself.[2] Thus in 1912 the amplifier circuit was constructed from the already existing triode vacuum tube in combination with other existing circuit components. The amplifier in turn made possible the oscillator (which could generate pure sine waves), and these with other components made possible the heterodyne mixer (which could shift signals' frequencies). These new components in combination with other standard ones went on to make possible continuous-wave radio transmitters and receivers. And these in conjunction with still other elements made possible radio broadcasting.

In its collective sense, technology forms a set or network of elements in which novel elements are continually constructed from existing ones.[3] Over time, this set bootstraps itself by combining simple elements to construct more complicated ones and by using few building-block elements to create many. This evolution is driven not just by the availability of previous technologies. It is driven by the large collection of human needs and also by needs brought into being by technologies themselves. Particular needs (in actual human history for food, transportation, cures for diseases, communication, and the drainage of fields and mines) are satisfied by simple technologies at first and then by more sophisticated ones that replace these simpler ones. Technologies that are replaced (think of horse transportation) become obsolete and in so doing may render other technologies that depend on them (carriage making and blacksmithing) obsolete, so that new elements not only add to the network but engender what Schumpeter called "gales of destruction" [1]. All this happens of course through the agency of the economy (which we

1. The idea that novel technologies are constructed from components—technologies—that already exist was observed by Ogburn in 1922 [8]. And Kaempffert in 1930 noted that novel technologies are "composites of mechanical elements that accumulated as part of the social heritage" [9]. See Arthur [10] for a fuller and more rigorous treatment of this idea.

2. We can therefore say that in its collective sense technology is self-producing, or autopoietic. (The term "autopoietic" was coined by Maturana and Varela [11].) This assertion that technology creates itself from itself requires a qualification. At bottom all technologies are created from harnessed phenomena [10, 12]. But phenomena are harnessed into use via existing physical devices and methods—by existing technologies. Thus, providing we think of phenomena as being harnessed by existing technologies and we bracket the human activities that create new technologies, we can say that technology creates itself.

3. This network is more properly defined by what brings what into existence—what makes what possible—and not just by what components are contained in each new technology.

can think of in shorthand as an organizational structure for arranging how technologies meet needs) and through the human agency of engineers, scientists, and developers.

It would be possible to explore this evolution of technology by historically examining its build-out piece by piece over the course of human history. In this article we take a different course. We model the build-out of technology by constructing a simple artificial world within the computer. In this world the technologies—the elements that build out—are logic circuits. (Logic circuits have the advantage that their function can be described exactly, and there are simple rules for forming them by combination.) We imagine that our artificial world has certain logical needs (for the ability to perform the exclusive-or function, say, or to be able to add 3-bit numbers), and these can be potentially satisfied by suitable logic circuits, providing they can be created. Starting from a primitive technology (in most of our experiments a simple NAND circuit), new circuits—new technologies—are constructed by randomly wiring together existing ones and testing the result to see whether they satisfy any existing needs. If a circuit proves useful—satisfies some need better than its competitors—it replaces the one that previously satisfied that need. It then adds to the active collection of technologies and becomes available as an element for the construction of still further circuits. In this way elements constantly add to the set of active technologies as they find uses and leave again if rendered obsolete by others. And in this way the collection of technologies bootstraps upward by first creating simple technologies that satisfy simple needs, then from these more complex technologies that satisfy more sophisticated needs.

We ask several questions. What are the properties of technology evolution in our artificial system? By what steps does the network of technology evolve? Do some technologies emerge as enabling ones (like ore smelting or the transistor) that have many uses in further combination, so that usefulness in generating further technologies is highly skewed? Do we see Schumpeterian gales of destruction? And if we start from a primitive technology, can our system artificially create combinations of elements that satisfy complex needs: that is, could our system evolve from one primitive circuit to satisfying a need say for 4- or 8-bit addition? (Note that our interest is in studying the evolution of complex artifacts and not in the engineering problem of generating efficient logic circuits for Boolean functions; that has been solved.)

We pay some attention to this last question. In real life, complex technologies are created both from the existence of simpler ones and from the particular needs that brought these simpler building blocks into being. Radar could not have been invented without the building blocks of electronic amplification and wave generation—and the needs that brought these simpler functions into existence. We should therefore not expect complicated circuits to appear without intermediate elements and without the simpler intermediate needs

Table 1. NEEDS ARE COMMON LOGIC FUNCTIONS FOR $2 \le n \le 15$, $1 \le k \le 8$, AND $2 \le m \le 7$

Name	Inputs	Outputs	Description
not	1	1	Negation
imply	2	1	Implication
n-way-xor	n	1	Exclusive or, addition mod 2
n-way-or	n	1	Disjunction n inputs
n-way-and	n	1	Conjunction n inputs
m-bitwise-xor	$2m$	m	Exclusive or on m input pairs
m-bitwise-or	$2m$	m	Disjunction on m input pairs
m-bitwise-and	$2m$	m	Conjunction on m input pairs
full-adder	3	2	Add 2 bits and carry
k-bit-adder	$2k$	$k + 1$	Addition
k-bit-equal	$2k$	1	Equality
k-bit-less	$2k$	1	Comparison

that generate these. There is a parallel observation in biology. Complex organismal features such as the human eye cannot appear without intermediate structures and "needs" or uses for these intermediate structures [2, 13].

We find that the collective of technology in our system can indeed bootstrap itself from extreme simplicity to surprisingly complicated circuits. We find, as we would expect, that most technologies created are not particularly useful as building blocks, but some turn out to be key in creating descendant technologies.

We find avalanches of replacement—Schumpeter's "gales of destruction." These follow a power law, so that the collective of technology shows evidence that it exists at self-organized criticality. And we find that the system arrives at complicated circuits only by first satisfying simpler needs and using the results as building blocks to bootstrap its way to satisfying more complex ones.

THE EXPERIMENTAL SYSTEM

We view each run of our artificial system as an experiment. Each experiment starts with only primitive components (usually one, an elementary logic gate), and the computer generates new circuits by randomly wiring together several components in a noncyclic way. A component can be a primitive logic gate or another circuit that has been created from this and has been encapsulated (think of it as a chip with designated input and output pins). We specify in Table 1 a set of *needs* or *goals*, useful logical functions to be achieved possible by the combinations. These are akin to the needs that drive technology evolution. Ideally we would like these needs to be generated by agents who occupy an artificial world in which logical functions such as adders or comparators have proved useful. But we avoid this complication and simply list a set of useful logical functionalities that suitable circuits, if they appear, might achieve.

Using an artificial system that asks for logical functionalities and provides ways for them to be realized has the advantage that needs and technologies can be easily compared. Each need for a particular logical functionality can be represented by a specific truth table: a set of desired output values for every possible set of input values presented. And each circuit created—each technology—provides a function that can also be represented as a truth table: for every set of binary values provided to its input pins it produces particular binary values on its output pins. Thus we can easily match experimental technologies with our list of needs. We can also think of a technology's behavior, its truth table, as the *phenotype* of this technology. Its *genotype* is the architecture or internal circuitry that realizes this function. Many different genotypes can generate the same phenotype.

Our computer model, then, consists of a set of primitives, a set of technologies or components constructed from primitives and from other components, and a set of needs to be fulfilled. [We normally use only one primitive, a NAND gate, with phenotype $\neg(x \wedge y)$.] The essence of the experiment is simple. In each evolutionary step novel circuits are created from existing ones by randomly wiring together between 2 and 12 circuits selected from all previously existing technologies according to a *choice function* that specifies probabilities of selection. Different phenotypic versions of the new circuit are created by selecting different internal wires in different orders as output pins. At each time there is a set of existing technologies that best match each of the needs or goals (have least incorrect entries in their truth tables). Each candidate circuit is tested against these to see if it improves upon them. It may do so by better matching a need's truth table, or if it has a function identical to that of an existing circuit, by costing less. (The cost of a circuit is determined by the number of its components and by *their* respective cost.) In either case it replaces the circuit it has improved upon both directly and in all circuits where that circuit is used as a component. It is also encapsulated: it becomes a new component that can serve as a building block for possible further combination. In this way the set of encapsulated technologies builds out. A need is *satisfied* if a new technology with its exact truth-table has been found. And a newly created circuit of course cannot replace one of its own components. Useful components are named (e.g., tech-256 or full-adder-121) and can be used in higher level technologies. Components that exactly implement a need are given mnemonic names describing that need (e.g., 3-bit-adder). Details of our implementation of these general algorithmic steps are listed in a section below.

The correspondence to the real world requires some comment. New technologies in the real world are indeed combinations of existing ones, but nowadays are rarely invented by randomly throwing together existing components. Loosely however we can think of each step in our process as a set of laboratory tests that investigates a novel idea. Or more exactly we can think of our process as corresponding to that used in modern combinatorial chemistry or synthetic biology, where new functionalities are created from random combinations and tested for their usefulness [3]. This process builds up a growing library of useful elements that can be exploited for further combination.

We can also think of this process more generally as an algorithm, not for solving a particular problem but for building up a library or repertoire of useful functionalities that can be combined to solve problems. The algorithm mimics the actual evolution of technology by first constructing objects that satisfy simple needs and using these as building blocks to construct objects of progressively higher complication.

EXPERIMENTAL RESULTS

The most complex circuits invented within 250,000 steps in our basic experimental design were as follows:

> 8-way-xor, 8-way-and, 8-way-or, 3-bitwise-xor, 4-bit-equal, 3-bit-less, and 4-bit-adder.

A more streamlined design, discussed below, created an 8-bit adder (which adds 8 bits to 8 bits correctly, a not uncomplicated achievement). Within the basic design different runs of the experiment invented circuits in different order and not all of these circuits evolved in the same experiment run.

Early in the experiment simple goals are fulfilled. We see from Figure 1, that even for simple circuits non-obvious implementations are invented. These circuits then become encapsulated for further use.

As the evolution proceeds more complicated circuits begin to construct themselves from simpler ones. The 2-bit-adder circuit shown in Figure 2 uses the supporting technology TECH-712. The latter circuit is an example of a technology that is useful toward satisfying a goal but that does not itself satisfy the goal 2-bit-adder (because the low-order (left) output bit is computed incorrectly). The circuit for 2-bit-adder is constructed from TECH-712 by adding circuitry to correct this error.

Some of our evolved circuits contain unused parts. The use of the 3-bit-adder on the right of Figure 3 is an example. In the course of the experiment such redundancies usually disappear because less "costly" circuits replace ones with needless complication.

Our experiment starts from the NAND primitive. In other versions of the experiment we used "implication" as the primitive. Similarly complicated

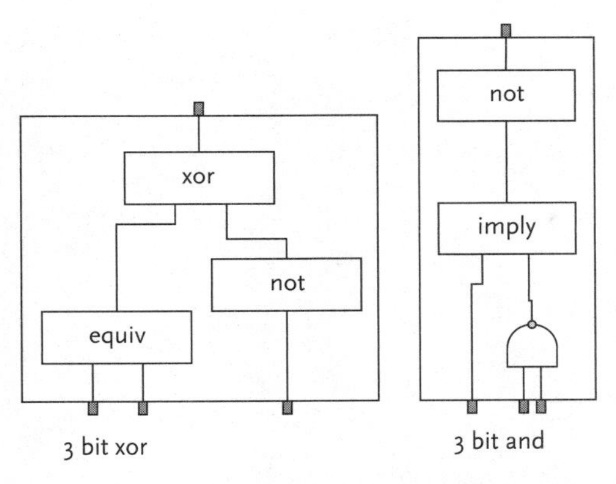

Figure 1:
Two circuits "invented" for simple goals.

circuits evolved. The process simply constructs the more elementary needs such as "not," "and," and "xor" from the new "implication" primitive and proceeds as before.

The emergence of circuits such as 8-bit adders may not seem particularly remarkable. But consider the combinatorics. If a component has n inputs and m outputs there are $(2^m)^{(2^n)}$ possible phenotypes, each of which could be realized in a practical way by a large number of different circuits. For example, an 8-bit adder is one of over $10^{177,554}$ phenotypes with 16 inputs and 9 outputs. The likelihood of such a circuit being discovered by random combinations in 250,000 steps is negligible. Our experiment—or algorithm—arrives at complicated circuits by first satisfying simpler needs and using the results as building blocks to bootstrap its way to satisfy more complex ones.

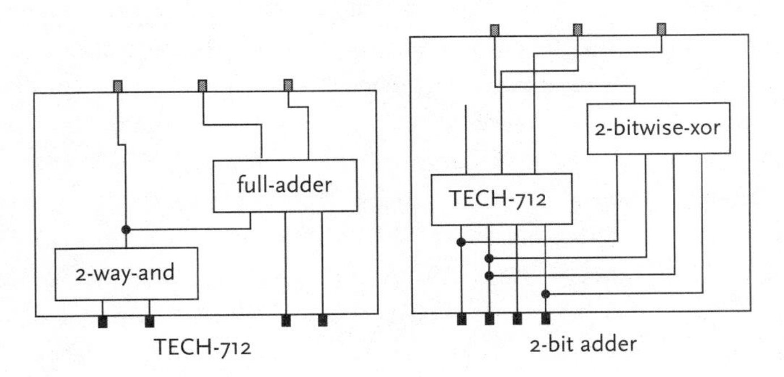

Figure 2:
TECH-712 is useful towards satisfying the "2-bit-adder" goal because the two high-order bits are computed correctly. (The low-order bit is on the left. For multi-bit adders, input bits are interleaved.)

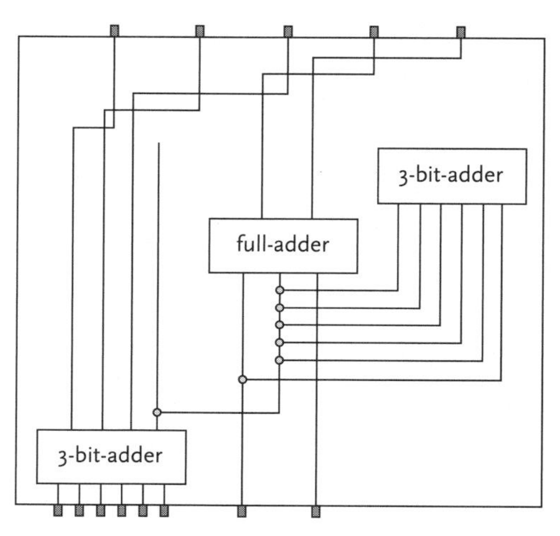

Figure 3:
A "4-bit-adder" circuit with an unconnected module.

THE BUILD-OUT OF TECHNOLOGIES

To talk about the build-out of technologies we need two definitions. The collection of all methods and devices (all circuits) ever used we call the *standing reserve*. The technologies that are currently viable—in current use—and have not yet been replaced, we call the *active repertoire*.

Figure 4 shows the growth over time of the standing reserve, the technologies ever invented. In contrast the growth of the active repertoire, the number of technologies actually in use, is not monotonic. This indicates that important inventions render older technologies obsolete. Figure 4 also shows that there is continual improvement in accomplishing truth function "needs" as indicated by growing number of replacements.

Tick marks along the time axis of Figure 4 indicate when one of the needs has been satisfied. Progress is slow at first: the experiment runs for some time without meeting any goals exactly, and then functional species begin to appear leading to further species. The evolution is not smooth. It is punctuated by the clustering of arrivals because from time to time key technologies—key building block components—are "discovered" that quickly enable other technologies. For example, after a circuit for OR is invented, circuits for 3-, 4-, and 5-bit OR and bitwise-OR operations follow in short order. This appearance of key building blocks that quickly make possible further technologies has analogies in the real world (think of the steam engine, the transistor, the laser) and with the build-out of species in biological evolution [2].

The order of invention makes a difference. Although "negation" is a simpler function than "implication," it happens that in some runs of the

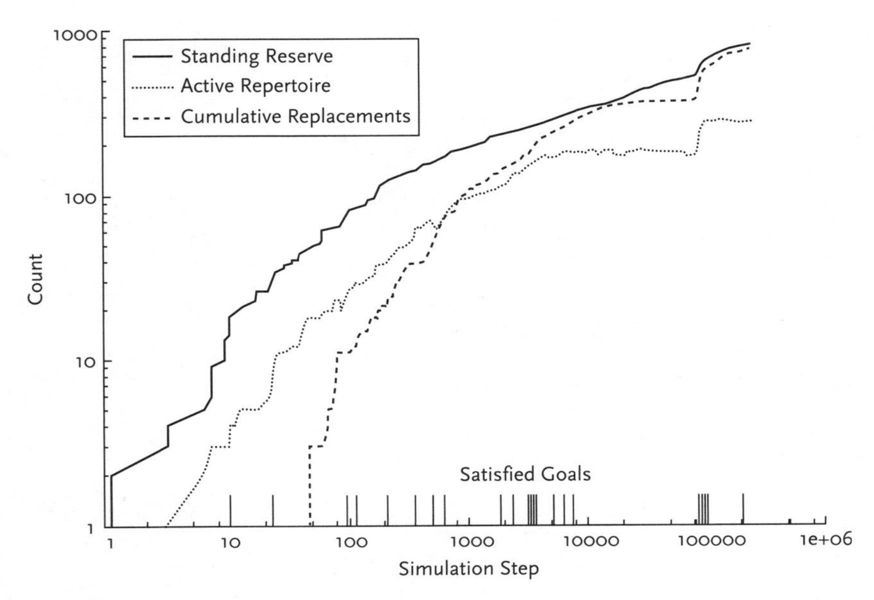

Figure 4:
The standing reserve, by definition, grows monotonically. The same is not true for the active repertoire because new inventions may improve upon and replace several existing ones.

experiment that the latter is invented first and is then used as a key building block.

Figure 5 shows the result of one such experiment. "Implication" was used in a large number of other technologies and became much more prevalent than "negation." But eventually, its usage as a component declined as negation and other, less costly components offered themselves for combination. For comparison, the figure shows a third technology, TECH-69, which also performs implication but has 3 additional redundant inputs and contains unneeded components. Eventually, all uses of TECH-69 are replaced with the functionally equivalent but more efficient implication.

There is a trade-off between the number of needs or goals posted and the creation of new technologies. To illustrate this, we performed an experiment masking some of the needs and retaining a subset that we considered useful for the construction of adders: ("not, imply, 2-way-or, 2-way-xor, full-adder," and "k-bit-adder" for $1 \leq k \leq 8$). (We can also streamline the process by adding more difficult needs, as measured by the number of inputs and outputs, to the experiment only after simpler ones have been satisfied.) An 8-bit adder evolved very quickly within 64,000 simulation steps. In contrast, using more general goals, some simulation runs took over 675,000 steps before even a 4-bit adder evolved. A large disparate set of needs leads to broad generation of functionalities within the circuit design space, but is slow in arriving at particular complex needs. Narrowly focused goals lead to a deep search that

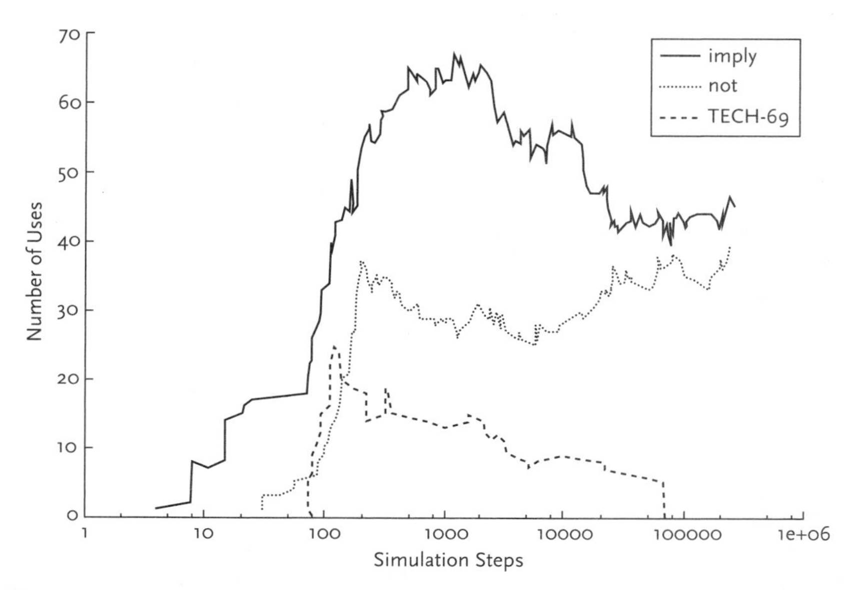

Figure 5:
"Implication," being invented before "negation" in this example, is used more heavily. Usage declines over time as better technologies are invented.

reaches particular complex needs quickly, but produces a narrow library of functionalities.

The algorithm does not produce complex circuits without intermediate needs present. If we start without these, the repertoire of necessary building blocks is missing. For instance, if the "full-adder" goal is omitted from the goals for adders listed above, not even a 2-bit adder was found in one million steps. When the "full-adder" goal is present, it occasionally happens that the 2-bit adder is found before the "full-adder" is invented. This is because the invention of technologies that build toward the "full-adder" goal are also useful for the 2-bit adder.

The fact that at each step only circuits combining fewer than 12 existing components are considered defines a set of possible experimental circuits at any time—a large number—which we can think as the *adjacent probable* [4]. We can think of this as a probabilistic cloud that surrounds the existing technologies and that gradually lead to new ones by being realized by points near intermediate goals. Thus if a goal is too complicated it cannot be reached—realized—with reasonable probability, and so if stepping stone goals are not present the algorithm does not work.

The technologies we have listed as needs or goals are well-ordered in the sense that the more complicated ones can be constructed from the more elementary ones by repeating these in simple patterns. For example, a complicated circuit such as a 4-bit adder can be constructed from simpler elements such as adders and half-adders that repeat in combination.

What if we choose complicated goals that are not easy to realize by repetitive patterns? We can do this by selecting random truth tables with n inputs and m outputs as needs. Not surprisingly we find that often these cannot be reached from our standard intermediate steps. By the same token, what if we replace our intermediate stepping-stone goals by random truth tables of the same intermediate size? Again, these also do not perform as well. The algorithm works best in spaces where needs are ordered (achievable by repetitive pattern), so that complexity can bootstrap itself by exploiting regularities in constructing complicated objects from simpler ones.

PROPERTIES OF THE NETWORK

Each technology (or encapsulated circuit) that is currently used to construct a technology is a node in the network of active technologies, and if two or more technologies are directly used to create a novel technology they show a (directed) link to this technology. A given technology A therefore links to its *user technologies*—the technologies it directly makes possible. As illustrated in Figure 6, some technologies have many links—are used very heavily to construct new ones—others have few. Usage approximates a power law (yielding a scale-free network) but by no means perfectly.

From time to time a new superior way of executing a certain functionality (or truth table function) is discovered. The new circuit may have fewer components or perform that function better. In this case the new circuit replaces

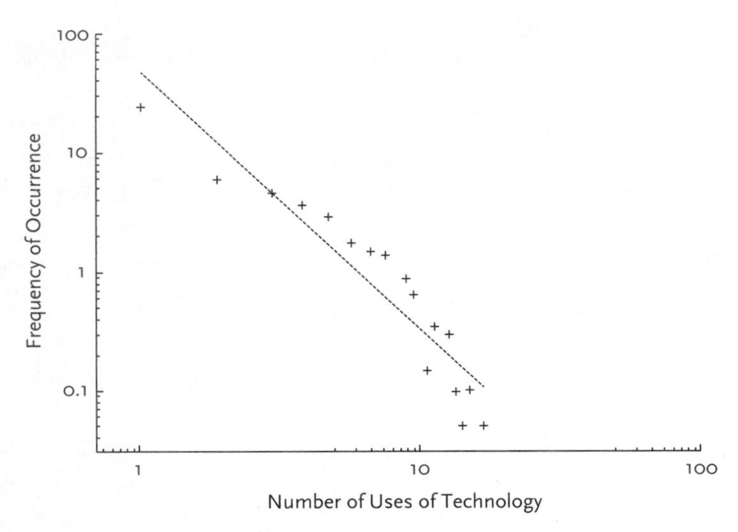

Figure 6:
Very few key technologies are used heavily to directly construct new ones. The plot shows the average over 20 experiments at their termination of 250,000 steps each.

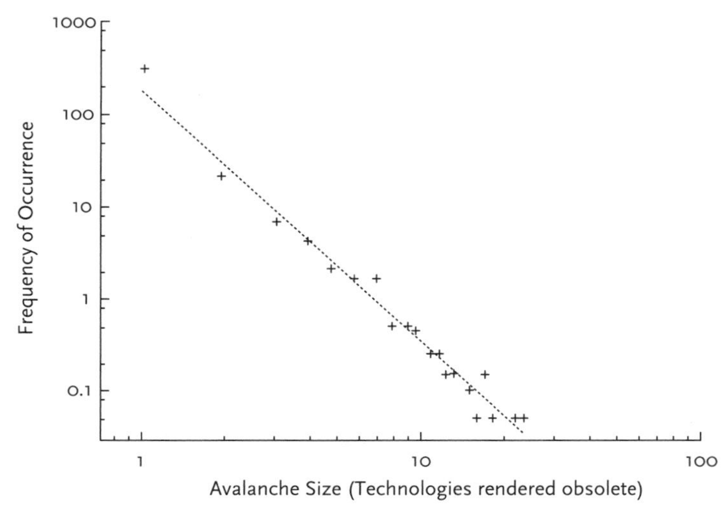

Figure 7:
Gales of destruction (or avalanches of collapse in use), average over 20 experiments.

the old one in all its *descendant* technologies (all the technologies below it in the network that use it directly or indirectly as a component). Replacement is immediate in our algorithm.

Replacement can also cause the collapse of technologies backward in the network. Suppose Tech 124 is used to construct Tech 136. Then, when a superior way to achieve Tech 136's functionality is found, Tech 124 may be left with no further use (it may neither satisfy any goal, nor be used in any active technology). In this case technology 124 disappears from the active set of technologies. In its disappearing, some of *its* component technologies may in turn be left with no further use. These also disappear from the active set. In this way technologies may be swept from active use in large or small avalanches of collapse—Schumpeter's "gales of destruction" [1].

Figure 7 shows that such sandpile avalanches of collapse follow a power law. The scale on the size axis does not extend far, however, because the number of technologies in the network is never large. We can take Figure 7 as suggestive that our system of technologies exists at self-organized criticality [5].

CONCLUSION

Using an artificial system, we have demonstrated how technology can bootstrap itself from extreme simplicity to a complicated level, both in terms of the numbers of objects created and their intricacy. In the real world, of course, novel technologies are not usually constructed by random combination, nor are the needs for which technologies are created specified in a posted list.

Nevertheless, all novel technologies are constructed by combining assemblies and components that already exist; the needs they satisfy are usually clearly signaled economically and technically; and existing technologies form a substrate or library of building blocks for future ones. The model captures certain phenomena we see in real life. Most technologies are not particularly useful as building blocks, but some (enabling technologies such as the laser or the transistor) are key in creating descendant technologies. Within our model, we find a strong indication that our collection of active technologies is subject to similar statistics as earthquakes and sand-piles: it exists at self-organized criticality. Our model also shows that the build-out of technology depends crucially on the existence of earlier technologies constructed for intermediate or simpler needs. This mirrors the finding of Lenski et al. in biological systems that complex features can be created, but only if simpler functions are first favored and act as stepping stones [2].

A COMMENT ON THE ALGORITHM

Just as biological evolution has been the model for genetic algorithms and genetic programming, technology-based evolution may inspire a new form of automatic programming and problem solving. The algorithm we develop here, viewed abstractly, operates by discovering objects of intermediate complexity and bootstraps complication by using these as building blocks in further combinations. It bears some semblance to other evolutionary algorithms such as genetic programming. But unlike these it does not attempt to solve a given single problem. Rather, it attempts to create a toolbox of useful functionalities that can be further used for further problem solving. In doing so it sets up no parallel population of trial solutions for a problem. Instead it creates a growing collection of objects that might be useful in solving problems of increasing complexity within the same class. In this sense it does not resemble standard programming methods inspired by genetic mechanisms; rather, it is an abstraction of methods already used as combinatorial chemistry or synthetic biology or software construction that build libraries of objects for the creation of further objects.

EXPERIMENTAL CONDITIONS

Our experimental system is implemented in Common Lisp. Different sets of goals can be added to the system manually. The detailed behavior of the system is controlled by a number of configuration parameters. (The values we give below are default ones.) Extensive experiments with different settings have shown that our results are not particularly sensitive to the choice of these parameters.

To construct new circuits, at each step a small number of components (up to a maximum of 12) is selected and combined. The selection is made each time by randomly drawing a component either from the set of primitives, or the constants 0 and 1, or the set of circuits encapsulated as technologies, with probabilities 0.5, 0.015, and 0.485, respectively (and then choosing with equal probability within these sets). (For the purpose of selection, components that satisfy a goal exactly are added to the primitives' set.) Selected components may then be combined randomly to each other two circuits at a time, or to combinations of each other, to form new circuits for testing. To combine two circuits C_1 and C_2, each input of C_1 becomes an input of the combination; each input of C_2 becomes an input of the combination with probability 0.2; otherwise it is connected to a random output of C_1. All outputs of C_1 and C_2 become outputs of the combination. The step stops when a useful circuit has been found, or when a limit to combinations tested has been reached.

The cost of a circuit is the sum of the costs of its components. The cost of a primitive component is 1. The cost of a circuit encapsulated as a new technology/component is the number of its components. Thus, the cost of a technology is less than the cost of the circuit it encapsulates, reflecting the idea that it becomes a commodity. We use the cost function to decide when to replace an existing technology by a cheaper one.

Logic functions are represented by binary decision diagrams (BDDs) [6, 7]. The phenotypes of goals and circuits are described by vectors of BDDs, one for each output wire. BDDs make it efficient to determine the equality of two logic functions. The representation also makes possible an efficient distance measure on logic functions, namely the number of input values for which two functions differ. We use this distance measure to define when one circuit C_1 better approximates a goal G than another circuit C_2. This is the case if for each output g of G circuit C_1 computes a function f that is closer to g than any of the functions computed by C_2. Note that this relation is a partial order, i.e., two circuits need not be comparable. A circuit C is encapsulated as a new technology if there is a goal G and no other circuit better approximates G than C. Only outputs of C appropriate for G become outputs of the new component, possibly making some parts of C redundant. In general, several circuits may approximate the same goal G at the same time, as when each circuit best satisfies some aspect (subset of the outputs) of the goal, but neither strictly dominates the other.

ACKNOWLEDGMENTS

This work was mainly carried out at and supported by Fuji Xerox Palo Alto Laboratory. We also thank the members of the Santa Fe Institute Workshop on Innovation in Natural, Experimental, and Applied Evolution (February

2004), for comments on an early version of these ideas. This workshop was supported by the Packard Foundation and the Thaw Charitable Trust. W.B.A. thanks Stuart Kauffman and John Holland for many discussions dating back to August 1987 on the notion of technologies creating technologies by combination. Both authors thank Eleanor Rieffel for helpful discussions in the early phases of this article, and Rob Carlson, Rich Lenski, and Peter Schuster for detailed comments.

REFERENCES

1. Schumpeter, J. A. *The Theory of Economic Development*; Transaction Publishers: New Brunswick, NJ, 1911/1934/1996.
2. Lenski, R. E.; Ofria, C.; Pennock, R. T.; Adami C. The evolutionary origin of complex features. *Nature* 2003, 423, 139–143.
3. Beck-Sickinger, A.; Weber, P. *Combinatorial Strategies in Biology and Chemistry*; Wiley: Chichester, England, 2001.
4. Kauffman, S. A. *Investigations*; Oxford University Press: New York, 2002.
5. Bak, P.; Wiesenfeld, K. Self-organized criticality: An explanation for *1/f noise*. *Phys Rev A* 1988, 38, 364.
6. Bryant, R. E. Graph-based algorithms for Boolean function manipulation. *IEEE Trans Comput* 1988, 35(8), 677–691.
7. Bryant, R. E. Symbolic Boolean manipulation with ordered binary-decision diagrams. *ACM Comput Surv* 1992, 24(3), 293–318.
8. Ogburn, W. F. *Social Change*; 1922 (Dell: New York, 1966).
9. Kaempffert, W. *Invention and Society*. Reading with a Purpose Series, 56, American Library Association: Chicago, 1930.
10. Arthur, W. B. *The Nature of Technology: What It Is and How It Evolves;* in preparation. (Appeared in 2009, The Free Press: New York.)
11. Maturana H.; Varela F. Autopoiesis and cognition: The realization of the living. *Boston Studies in the Philosophy of Science* 42; Cohen, R. S; Wartofsky, M. W., Eds.; D. Reidel Publishing: Dordrecht, 1973.
12. Arthur, W. B. *The Logic of Invention*. Santa Fe Institute Working Paper 2005-12-045; Santa Fe Institute: Santa Fe, NM, 2005.
13. Gehring, W. J. The genetic control of eye development and its implications for the evolution of the various eye-types. *Int J Dev Biol* 2002, 46, 65–73.

CHAPTER 8
The Economy Evolving as Its Technologies Evolve

W. BRIAN ARTHUR

New technologies entering an economy cause it not only to grow and become more productive; if significant, they cause it to change in structure—to change in how it is organized. How does such structural change happen? How does an economy evolve as its technologies evolve?

This chapter argues that the appearance of a novel technology triggers a cascade of further events. The new technology becomes available as a possible building-block for further new technologies, and it creates opportunity niches in the form of needs for supporting technologies, for novel forms of organization to accommodate it, and for novel institutions. It may also bring social and economic challenges, which call for further technologies to resolve these. A new technology therefore brings a train of further technologies, and the economy thereby continually changes its character or internal structure. The chapter is a slightly rewritten version of chapter 10, "The Economy Evolving as its Technologies Evolve," from my book *The Nature of Technology: What It Is and How It Evolves* (The Free Press, New York, 2009).

We have been looking very directly at the evolution of technology in the previous chapter [of my book, *The Nature of Technology: What It Is and How It Evolves* (2009)].[1] There is an alternative way to perceive this evolution, and that is through the eyes of the economy. An economy mirrors the changes in its technologies, the additions and replacements I have been talking about. And it does this not merely by smoothly readjusting its patterns of production

1. The Free Press, New York. This is chapter 10 of that book.

and consumption or by creating fresh combinations, as we saw in chapter 8. It alters its structure—alters the way it is arranged—as its technologies evolve, and does this at all times and at all levels.

So I want to go back to the steps in the evolution of technology and look at how they play out from the viewpoint of the economy. What we will see is a natural process of structural change in the economy driven by the evolutionary processes we have just delved into. To explore this we will first need to think of the economy in a way that differs from the standard one.

THE ECONOMY AS AN EXPRESSION OF ITS TECHNOLOGIES

The standard way to define the economy—whether in dictionaries or economics textbooks—is as a "system of production and distribution and consumption" of goods and services.[2] And we picture this system, "the economy," as something that exists in itself as a backdrop to the events and adjustments that occur within it. Seen this way, the economy becomes something like a gigantic container for its technologies, a huge machine with many modules or parts that are its technologies—its means of production. When a new technology (the railroad for transportation, say) comes along it offers a new module, a new upgrade, for a particular industry: the old specialized module it replaces (canals) is taken out and the new upgrade module is slid in. The rest of the machine automatically rebalances and its tensions and flows (prices and goods produced and consumed) readjust accordingly.

This view is not quite wrong. Certainly it is the way I was taught to think about the economy in graduate school, and it is very much the way economic textbooks picture the economy today. But it is not quite right either. To explore structural change, I want to look at the economy in a different way.

I will define the economy as *the set of arrangements and activities by which a society satisfies its needs*. (This makes economics the study of this.) Just what are these arrangements? Well, we could start with the Victorians economists' "means of production," the industrial production processes at the core of the economy. Indeed, my definition would not have surprised Karl Marx. Marx saw the economy as issuing from its "instruments of production," which would have included the large mills and textile machinery of his day.

But I want to go beyond Marx's mills and machinery. The set of arrangements that form the economy include all the myriad devices and methods and all the purposed systems we call technologies. These include hospitals and surgical procedures. And markets and pricing systems. And trading arrangements, distribution systems, organizations, and businesses. And financial

2. The definition is from Dictionary.com. WordNet® 3.0. Princeton University, 2008.

systems, banks, regulatory systems and legal systems. All these are arrangements by which we fulfill our needs, all are means to fulfill human purposes. Now, earlier in the book [Arthur, 2009] I defined technologies as means to human purposes, so all these are "technologies," or purposed systems. So if we allow that the New York Stock Exchange and the specialized provisions of contract law are as much means to human purposes as are steel mills and textile machinery, we can say that they too are in a wide sense technologies.

If we include all these "arrangements" in the collective of technology, we begin to see the economy not as a container for its technologies, but as something constructed from its technologies. The economy is a set of activities and behaviors and flows of goods and services, mediated by—draped over—its technologies. It follows that the methods, processes, and organizational forms I have been talking about *form* the economy.

The economy is an expression of its technologies.

I am not saying that an economy is identical to its technologies. There is more to an economy than this. Strategizing in business, investing, bidding, and trading—these are all activities and not purposed systems. What I *am* saying is that the structure of the economy is formed by its technologies, that technologies if you like form the economy's skeletal structure. The rest of the economy—the activities of commerce, the strategies and decisions of the various players in the game, the flows of goods and services and investments that result from these—form the muscle and neural structure and blood of the body-economic. But these parts surround and are shaped by the set of technologies, the purposed systems, that form the structure of the economy.

The shift in thinking I am putting forward here is not large; it is subtle. It is like seeing the mind not as a container for its concepts and habitual thought processes but as something that emerges from these. Or seeing an ecology not as containing a collection of biological species, but as forming from its collection of species. So it is with the economy. The economy forms an ecology for its technologies, it forms out of them, and this means it does not exist separately. And as with an ecology, it forms opportunity niches for novel technologies and fills these as novel technologies arise.

This way of thinking carries consequences. It means that the economy emerges—wells up—from its technologies. It means that the economy does more than readjust as its technologies change, it continually forms and re-forms as its technologies change. And it means that the character of the economy—its form and structure—change as its technologies change.

In sum, we can say this: As the collective of technology builds, it creates a structure within which decisions and activities and flows of goods and services take place. It creates something we call "the economy." The economy in this way emerges from its technologies. It constantly creates itself out of its technologies and decides which new technologies will enter it. Notice the circular causality at work here. Technology creates the structure of the economy, and the economy mediates the creation of novel technology (and therefore its own creation). Normally we do not see this technology-creating-the-economy-creating-technology. In the short term of a year or so the economy appears given and fixed; it appears to be a container for its activities. Only when we observe over decades do we see the arrangements and processes that form the economy coming into being, interacting, and collapsing back again. Only in the longer reaches of time do we see this continual creation and re-creation of the economy.

STRUCTURAL CHANGE

What happens to this system that forms from its technologies as new technologies enter? We would still see the same adjustments and fresh combinations I spoke about in chapter 8 of course; they are perfectly valid. But we would see something more: the addition of new technologies setting in motion a train of changes to the structure of the economy, to the set of arrangements around which the economy forms.

We are coming into territory here—that of structural change—that economic theory does not usually enter. But this is not empty territory. It is inhabited by historians, in our case by economic historians. Historians see the introduction of new technologies not simply as causing readjustments and growth, but as causing changes in the composition of the economy itself—in its structure. But they proceed for the most part on an ad-hoc, case-by-case basis. Our way of thinking about the economy and technology by contrast gives us a means to think abstractly about structural change.

In practice a new technology may call forth new industries; it may require that new organizational arrangements be set up; it may cause new technical and social problems and hence create new opportunity niches; and all these themselves may call forth further compositional changes. We can capture this sequence of changes if we borrow the steps in the evolution of technology from the previous chapter, but now see them through the eyes of the economy. So let us do this.

We can start by supposing that a candidate novel technology appears. It has been made possible by a combination of previous technologies and has bested its rivals for entry into the economy. Six events or steps then follow. We can think of these as the legitimate moves that can be made in the technology buildout game. I will state them abstractly, but the reader might find it helpful to have an example technology in mind: the railroad, say, or the automobile, or the transistor.

1. The novel technology enters the active collection as a novel element. It becomes a new element in the active collection.

2. The novel element becomes available to replace existing technologies and components in existing technologies.
3. The novel element sets up further "needs" or opportunity niches for supporting technologies and organizational arrangements. In particular such needs may arise from the new technology causing novel technical, economic, or social problems. And so, the new technology sets up needs for further technologies to resolve these.
4. If old displaced technologies fade from the collective, *their* ancillary needs are dropped. The opportunity niches they provide disappear with them, and the elements that in turn fill these may become inactive.
5. The novel element becomes available as a potential component in further technologies—further elements. In doing so it acts to call forth other technologies that use and accommodate it. In particular it may give rise to novel organizations that contain it.
6. The economy—the pattern of goods and services produced and consumed—readjusts to these steps. Costs and prices (and therefore incentives for novel technologies) change accordingly.

I have really just stated in economic terms the steps described in the previous chapter that form the mechanism by which the collective of technology evolves. But I am interpreting these steps to describe how a new structure for the economy forms. When a novel technology enters the economy, it calls forth novel arrangements—novel technologies and organizational forms. The new technology or new arrangements in turn may cause new problems. These are answered by further novel arrangements (or by existing technologies modified for the purpose), which in their turn may open needs for yet more novel technologies. The whole moves forward in a sequence of problem and solution—of challenge and response—and it is this sequence we call structural change. In this way the economy forms and re-forms itself in spates of change, as novelty, new arrangements to accommodate this, and the opening of resulting opportunity niches follow from each other.

Let me make this concrete with a particular example. When workable textile machinery began to arrive around the 1760s in Britain, it offered a substitute for the cottage-based methods of the time, where wool and cotton were spun and woven at home by hand in the putting-out system.[3] But the new machinery at first was only partly successful; it called for a larger scale of organization than did cottage hand-work. And so it presented an opportunity for—and became a component in—a higher level organizational arrangement, the textile factory or mill. The factory itself as a means of organization—a

3. For accounts of the industrial revolution, see Landes (1969), Mokyr (1990), and Ashton (1968).

technology—in turn required a means to complement its machinery: it called for factory labor. Labor of course already existed in the economy, but it did not exist in sufficient numbers to supply the new factory system. The necessary numbers were largely drawn from agriculture, and this in turn required accommodation near the mills. Worker dormitories and worker housing were therefore provided, and from the combination of mills, workers, and their housing, industrial cities began to grow. A new set of societal means of organization had appeared—a new set of arrangements—and with these the structure of the Victorian industrial economy began to emerge. In this way the character of an era—a set of arrangements compatible with the superior technology of industrial machinery—fell into place.

But an era is never finished. Manufacturing laborers, many of them children, worked often in Dickensian conditions. This presented a strongly felt need for reform, not only of "the moral conditions of the lower classes" but of their safety as well.[4] In due course the legal system responded with further arrangements, labor laws designed to prevent the worst of the excesses. And the new working class began to demand a larger share of the wealth the factories had created. They made use of a means by which they could better their conditions: trade unions. Labor was much easier to organize in factories than in isolated cottages, and over the course of decades it became a political force (Chase, 2000; and Fraser, 1999).

In this way the original arrival of textile machinery not only replaced cottage hand manufacturing, it set up an opportunity for a higher-level set of arrangements—the factory system—in which the machinery became merely a component. The new factory system in turn set up a chain of needs—for labor and housing—whose solutions created further needs, and all this in time became the Victorian industrial system. The process took a hundred years or more to reach anything like completion.

The reader might object that this makes structural change appear too simplistic—too mechanical. Technology *A* sets up a need for arrangements *B*; technology *C* fulfills this, but sets up further needs *D* and *E*; these are resolved by technologies *F* and *G*. Certainly such sequences do form the basis of structural change, but there is nothing simple about them. If we invoke recursion these new arrangements and technologies themselves call for sub-technologies and sub-arrangements. The factory system itself needed means of powering the new machinery, systems of ropes and pulleys for transmitting this power, means of acquiring and keeping track of materials, means of bookkeeping, means of management, means of delivery of the product. And these in turn were built from other components, and had their own needs. Structural

4. The quote is from M. E. Rose (1981). See also P. W. J. Bartrip and S. B. Burman (1983).

change is fractal, it branches out at lower levels, just as an embryonic arterial system branches out as it develops into smaller arteries and capillaries.

And some of the responses are not economic at all. The very idea that hand craft could be mechanized spread from textiles to other industries and led to new machinery there. And again psychologically, factories created not just a new organizational set of arrangements but called for a new kind of person. Factory discipline, says historian David Landes, "required and eventually created a new breed of worker.... No longer could the spinner turn her wheel and the weaver throw his shuttle at home, free of supervision, both in their own good time. Now the work had to be done in a factory, at a pace set by tireless, inanimate equipment, as part of a large team that had to begin, pause, and stop in unison—all under the close eye of overseers, enforcing assiduity by moral, pecuniary, occasionally even physical means of compulsion. The factory was a new kind of prison; the clock a new kind of jailer." The new technology caused more than economic change; it caused psychological change.

In talking about structural change then, we need to acknowledge that the set of changes may not all be tangible and may not all be "arrangements." And we need to keep in mind that changes may have multiple causes and a high multiplicity of effects. Nevertheless, I want to emphasize that we can think of the process of structural change in logical terms—theoretically if you like—using the steps laid out for the evolution of technology. Structural change in the economy is not just the addition of a novel technology and replacement of the old, and the economic adjustments that follow these. It is a chain of consequences where the arrangements that form the skeletal structure of the economy continually call forth new arrangements.

There is of course nothing inevitable—nothing predetermined—about the arrangements that fall into place and define the structure of the economy. We saw earlier that very many different combinations, very many arrangements, can solve the problems posed by technology. Which ones are chosen is in part a matter of historical small events: the order in which problems happen to be tackled, the predilections and actions of individual personalities. The actions, in other words, of chance. Technology determines the structure of the economy and thereby much of the world that emerges from this, but which technologies fall into place is not determined in advance.

PROBLEMS AS THE ANSWER TO SOLUTIONS

I have talked about this unfolding of structure as a constant remaking of the arrangements that form the economy; one set of arrangements sets up conditions for the arrival of the next. There is no reason once set in motion this remaking should come to an end. The consequences of even one novel technology—think of the computer or the steam engine—can persist without letup.

It follows in turn that the economy is never quite at stasis. At any time its structure may be in some high degree of mutual compatibility, and hence close to unchanging. But within this stasis lie the seeds of its own disruption, as Schumpeter (1912) pointed out a hundred years ago. The cause is the creation of novel combinations—novel arrangements—or for Schumpeter the new "goods, the new methods of production or transportation, the new markets, the new forms of industrial organization" that set up a process of "industrial mutation" that "incessantly revolutionizes the economic structure *from within*, incessantly destroying the old one, incessantly creating a new one."

From within, the system is always poised for change.

But the argument I am giving implies more—quite a bit more—than Schumpeter said. The coming of novel technologies does not just disrupt the status quo by finding new combinations that are better versions of the goods and methods we use. It sets up a train of technological accommodations and of new problems, and in so doing it creates new opportunity niches that call forth fresh combinations which in turn introduce yet further technologies—and further problems.[5]

The economy therefore exists always in a perpetual openness of change—in perpetual novelty. It exists perpetually in a process of self-creation. It is always unsatisfied. We can add to this that novel technologies of all degrees of significance enter the economy at any time alongside each other. The result is not just Schumpeter's disturbance of equilibrium, but a constant roiling of simultaneous changes, all overlapping and interacting and triggering further change. The result is change begetting change.

Curiously, we may not be very conscious of this constant roiling at any time. This is because the process of structural change plays out over decades, not months. It is more like the slow geological upheavals that take place under our feet. In the short term the structure in place has a high degree of continuity; it is a loosely compatible set of systems within which plans can be made and activities can take place. But at all times this structure is being altered. The economy is perpetually constructing itself.

Could this process of constant evolution of technology and remaking of the economy ever come to a halt? In principle, it could. But only in principle. This could only happen if no novel phenomena from which to create technologies in the future were to be uncovered; or if the possibilities for further combinations were somehow exhausted. Or if our practical human needs were somehow fulfilled by the available technologies we possessed. But each of these

5. See Rapp (1989) for a similar idea.

possibilities is unlikely. Ever-open needs and the likely discovery of new phenomena will be sufficient to drive technology forward in perpetuity, and the economy with it.

Coming to a halt is unlikely for another reason. I have been stressing that every solution in the form of a new technology creates some new challenge, some new problem. Stated as a general rule, *every technology contains the seeds of a problem,* often several. This is not a "law" of technology or of the economy, much less one of the universe. It is simply a broad-based empirical observation—a regrettable one—drawn from human history. The use of carbon-based fuel technologies has brought global warming. The use of atomic power, an environmentally clean source of power, has brought the problem of disposal of atomic waste. The use of air transport has brought the potential of rapid worldwide spread of infections. In the economy, solutions lead to problems, and problems to further solutions, and this dance between solution and problem is unlikely to change at any time in the future. If we are lucky we experience a net benefit that we call progress. Whether or not progress exists, this dance condemns technology—and the economy as a result—to continuous change.

What I have been talking about in this chapter is really the evolution of technology seen through the eyes of the economy. Because the economy is an expression of its technologies, it is a set of arrangements that forms from the processes, organizations, devices, and institutional provisions that comprise the evolving collective; and it evolves as its technologies do. And because the economy arises out of its technologies, it inherits from them self-creation, perpetual openness, and perpetual novelty. The economy therefore arises ultimately out of the phenomena that create technology; it is nature organized to serve our needs.

There is nothing simple about this economy. Arrangements are built one upon another: the commercial parts of the legal system are constructed on the assumption that markets and contracts exist; and markets and contracts assume that banking and investment mechanisms exist. The economy therefore is not a homogeneous thing. It is a structure—a magnificent structure—of interacting, mutually supporting arrangements existing at many levels that has grown itself from itself over centuries. It is almost a living thing, or at least an evolving thing, that changes its structure continually as its arrangements create further possibilities and problems that call forth further responses—yet further arrangements.

This evolution of structure is a constant remaking of the arrangements that form the economy, as one set of arrangements sets up the conditions for the arrival of the next. This is not the same as readjustment within given arrangements or given industries, and it is not the same as economic growth. It is continual, fractal, and inexorable. And it brings unceasing change.

Is there anything constant about structural change? Well, the economy forms its patterns always from the same elements—the predilections of human behavior, the basic realities of accounting, and the truism that goods bought must equal goods sold. These underlying base "laws" always stay the same. But the means by which they are expressed change over time, and the patterns they form change and re-form over time. Each new pattern, each new set of arrangements, then, yields a new structure for the economy and the old one passes, but the underlying components that form it—the base laws—remain always the same.

Economics as a discipline is often criticized because, unlike the "hard sciences" of physics or chemistry, it cannot be pinned down to an unchanging set of descriptions over time. But this is not a failing, it is proper and natural. The economy is not a simple system; it is an evolving, complex one, and the structures it forms change constantly over time. This means our interpretations of the economy must change constantly over time. I sometimes think of the economy as a World War I battlefield at night. It is dark, and not much can be seen over the parapets. From a half mile or so away, across in enemy territory, rumblings are heard and a sense develops that emplacements are shifting and troops are being redeployed. But the best guesses of the new configuration are extrapolations of the old. Then someone puts up a flare and it illuminates a whole pattern of emplacements and disposals and troops and trenches in the observers' minds, and all goes dark again. So it is with the economy. The great flares in economics are those of theorists like Smith or Ricardo or Marx or Keynes. Or indeed Schumpeter himself. They light for a time, but the rumblings and redeployments continue in the dark. We can indeed observe the economy, but our language for it, our labels for it, and our understanding of it are all frozen by the great flares that have lit up the scene, and in particular by the last great set of flares.

REFERENCES

Ashton, T. S., *The Industrial Revolution*, Oxford University Press, New York, 1968.

Bartrip, P. W. J. and S. B. Burman, *The Wounded Soldiers of Industry*, Clarendon Press, Oxford, UK, 1983.

Chase, M., *Early Trade Unionism*, Ashgate, Aldershot, UK, 2000.

Fraser, W. H., *A History of British Trade Unionism 1700–1998*, Macmillan, London, 1999.

Landes, David, *The Unbound Prometheus*, Cambridge University Press, Cambridge, UK, 1969.

Mokyr, Joel, *The Lever of Riches*, Oxford University Press, New York, 1990.

Rapp, Friedrich, in Paul. T. Durbin, ed., *Philosophy of Technology*, Kluwer Academic Publishers, Norwell, MA, 1989.

Rose, M. E., "Social Change and the Industrial Revolution," in *The Economic History of Britain since 1700*, Vol. 1, R. Floud, and D. McCloskey, eds., Cambridge University Press, Cambridge, UK, 1981.

Schumpeter, Joseph, *The Theory of Economic Development*. 1912. Reprinted, Harvard University Press, Cambridge, MA, 1934.

CHAPTER 9
On the Evolution of Complexity

W. BRIAN ARTHUR

We often take for granted that systems evolving over time tend to become more complicated. In 1994, when this paper was written, little was understood about what mechanisms might cause evolution to favor increases in complication. This paper proposes three means by which complication tends to grow as systems evolve. In coevolutionary systems it may grow by increases in "species" diversity: under certain circumstances new species may provide further niches that call forth further new species in a steady upward spiral. In single systems it may grow by increases in structural sophistication: the system steadily cumulates increasing numbers of internal subsystems or sub-functions or subparts to break through performance limitations, or to enhance its range of operation, or to handle exceptional circumstances. Or, it may suddenly increase by "capturing software": the system captures simpler elements and learns to "program" these as "software" to be used to its own ends.

Growth in complication in all three mechanisms is intermittent and epochal. And in the first two it is reversible; collapses in complexity may occur randomly from time to time. Illustrative examples are drawn not just from biology, but from economics, adaptive computation, artificial life, and evolutionary game theory. This paper appeared in the book *Complexity: Metaphors, Models, and Reality*, edited by G. Cowan, D. Pines, and D. Meltzer, Perseus Advanced Book Classics, Cambridge, MA, 1994.

It is a commonly accepted belief—a folk theorem, almost—that as systems evolve over time they tend to become more complex. But what is the evidence for this? Does evolution, in fact, favor increases in complexity and, if so, why? By what mechanisms might evolution increase complexity over time? And can the process go in the other direction, too, so that complexity diminishes from time to time? In this chapter I will discuss these questions and, in particular, three different ways in which evolution tends to increase complexity in general systems.

In the biological literature, there has been considerable debate on the connection between evolution and complexity.[1,11] But much of this discussion has been hampered by the fact that evolutionary innovations typically come in the form of smooth changes or continuous, plastic modifications: in the size of organism,[1] in the morphology of body parts,[13] or in animal behavior,[1] so that increases in "complexity" are difficult both to define and discern. As a result, while most biologists believe that complexity does indeed increase with evolution, and particular mechanisms are often cited, the question remains muddied by problems of definition and observation, so that some biologists have expressed doubts about any linkage between evolution and complexity at all.[11]

Fortunately, of late we are beginning to cumulate experience in evolutionary contexts that are not necessarily biological. These contexts include those of competition among technologies and firms in the economy, of self-replicating computer programs, of adaptive computation, of artificial life systems, and of computer-based "ecologies" of competing game strategies. Used as alternatives to biological examples, these have two advantages. Their alterations and innovations are very often discrete and well-marked, so that in these contexts we can define and observe increases in complexity more easily. And many are computer based. Thus, they can provide "laboratories" for the real-time measurement and replication of changes in complexity in the course of evolution.

In discussing complexity and evolution in this chapter, I will draw examples from the economy and from several of the other contexts mentioned above, as well as from biology. I will be interested in "complexity" seen simply as complication. Exactly what "complication" means will vary from context to context; but it will become clear, I hope, in the mechanisms as they are discussed. And I will use the term "evolution" often in its phylogenetic sense, as development in a system with a clear lineage of inherited structures that may change over time. Thus, we can talk about the evolution of a language, or of a technology, without having to assume that these necessarily reproduce in a population of languages or technologies.

GROWTH IN COEVOLUTIONARY DIVERSITY

The first mechanism whereby complexity increases as evolution takes place, I will call *growth in coevolutionary diversity*. It applies in systems where the individuals or entities or species or organisms coexist together in an interacting population, with some forming substrates or niches that allow the existence of others. We may, therefore, think of such coevolving systems as organized into loose hierarchies or "food webs" of dependence, with individuals further down a hierarchy depending for their existence on the existence of more fundamental ones nearer the base of the hierarchy.

When the individuals (and their multiple possibilities in interaction) in such systems create a variety of niches that are not closed off to further newly generated individuals, diversity tends to grow in a self-reinforcing way. New individuals that enter the population may provide new substrates, new niches. This provides new possibilities to be filled or exploited by further new entities. The appearance of these, in turn, may provide further new niches and substrates. And so on. By this means, complexity in the form of greater diversity and a more intricate web of interactions tends to bootstrap itself upward over time. Growth in coevolutionary diversity may be slow and halting at first, as when the new individuals merely replace uncompetitive, preexisting ones. But over time, with entities providing niches and niches making possible new entities, it may feed upon itself; so that diversity itself provides the fuel for further diversity.

Growth in coevolutionary diversity can be seen in the economy in the way specialized products and processes within the computer industry have proliferated in the last two decades. As modern microprocessors came into existence, they created niches for devices such as memory systems, screen monitors, and bus interfaces that could be connected with them to form useful hardware—computing devices. These, in turn, created a need, or niche, for new operating system software and programming languages, and for software applications. The existence of such hardware and software, in turn, made possible desktop publishing, computer-aided design and manufacturing, electronic mail, shared computer networks, and so on. This created niches for laser printers, engineering-design software and hardware, network servers, modems, and transmission systems. These new devices, in turn, called forth further new microprocessors and system software to drive them. And so, in about two decades, the computer industry has undergone an explosive increase in diversity: from a small number of devices and software to a very large number, as new devices make possible further new devices, and new software products make possible new functions for computers, and these, in turn, call forth further new devices and new software.

Of course, we should not forget that as new computer products and functions for computers appear, they are often replacing something else in the economy. Computer-aided design may eventually replace standard drawing board and T-square design. And so the increase in diversity in one part of a system may be partially offset by loss of diversity elsewhere. Occasionally, in a coevolving system, this replacement of an existing function can cause a *reversal* in the growth of coevolutionary diversity. This happens when the new entity replaces a more fundamental one in the system and the niches dependent on this disappear. In the economy of the last century, for example, there was a steady increase in the numbers of specialized, interconnected "niche firms" in the horse-drawn transportation industry; so that by the end of the century very many different types of coach builders, harness makers, smithy shops, and horse breeders coexisted. The appearance of the automobile caused all this to collapse, to be replaced, in turn, by a slow-growing network of interconnected niche manufacturers dependent on gasoline technology, oil exploration and refining, and the internal combustion engine. Thus, complexity—diversity in this case—may, indeed, tend to grow in coevolving systems, but it may also fluctuate greatly over time.

Growth in diversity can be observed in several artificial evolution contexts: for example, Tom Ray's Tierra system,[14] John Holland's ECHO system,[6] and Stuart Kauffman's various chemical evolution systems.[7] To take the Tierra example, Ray sets up an artificial world in which computer programs compete for processor time and memory space in a virtual computer. He begins with a single "organism" in the form of a set of self-replicating machine language instructions that can occasionally mutate. This forms a niche or substrate for the appearance of parasitic organisms that use part of its code to replicate—that "feed" on its instructions. Further organisms appear that are immune to the parasites. The parasites in turn form a substrate for hyper parasites that feed on them. Hyper-hyper parasites appear. And so on. New "organisms" continually appear and disappear, in a rich ecosystem of symbiotic and competing machine-language programs that shows a continual net growth of diversity. In several days of running this system, Ray found no endpoint to the growth of diversity. Starting from a single genotype, over 29,000 different self-replicating genotypes in 300 size classes (equivalent to species in this system) accumulated in this coevolving computer ecology.

At this point I want to note several things that apply to this mechanism.

First, the appearance of new entities may, in some cases, depend not so much on the existence of previous entities as on their possibilities in interaction. For example, in the economy, a new technology such as the computer laser printer mentioned above is possible only if lasers, xerography, and computers are previously available as technologies. In these cases, symbiotic clusters of entities—sets of entities whose collective activity or existence is important—may form many of the niches. We could predict that where collective existence is important in forming niches, growth in coevolutionary diversity would be slow at first—with few entities there would be few possibilities in combination and, hence, few niches. But as more single entities enter, we would see a very rapid increase in niche possibilities, as the number of possible niche clusters that can be created undergoes a combinatorial explosion.

Second, collapses will be large if replacement by a new entity happens near the base of the dependency hierarchy; small if near the endpoints. Therefore, the way in which expansion and collapse of diversity actually work themselves out in a coevolutionary system is conditioned heavily on the way dependencies are structured.

Third, two positive feedbacks—circular causalities—are inherent in this mechanism. The generation of new entities may enhance the generation of new entities, simply because there is new "genetic material" in the system available for further "adaptive radiation." And the appearance of new entities provides niches for the appearance of further, new entities. In turn, these mean that where few new entities are being created, few new entities can appear; thus, few new niches will be created. And so the system will be largely quiescent. And where new entities are appearing rapidly, there will be a rapid increase in new niches, causing further generation of entities and further new niches. The system may then undergo a "Cambrian explosion." Hence, we would expect that such systems might lie dormant in long periods of relative quiescence but burst occasionally into periods of rapid increase in complexity. That is, we would expect them to experience punctuated equilibria.

This mechanism, whereby complexity increases via the generation of new niches, is familiar to most of us who study complex systems. Certainly Stuart Kauffman has written extensively on various examples of self-reinforcing diversity. Yet strangely it is hard to find discussion of it in the traditional biological literature. Bonner's 1988 book, *The Evolution of Complexity,* does not mention it, for example, although it devotes a chapter to a discussion of complexity as diversity. Waddington[16] comes somewhat closer when he suggests that niches become more complex as organismal diversity increases. The more complex niches, he suggests, are then filled by more complex organisms, which in turn increases niche complexity. But he seems to have in mind an upward spiral of internal structural complexity, and not of ecological diversity. An intriguing mention of this mechanism—or something tantalizingly close to it—comes from Darwin's notebooks,[3] p. 422.

"The enormous number of animals in the world depends, of their varied structure and complexity... hence as the forms became complicated, they opened fresh means of adding to their complexity."[1]

But once again this could be read as having to do with internal structural complexity, rather than ecological diversity.

STRUCTURAL DEEPENING

A second mechanism causing complexity to increase over time I will call *structural deepening*. This applies to single entities—systems, organisms, species, individuals—that evolve against a background that can be regarded as their "environment." Normally, competition exerts strong pressure for such systems to operate at their limits of performance. But they can break out of these

[1] I am grateful to Dan McShea for pointing out this quotation to me.

limits by adding functions or subsystems that allow them to (a) operate in a wider or more extreme range, (b) sense and react to exceptional circumstances, (c) service other systems so that they operate better, and (d) enhance their reliability. In doing so, they add to their "structural depth" or design sophistication. Of course, such functions or subsystems, once added, may operate at *their* limits of performance. Once again they can break through these limits by adding sub-subsystems according to (a)–(d) above. By this process, over time the original system becomes encrusted with deeper functions and subfunctions. It may improve greatly in its performance and in the range of environment it can operate in. But in doing so, it becomes internally complex.

The history of the evolution of technology provides many examples of structural deepening. The original gas-turbine (or jet) aero engine, designed independently by Frank Whittle and Hans von Ohain in the 1930s, for example, was simple.[2] It compressed intake air, ignited fuel in it, released the exploding mixture through a turbine that drove the compressor, and then exhausted the air mass at high velocity to provide thrust. Whittle's original prototype had one moving part, the compressor-turbine combination. But over the years, competitive pressures felt by commercial and military interests led to constant demands for improvement. This forced designers to overcome limits imposed by extreme stresses and temperatures, and to handle exceptional situations, sometimes by using better materials, but more often by adding subsystems.

And so, over time, higher air-compression ratios were achieved by using not one, but an assembly—a system—of many compressors. Efficiency was enhanced by a variable position guide-vane control system that admitted more air at high altitudes and velocities and lowered the possibility of the engine stalling. A bleed-valve control system was added to permit air to be bled from critical points in the compressor when pressures reached certain levels. This also reduced the tendency of the engine to stall. A secondary airflow system was added to cool the red-hot turbine blades and pressurize sump cavities to prevent lubrication leakage. Turbine blades were also cooled by a system that circulated air inside them. To provide additional thrust in military air combat conditions, afterburner assemblies were added. To handle the possibility of engine fires, sophisticated fire-detection systems were added. To prevent the build up of ice in the intake region, deicing assemblies were added. Specialized fuel systems, lubrication systems, variable exhaust-nozzle systems, and engine-starting systems were added.

But all these required further subsystems, to monitor and control *them* and to enhance their performance when they ran into limitations. These subsystems, in turn, required sub-subsystems to enhance their performance. A modern, aero gas turbine engine is 30 to 50 times more powerful than Whittle's and a great deal more sophisticated. But Whittle's original simple system is now encrusted with subsystem upon subsystem in an enormously complicated array of interconnected modules and parts. Modern jet engines have upwards of 22,000 parts.[2]

And so, in this mechanism, the steady pressure of competition causes complexity to increase as functions and modifications are added to a system to break through limitations, to handle exceptional circumstances, or to adapt to an environment itself more complex. It should be evident to the reader after a little thought that this increase of structural sophistication applies not just to technologies, but also to biological organisms, legal systems, tax codes, scientific theories, and even to successive releases of software programs.

One laboratory for observing real-time structural deepening is John Holland's genetic algorithm.[5] In the course of searching through a space of feasible candidate "solutions" using the genetic algorithm, a rough ballpark solution—in Holland's jargon, a coarse schema—appears at first. This may perform only somewhat better than its rivals. But as the search continues, superior solutions begin to appear. These have deeper structures (finer subschemas) that allow them to refine the original solution, handle exceptional situations, or overcome some limitation of the original solution. The eventual solution-formulation (or schemata combination) arrived at may be structurally "deep" and complicated. Reversals in structural depth can be observed in the progress of solutions provided by the genetic algorithm. This happens when a coarse schema that has dominated for some time and has been considerably elaborated upon is replaced by a newly "discovered," improved coarse schema. The hierarchy of subschemas dependent on the original coarse schema then collapses. The search for good solutions now begins to concentrate upon the new schema, which in its turn begins to be elaborated upon. This may happen several times in the course of the algorithmic search.

John Koza's genetic programming algorithm, in which algebraic expressions evolve with the purpose of solving a given mathematical problem, provides a similar laboratory.[8] In Koza's setup, we typically see the algorithmic parse trees that describe the expressions grow more and more branches as increasing "depth" becomes built into the currently best-performing algebraic expression.

In Figure 1 I show the growth of structure as the search for good "solutions" progresses in one of Koza's examples. As we can see, once again this mechanism is not unidirectional. Reversals in structural depth and sophistication occur when new symbolic expressions come along that allow the replacement of ones near the "root base" of the original system. On the whole, depth increases, but with intermittent reversals into relatively simpler structures along the way.

[2] Personal communication from Michael Bailey, General Electric Aircraft Engines.

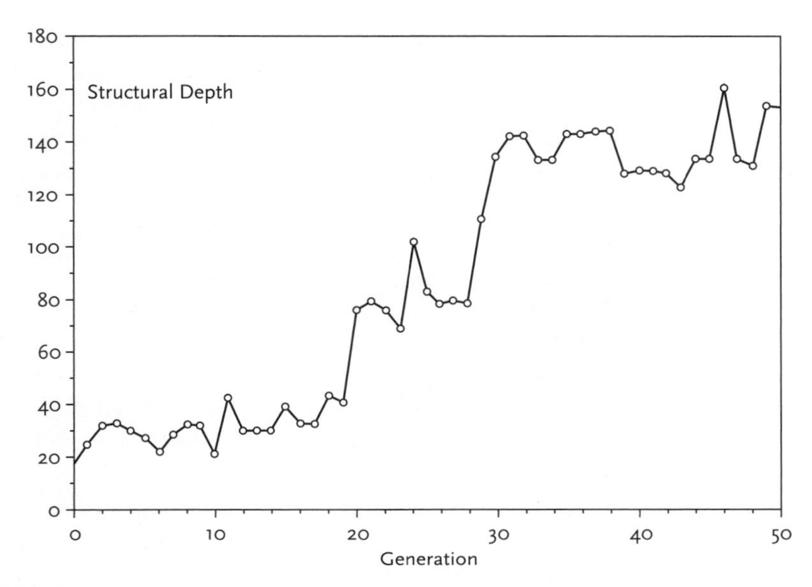

Figure 1:
Structural depth (number of parts in parse tree) of the currently best expression plotted against number of generations of search in the problem of finding a Fourier series expression to match a given function (from Koza,[8] p. 502).

Collapse near the base of a system can be seen in a very different context, the history of science, when new theories suddenly replace old, elaborate ones. An example is the collapse of Ptolemaic astronomy caused by the Kepler-Newton version of the Copernican theory. This novel system, that explained planetary orbits using only a few simple laws, struck at the root base of the hugely complicated Ptolemaic system; and it had such superior explanatory power that the Ptolemaic system never recovered. Similarly, Whittle's jet engine, with its extraordinarily simple propulsion principle, largely replaced the piston aero engine of the 1930s, which had become incurably complicated in attempts to overcome the limitations in operating internal combustion engines at high speed in the very thin air of higher altitudes.[4] And so in evolving systems, bursts of simplicity often cut through growing complexity and establish a new basis upon which complication can again grow. In this back-and-forth dance between complexity and simplicity, complication usually gains a net edge over time.

So far I have described two apparently separate mechanisms. In the first, ecosystems—collections of many individuals—become more complex, more diverse, in the course of evolution; in the second, individuals within ecosystems become internally more complex, structurally deeper, in the course of evolution. In many systems, of course, these mechanisms operate simultaneously, and they may interact, alternate, and even compete.

This can be seen clearly in Kristian Lindgren's study of strategies that evolve in a game-theoretic setting.[10] Lindgren sets up a computerized model populated by strategies that meet randomly and cumulate profit by playing, one-on-one, a finite version of the iterated prisoners' dilemma. The competing strategies are described as coded bit-strings, where the bits represent memory of previous plays that the strategies can take account of. The strategies can occasionally mutate. Successful ones proliferate in this coevolutionary environment; unsuccessful ones die out. In Lindgren's world, it can clearly be seen that the diversity of strategies increases as new coevolving strategies provide niches that can be exploited by fresh, new strategies, exactly as in the first mechanism I have discussed. But the strategies themselves also become increasing "deep"—their code string or memory lengthens—as competition rewards increasingly subtle strategies, as in the second mechanism. In fact, the two mechanisms interact in that the arrival of a new, successful, deeper strategy eliminates many of the previous, simpler strategies. Diversity collapses, and with it many of the niches it provides. There follows a phase in which the newer, deeper strategies mutate and proliferate, so that diversity increases again. And so new depth can both destroy old diversity and feed a new round of increased diversity among newer, deeper strategies. In this way, the growth of coevolutionary diversity alternates in a sporadic way with the growth of structural depth in the strategies. This process has obvious parallels in the history of biological evolution. Some biologists suggest, for example, that increased "depth" in the form of the appearance of multicellular, eukaryotic organisms fueled the Cambrian explosion of diversity 600 million years ago.[15]

CAPTURING SOFTWARE

The third mechanism in the growth of complexity that I will propose is completely different from the first two. Actually it has more to do with the rapid emergence of complexity than with any slow growth. It is a phenomenon I will call *capturing software*. This is the taking over and "tasking" of simpler elements by an outside system for its own (usually informational) purposes. Typically the outside system "discovers" the simpler elements and finds it can use them for some elementary purposes. The elements turn out to have a set of rules that govern how they may be combined and used—an "interactive grammar." This grammar typically allows many combinations of the simple elements; and as the outside system begins to learn this grammar, it also learns to take advantage of the elements in combination. At full fruition, the outside system learns to use this interactive grammar to "program" the simple elements and use them in complicated combinations for its own multipurpose ends.

This mechanism may sound somewhat strange and unfamiliar; so let me clarify it by some examples. A very simple one would be electronics, taken as a technology. As humans, we have learned over the last couple of centuries to "task" electrons to carry out such activities as transmitting sound and vision, controlling sophisticated machinery, and computing. Originally, in the days of Faraday and Franklin, the workings of electrons and of static electricity were poorly understood. And so, uses were few. But in the last century and in the early decades of this one, we began to learn the "grammar" of electricity—the set of operational rules involving induction, capacitance, and impedance that govern the movements of electrons and amplification of their flow. And so we slowly learned to "capture" and "program" electrons for our own use. In this case the simple elements referred to above are electrons. The outside system is ourselves, the human users. The grammar is the laws of electromagnetism. And the programmable outputs are the various technical uses to which electronics are put. At the output level, there is swift "adaptation." The various technological purposes in which we use electrons as a "programmable software" shift and expand rapidly. But at the grammar and carrier level, in this case, adaptation is absent. The behavior of electricity and of electrons is fixed by physical laws that are, within the human time frame at least, immutable.

Sometimes with capturing software, the interactive grammar is not laid down unalterably, but can itself change and evolve in the process of "capturing" the software. An example is the way in which human language evolved. Early humans learned perhaps several hundred thousand years ago that crude, emitted sounds could be used for communicating warnings, pleasure, or simple needs. Very slowly, and comparatively recently on an evolutionary time scale, elementary rules—a grammar—began to emerge to organize these into simple concatenated expressions. Eventually, over many thousands of years, these sounds or phonemes plus grammar evolved into a complex interactive system—a language. This could be "programmed" to form statements, queries, and commands that conveyed a high degree of nuance and subtlety.

In this example, the simple, carrier elements are the sounds or phonemes of human speech. The outside system is the human community that "captures" and makes them into a software, a language. And the grammar is the syntactical system that develops to ensure consistency and commonality of meaning. Of course, there is no single syntactical grammar for all human languages. A grammar must emerge by the slow evolution of a social convention, with constraints exercised by the need for linguistic efficiency and consistency, and by the way linguistic activities are organized in the human brain.[9] (Of course, both the human vocal anatomy and brain also changed as a response to the evolution of language.) The overall language that results from this evolutionary process is a programmable software whose potential output we may think of as the set of all meaningful sentences or statements the language can express.

Adaptation in this case can occur at all levels. At the program output level, adaptation is instantaneous. We can think of a sentence uttered as a one-off, extremely rapid adaptation of software output to the purpose of what the sentence is intended to communicate. At the grammar level, adaptation implies change in the language itself. This commonly takes the form of drift, and it happens slowly and continuously. This is because any abrupt alteration or large deviation in grammar would invalidate current "output programs." At the phoneme or simple element level, adaptation—or change and drift—is slowest of all. Slight changes at this carrier level, if not subtle and continuous, might upset all that is expressed in the system. Slow drift may occur, as when vowels shift over the course of a generation or two; but there is a powerful mechanism acting to keep the carrier elements locked-in to a constant way of behaving.

A particularly telling example of capturing software is the way in which sophisticated derivatives have arisen and are used in recent years in financial markets. In this case the outside system is the financial community. It begins by the simple trading of something of value—soybeans, securities, foreign currencies, municipal bonds, Third World debt, packages of mortgages, Eurodollars—anything to which title can be held. Such items may fluctuate in value and can be swapped and traded. They are called underlyings in financial jargon, and they form the simple, carrier elements of the system I want to consider now.

In early days of such markets, typically an underlying is simply held and traded for its intrinsic value. But over time, a grammar forms. Traders find they can: (a) usefully arrange *options* associated with contingent events that affect the underlying; (b) put several underlyings together to create an associated *index,* as with a stock index; (c) issue *futures* contracts to deliver or obtain an underlying at some time, say, 60 days or one year, in the future; and (d) issue *securities* backed by the underlying. But notice that such "derivatives" as contingent-event options, indices, futures, and securities are themselves elements of value. Thus, they, too, can become *underlyings,* with their own traded values. Once again the market could apply (a), (b), (c), or (d) to these new underlyings. We may then have options on securities, index-futures, options on futures, securities indices, and so on, with trades and swaps of all these.

With such a grammar in place, derivatives experts "program" these elements into a package that provides a desired combination of financing, cash-flow, and risk exposure for clients with highly particular, sophisticated financial needs. Of course, financial markets did not invent such programming all at once. It evolved in several markets semi-independently, as a carrier element was used, simply at first and then in conjunction with the natural grammar of finance.

From the examples I have given, it may seem that the system that uses and captures simple elements to its own uses is always a human one. But, of course, this is not the case. Let me point out two examples in the biological sphere. One is the formation of neural systems. As certain organisms evolved, they began to "task" specialized cells for the simple purposes of sensing and modulating reactions to outside stimuli. These specialized cells, in turn, developed their own interactive grammar; and the overall organism used this to "program" this interconnected neural system to its own purposes. Similarly, the ancestors of the cells found in the immune systems of higher organisms were used originally for simple purposes. Over time, these, too, developed useful rules of interaction—an interactive grammar—thereby eventually becoming a highly programmable system that could protect against outside antigens.

Biological life itself can be thought of in this way. Here the situation is much more complicated than in the previous examples. Biological organisms are built from modules—cells mainly—that in turn are built from relatively small and few (about 50 or so), fairly simple molecules.[12] These molecules are universal across all terrestrial life and are the carriers of biological construction. They are combined into appropriate structures using a grammar consisting of a relatively small number of metabolic chemical pathways. This metabolic grammar, in turn, is modulated or programmed by enzymes. The enzymes doing the programming of course have no conscious purpose. In fact they themselves are the carriers in a second programmed system. They are governed by a complicated gene-expression "grammar," which switches on or inhibits their production from the genes or DNA that code for them, according to feedback received from the state of the organism they exist in. And so we have one captured software system, the programming of the simple metabolic pathways via proteins or enzymes to form and maintain biological structures, modulated by another captured software system, the programming of proteins or enzymes via nucleic acids and the current state of the organism.

In this case the entire system is closed—there is no outside system programming the biological one to its own purposes. In the short term each organism programs itself according to its current development and current needs. In the long term the overall system—the resulting biospheric pattern of organisms that survive, interact, and coevolve—together with environmental and climatic influences, becomes the programmer, laying down its code in the form of the collection of gene sequences that survive and exist at any time. Of course, without an outside system, we cannot say these programmable systems were ever "captured." Instead they emerged and bootstrapped themselves, developing carriers, grammar, and software as they went. Viewed this way, the origin of life is very much the emergence of a software system carried by a physical system—the emergence of a programmable system learning to program itself.

Capturing software in all the cases discussed here is an enormously successful evolutionary strategy. It allows the system to adapt extremely rapidly by merely reprogramming the captured system to form a different output. But because changes in grammars and in carriers would upset existing "programs," we would expect them to be locked in and to change slowly if at all. This explains why a genetic sequence can change easily, but the genetic code can not; why new organisms can appear, but the cell and metabolic chemistry remain relatively fixed; why new financial derivatives are constantly seen, but the securities-and-exchange rules stay relatively constant.[3]

CONCLUSION

In this chapter, I have suggested three ways in which complexity tends to grow as evolution takes place. It may grow by increases in diversity that are self-reinforcing; or by increases in structural sophistication that break through performance limitations; or by systems "capturing" simpler elements and learning to "program" these as "software" to be used to their own ends. Of course, we would not expect such growth in complexity to be steady. On the contrary, in all three mechanisms we would predict it to be intermittent and epochal. And we would not expect it to be unidirectional. The first two mechanisms are certainly reversible, so we would expect collapses in complexity to occur randomly from time to time.

As we study evolution more deeply, we find that biology provides by no means all of the examples of interest. Any system with a lineage of inherited, alterable structures pressured to improve their performance shows evolutionary phenomena. And so, it is likely that increasingly we will find connections between complexity and evolution by drawing examples not just from biology, but from the domains of economics, adaptive computation, artificial life, and game theory. Interestingly, the mechanisms described in this chapter apply to examples in all of these evolutionary settings.

ACKNOWLEDGMENTS

This paper was originally presented at the Santa Fe Institute's Integrative Themes Workshop in July 1992. I thank Dan McShea, Brian Goodwin, and the workshop participants for useful comments. I am grateful to Harold Morowitz in particular for several conversations on the themes of this essay.

[3] Carriers do change, of course, if they can be substituted for one another easily. For example, options can be built on any underlying; and so, in this case, carriers can and do change rapidly. But the essential property of underlyings—that of being an object that carries uncertain value—remains necessary in all cases and does not change.

REFERENCES

1. Bonner, J. T. *The Evolution of Complexity*. Princeton: Princeton University Press, 1988.
2. Constant, E. W. *Origins of the Turbojet Revolution*. Baltimore: Johns Hopkins University Press, 1980.
3. Darwin C. *From Charles Darwin's Notebooks*, edited by P. H. Barrett et al., 422. Ithaca: Cornell University Press, 1987.
4. Heron, S. D. *History of the Aircraft Piston Engine*. Detroit: Ethyl Corp., 1961.
5. Holland, J. *Adaptation in Natural and Artificial Systems*, 2nd ed. Cambridge: MIT Press, 1992.
6. Holland, J. "Echoing Emergence: Objectives, Rough Definitions, and Speculation for Echo-Class Models." Mimeograph, University of Michigan, 1993.
7. Kauffman, S. "The Sciences of Complexity and Origins of Order." Working Paper 91-04-021, Santa Fe Institute, 1991.
8. Koza, J. *Genetic Programming*. Cambridge, MA: MIT Press, 1992.
9. Lieberman, P. *The Biology and Evolution of Human Language*. Cambridge, MA: Harvard University Press, 1984.
10. Lindgren, K. "Evolutionary Phenomena in Simple Dynamics." In *Artificial Life II*, edited by C. Langton, C. Taylor, J. D. Farmer, and S. Rasmussen. Santa Fe Institute Studies in the Sciences of Complexity, Vol. X, 295–312. Reading, MA: Addison-Wesley, 1991.
11. McShea, D. "Complexity and Evolution: What Everybody Knows." *Bio. & Phil.* 6 (1991): 303–324.
12. Morowitz, H. *Beginnings of Cellular Life*. New Haven: Yale University Press, 1992.
13. Müller, G. B. "Developmental Mechanisms at the Origin of Morphological Novelty: A Side-Effect Hypothesis." In *Evolutionary Innovations*, edited by Matthew Nitecki, 99–130. Chicago: University of Chicago Press, 1990.
14. Ray, T. S. "An Approach to the Synthesis of Life." In *Artificial Life II*, edited by C. Langton, C. Taylor, J. D. Farmer, and S. Rasmussen. Santa Fe Institute Studies in the Sciences of Complexity, Vol. X, 371–408. Reading, MA: Addison-Wesley, 1991.
15. Stanley, S. M. "An Ecological Theory for the Sudden Origin of Multicellular Life in the Late Precambrian." *Proc. Nat. Acad. Sci.* 70 (1979): 1486–1489.
16. Waddington, C. H. "Paradigm for an Evolutionary Process." In *Towards a Theoretical Biology*, edited by C. H. Waddington, Vol. 2, 106–128. New York: Aldine, 1969.

CHAPTER 10

Cognition

*The Black Box of Economics**

W. BRIAN ARTHUR

Most economists agree that when human agents face decision problems of complication or ones that contain fundamental uncertainty they don't use deductive rationality. But what do they use in its place? Cognitive science tells us that in such situations we think associatively—we find similar situations from our repertoire of experiences and fit these to the problem in question, then derive implications from there. This essay explores the consequences for economics of this type of reasoning and it suggests ways such reasoning can be built into economic models. It argues that because a wide collection of memories and experiences of situations is necessary to our reasoning, economics students should be deeply versed in economic history, not just economic theory.

The essay appeared in *The Complexity Vision and the Teaching of Economics*, edited by David Colander, Edward Elgar Publishers, Cheltenham, UK, 2000.

In his autobiography Bertrand Russell tells us he dropped his interest in economics after half a year's study because he thought it was too simple. Max Planck dropped his involvement with economics because he thought it was too difficult. I went into economics because I had been trained in mathematics and I thought, as Russell did, that economics looked easy. It took me several years to get from Russell's position to Planck's. Economics is inherently difficult. In this chapter I will explain one path by which I came to that view.

* Editor's note: this is adapted from the conference keynote address upon which this volume is based. I asked Brian to keep the informal style as part of the chapter.

Whether one sees economics as inherently difficult or as simple depends on how one formulates economic problems. If one sets up a problem and assumes rationality of decision making, a well-defined solution normally follows. Economics here is simple: from the problem follows the solution. But how agents get from problem to solution is a black box; and whether indeed agents can arrive at the solution cannot be guaranteed unless we look into this box. If we open this box economics suddenly becomes difficult.

Once in a while as economists, we do justify our assumed connection between problem and solution. In a well-known paper, Rust (1987) tells the story of Harold Zurcher, the superintendent of maintenance at the Madison (Wisconsin) Metropolitan Bus Company. For 20 years Zurcher scheduled bus engine replacement of a large fleet of buses—a complicated problem that required him to balance two conflicting objectives: minimizing maintenance costs versus minimizing unexpected engine failures. Rust figured out the solution to this combinatorial optimization problem by stochastic dynamic programming, and matched that optimization against Zurcher's. He found a reasonably close fit. The point of Rust's article was that although this was an enormously complicated problem, Harold Zurcher found the solution and therefore, at least in this case, the economists' assumption that individuals find optimal solutions to complex questions is not a bad assumption.

The Zurcher example leaves us with a broad question: Can the assumption that individuals find optimal solutions to economic problems be justified so that we can avoid studying the details of the decision process? In simple cases the answer is yes. In most cases, however, it is no. Think of an ocean that contains all the well-defined problems that interest us in the economy, with ever more difficult problems at greater depths. Near the surface lie problems like tic-tac-toe. Below that are problems at the level of checkers, and deeper still are problems like chess and Go. We might know theoretically that a solution to chess exists, say in mixed Nash strategy form, but we can't guarantee that human agents would arrive at it. So the problems that are solvable the way tic-tac-toe is solvable lie within two or three inches of the surface, but at levels deeper than this, problems cannot be guaranteed a solution. We can add to these the many problems agents face, perhaps the majority they face, that are *not* well specified. Zurcher's problem lies on the boundary of what economic agents can accomplish by way of a "rational" solution. Deeper than this, economic "solutions" may not match "rationality" or may not exist.

What happens at these deeper levels? Human decision-makers do not back off from a problem because it is difficult or unspecified. We might say that when problems are too complicated to afford solutions, or when they are not well-specified, agents face not a problem but a situation. They must deal with that situation; they must frame the problem, and that framing in many ways is the most important part of the decision process. To consider that framing you have to consider what lies between the problem and the action taken.

And between the problem and the action lies cognition. Between the problem and the solution there's a lot going on, and if one considers what is going on, economics becomes difficult. To paraphrase my question then: How do people make sense of a problem? How do individuals handle these more complicated problems? How do we really cognize?

In this chapter I want to consider cognition as a cognitive psychologist might look at it, and apply the findings to thinking about two different issues: economic modeling and the education of graduate students.

NOTIONS OF THE MIND

In economics we have a simple and old notion of mind. Mind is a container that holds data. The data are constantly updated by interaction with the world; and mind performs deductions based upon these data. All of this of course is implicit; in economics we don't talk about "mind." But we do view mind—or that which gives rise to ratiocination—as deduction upon collections of data sets. In economic theory this is reflected in treating beliefs about the world as expectations of variables conditioned upon current data (or sigma fields)—current information—and in formulating solutions based upon these. This is a shorthand, the sort of reasonable abstraction that any science makes that works well in many cases. But we need to get beyond it when we go deeper than two or three inches into the ocean of problems.

Let me look at mind and the cognitive process then from a deeper viewpoint—that of cognitive science. Imagine that at night you are reading a novel, say Haldór Laxness's *Independent People* and you're enjoying it. What is actually going on? Actually, that's complicated. The black and white marks on the page are focused onto the light sensors or pixels at the back of your retina. These sensory perceptions are transmitted to the rear part of your brain, and map into certain visual structures there. Somehow letters and words are parsed out, and somehow these fit together via an understanding of syntax. (Where I say "somehow" I mean that cognitive scientists do not know the exact mechanism of what is happening.) From syntax somehow "meaning" emerges. But what is meaning? Meaning in this case is a set of associations. You might read a sentence about rain: "Smoothly, smoothly it fell, over the whole shire, over the fallen marsh grass, over the troubled lake, the iron-gray gravel flats, the somber mountain above the croft, smudging out every prospect." These words trigger associations—associated memories really—and you form a picture, or a set of pictures. These associated memories and pictures in turn trigger what you might call "affect," or feelings. The feelings are often subtle, the kind of feelings of what it might be like to be in Laxness's world—the gloom of the rain, the dreariness of the gravel flats, the oppressiveness of the mountain, the smell of the croft in the dampness. These are subtle feelings, and these feelings actually are our intelligence, are part of our cognition. They're part of the meaning that we give to symbols. Reading and making sense of what is read consist of associated memories and associated feelings. How all this happens is not well understood by cognitive scientists; it's what French thinker Henri-Jean Martin calls a mysterious alchemy.

Here's how the Princeton cognitive psychologist Julian Jaynes (1976, p. 1) expresses this alchemy of mind:

> O, what a world of unseen visions and heard silences, this insubstantial country of the mind! What ineffable essences, these touchless rememberings and unshowable reveries! And the privacy of it all! A secret theater of speechless monologue and prevenient counsel, an invisible mansion of all moods, musings, and mysteries, an infinite resort of disappointments and discoveries. A whole kingdom where each of us reigns reclusively alone, questioning what we will, commanding what we can. A hidden hermitage where we may study out the troubled book of what we have done and yet may do. An introcosm that is more myself than anything I can find in a mirror. This consciousness that is myself of selves, that is everything, yet nothing at all—what is it? And where did it come from? And why?

The point I want to make here is the meaning that's abstracted from the book is not *in* the book; it is in the mind. It's a point that starts to get recognized in philosophy in the 1700s by Kant, but isn't fully articulated until the twentieth century. We construct meaning by the associations we make. If this seems strange, imagine a page in Russian of Dostoyevsky shown to a Russian reader and a non-Russian reader. Each gets exactly the same data, but the Russian has the associations to parse the Cyrillic script and make the written sense data come alive. The non-Russian sees exactly the same data; but his associations if he does not speak the language are nil and there is no meaning. Meaning therefore is imposed. It emerges by our imposing associations. It's not Dostoyevsky or the book *Independent People* that brings meaning to me—that's an illusion. It's *me* that brings meaning to *Independent People. I*'m making sense, *I*'m imposing associations, *I* impose meaning on what I'm seeing. Not just any old meaning, but the meaning that emerges from the associations the book makes with my neural memory.

Let me give you another example because I want to hammer on this point and derive a few things from it. There's a Yeats poem that goes something like this: "Down by the salley gardens my love and I did meet; she passed the salley gardens on little snow-white feet. She bid me to take life easy, like the grass grows on the weirs, but I was young and foolish, and now am full of tears."[1]

1. Editor's note: The lines are lines 1, 2, 7, and 8 of an eight-line poem, 'Down by the Salley Gardens', by W. B. Yeats. From *W. B. Yeats, the Poems,* ed. Richard J. Finneran, New York; Macmillan, 1983 (p. 20). Down by the salley gardens my love and I did meet;

These words will have different effects on different people—different meanings. Ask yourself what meaning you get out of weirs. For me this has enormous meaning because I and my friends played near weirs as children. (Weirs are little dams in a stream, usually covered with algae and some form of green trailing grass.) I also know what salley gardens are. But those who are not Irish will probably be affected differently. They may wonder: what are salley gardens anyway? Maybe Salley had a garden. Maybe there's such a thing as the Salley Gardens—maybe they exist on some estate near Dublin. In the absence of knowing what salley gardens are, you probably have an image of a garden well kept, surrounded by flowers and tended by keepers. But it's not that. The word in Gaelic is s-a-i-l-e-a-c-h, and it means "willow." So Yeats is near willows, and therefore likely near water. If there's a weir, the water is a stream or river. Once one has these associations, immediately the initial picture shifts. My point is that different meanings can be imposed on the same data. Different meanings that come from different associations.

Data—literary or economic—have no inherent meaning. They acquire meaning by our bringing meaning to them. And different people, with different experiences, will construct different meanings.

THE MIND AS A FAST PATTERN COMPLETER

What conclusions does modern cognitive psychology draw from such examples? The first conclusion is that our brains are "associative engines" to use a phrase of Andy Clark, a philosopher and cognitive scientist from Washington University in St. Louis (Clark, 1993). We're wonderful at association, and in fact, in cognition, association is just about all we do. In association we impose intelligible patterns. To use another of Clark's labels, we are fast pattern completers. If I see a tail going around a corner, and it's a black swishy tail, I say, "There's a cat!" But it could be a small boy with a tail on the end of a stick who's trying to fool me. But I don't do that. My mind is not built to do that. If I were strongly skeptical, I *could* do that, or if I saw some small boy playing pranks I could say, "Well, it's either a cat or a small boy." But in the absence of a small boy, all I'm really saying is, "Hey! I see a cat." But I didn't see a cat. I saw a black tail. A famous Bertrand Russell story makes the same point. A schoolboy, a parson and a mathematician are crossing from England into Scotland in a train. The schoolboy looks out and sees a black sheep and says,

/She passed the salley gardens on little snow-white feet. / She bid me take love easy, as the leaves grow on the tree, / But I, being young and foolish, with her would not agree. / In a field by the river my love and I did stand, / As on my leaning shoulder she laid her snow-white hand. / She bid me take life easy, as the grass grows on the weirs; / But I was young and foolish, and now am full of tears.'

"Oh! Look! Sheep in Scotland are black!" The parson, who is learned, says, "No. Strictly speaking, all we can say is there is one sheep in Scotland that is black." The mathematician says, "No, still not correct. All we can really say is that we know that in Scotland there exists at least one sheep, at least one side of which is black."

Cognitive science repeatedly tells us that we don't think deductively as the mathematician did, we think associatively as the schoolboy did. And for a very good reason: evolution has made it so. Our ability as humans a hundred thousand years ago to sniff the air and associate a fleeting humidity with the presence of water a few miles away had real survival value. Completing patterns fast, surmising the presence of water from the faintest of clues, helped us survive. Deductive logic did not; and in all but the most trivial of cases we do not use it at all. In fact, cognitive psychologists tell us that deductions themselves are primarily associative. I may say I can solve such-and-such a problem: it's a problem in spherical trigonometry. I then associate the problem with this framework. From there I associate structures and symbols with the sense data of the problem. And I proceed by such associations, stitching them together into a pattern. I'm not saying that association is all the human brain does, but cognitively, association is the main thing we do. And we do it fast. Our neural system searches fast over many associations before settling on one as a "meaning." Occasionally this process slows and we can see it in action, as with the three-dimensional optical-illusion pictures that were popular a few years ago that appear flat and two-dimensional until after staring for half a minute a 3-D picture "leaps out." So our brains process a large collection of associations into patterns—and a large set of metaphors which are merely more complicated associations with entailments. With metaphors we compare this to this and that to that, and if the comparison is good, we expect such and such to follow. Metaphor is a form of pattern association, and we process much information through metaphors. In sum, we have many different forms of associations: pictures; memories; metaphors; and theories, which are really elaborated metaphors. And this collection when it's fully operating, along with the rules for combining these (which are also associations), we call the mind.

Our minds then are extremely good at associating things, using metaphors, memories, structures, patterns, theories. In other words, the mind is not given. It's not an empty bucket for pouring data in. The mind itself is emergent. This idea is new in Western thinking but there's plenty of precedent for it in the East. The Neo-Confucian philosopher brothers Ch'eng Yi and Ch'eng Hao, writing during the Sung Dynasty about 900 years ago, both saw mind as emergent. They did not see the mind as a container, but rather as sets of ideas built one upon the other. The mind doesn't contain our ideas. It's these ideas—these associations—that instead contain the mind or constitute the mind. The mind is not fixed in any way; it consists in its associations and the apparatus to manipulate these. In this sense it's emergent. So strictly speaking I shouldn't say as I did earlier that meaning resides in the mind, because deep enough within cognitive philosophy the concept of mind itself dissolves. Meaning resides in associations which our neural apparatus connects with the data presented. We are now far from seeing reasoning as deduction that takes place in a container of variables whose values are updated by "information." If reasoning is largely association, it depends on the past experiences of the reasoner. The framing of a situation, the "sense" made of it, are therefore dependent on the reasoner's history. And so is the outcome.

One final point about cognition. Sometimes we can say roughly that there is a "correct" meaning—a single, correct association. More often, in any situation of complication, there are multiple interpretations. We may hold one or we may hold many. Often, if we are trying to solve a puzzle, or to come to a decision such as the next move in a chess game, we make many hypothetical associations and search over these, perhaps retaining more than one until further evidence presents itself. In the black tail example, if I had indeed seen a small boy a few minutes earlier, I might hold in mind both "cat" and "prank" until further evidence arrived.

MODELING THE COGNITIVE PROCESS

All this is fine. But as economists how do we make use of it? How might we model the thinking process in problems that are complicated or ill-defined?

I would suggest the following, by way of distillation of the observations above: in problems of complication, as decision makers, economic agents look for ways to frame the situation that faces them. They try to associate temporary internal models or patterns or hypotheses to frame the situation. And they work with these. They may single out one such pattern or model and carry out simplified deductions (at the level of tic-tac-toe) on it, if they seek guidance for action. As further evidence from the environment comes in, they may strengthen or weaken their beliefs in their current models or hypotheses. They may also discard some when they cease to perform, and replace them as needed with new ones. In other words, where agents face problems of complication or ill-definition, they use clues from the situation to form hypothetical patterns, frameworks and associations. These hypothetical patterns fill the gaps in the agent's understanding.

Such a procedure enables us as humans to deal with complication: we construct plausible, simpler models that we can cope with. It enables us to deal with ill-definedness: where we have insufficient definition, we use working models to fill the gap. Such behavior is inductive. It may appear ad hoc and messy, but it is not antithetical to "reason," or to science for that matter. In fact, it is the way science itself operates and progresses.

More practically then, in a typical economics problem that plays out over time, we might set up a collection of agents, probably heterogeneous, and assume they make associations in the form of mental models, or hypotheses, or subjective beliefs. These beliefs might themselves take the form of simple mathematical expressions that can be used to describe or predict some variable or action; or of statistical hypotheses; or of condition/prediction rules (if situation Q is observed/predict outcome or action D). These will normally be subjective—they will differ among the agents. An agent may hold one in mind at a time, or several simultaneously, keeping track of the performance of each. When the time comes to make choices, the agent acts upon his currently most credible (or possibly most profitable) one. The others he keeps at the back of his mind, so to speak. As economists we will be tempted to say the agent rationally combines his several hypotheses. But cognitive psychology tells us we don't do this, we hold in mind many hypotheses at a time and act on the one currently most plausible. Once actions are taken the aggregative picture is updated, and agents update their confidence in each of their hypotheses.

This scheme I'm suggesting is of course also a simplification and abstraction. But it captures the idea that the agent is *imposing* meaning on the problem situation, or making sense of it by associating multiple frameworks, or belief structures, or hypotheses with it and allowing these to "compete." This is also a system in which learning takes place. Agents "learn" which of their hypotheses work, and they "learn" also in the acts of discarding poorly performing hypotheses and generating new "ideas" to put in their place. Notice there is a built-in hysteresis: agents linger with their currently most believable hypothesis or belief model, but drop it when it no longer performs, in favor of a better one. A hypothesis or association or belief model is clung to not because it is "correct"—there is no way to know this—but rather because it has worked in the past and must cumulate a record of failure before it is worth discarding.

A key question remains. Where do the hypotheses or mental models come from? How are they generated? Behaviorally, this is a deep question in psychology, having to do with object representation, and pattern recognition. I will not go into it here. But there are some simple and practical options for modeling. Sometimes we might endow our agents with focal models—patterns or hypotheses that are obvious, simple and easily dealt with mentally. We might generate a "bank" of these and distribute them among the agents. Other times, given a suitable model-space, we might allow some similar intelligent search device such as the genetic algorithm to generate suitable models. The reader should note that whatever option is taken, the framework I've described is independent of the specific hypotheses or beliefs used, just as the consumer theory framework is independent of particular products chosen among.

Can such a scheme be put in practice in economics? The answer is yes. There is now a growing body of examples: the work of Sargent (1993); the El Farol problem (Arthur 1994); the Santa Fe stock market study (Arthur et al. 1997). This type of study typically finds that "solutions"—patterns of beliefs and actions predicated upon these—need to be generated by computation because of the increased complication of heterogeneous beliefs. It also typically finds a richer world, a psychological world, where an ecology of beliefs about the problem in question emerges. Sometimes this ecology of hypotheses converges to some standard equilibrium of beliefs. More often it remains open-ended, always discovering new hypotheses, new ideas.

COGNITION AND GRADUATE ECONOMIC EDUCATION

Let me turn from modeling in economics to quite a different area that can benefit from the insights of cognitive science: the education of economists.

I want to start here by drawing attention to two ways in which we make sense: two types of association, not completely different and at opposite ends of a spectrum. Let me call one "theory" and the other "experience."

Theories are metaphors with entailments. If in 1705, Edmond Halley subscribed to Newton's gravitational theory and applied it to a comet that had previously appeared in 1531, 1607 and 1682, one entailment was that the comet would return in the year 1759. In using Newton's theory, Halley was making an association between a comet and the heavenly bodies Newton dealt with; and the entailments of the association allowed Halley to predict. I want to suggest that theories are *thin* associations: the theory fits if a narrow and precise set of conditions is fulfilled; and the entailments are also narrow and precise. Providing the theory fits correctly—is a good association—and is consistent within itself, then the entailments can be relied upon. Narrow fit, narrow entailments. Theories are in this way thin but powerful associations.

Experience is different. Suppose I'm an executive sent to Korea, and I've never done business there. I arrive in Korea and I'm wondering how I shall act. I have no idea of how many times I should bow to my host, or if anybody bows to the host, or whether I should take my shoes off, or if I want to close the deal do I wait till the end of dinner or do I try to close the deal up front? But I do have a lot of experience in Japan and in China, and so I use these. In this case hundreds of pictures are going through my mind. This sort of association is more dream-like. It's richer. It covers a wider set of cases. It is suggestive of what will follow given what is. But it's much less accurate and less precise and less reliable than theory. So experience in the form of a wide collection of memories and pictures of situations—*thick* association—is also powerful. Its power lies in its width of coverage and its suggestiveness. Such experience is what we seek from human conversation and from taking in stories and novels and plays. We seek to draw into ourselves other people's experiences, to make their situations into our memory pictures that we can use later. In this way we construct and conjure a whole dream-like world where logic doesn't matter and precision doesn't matter, but where suggestiveness and coverage give power.

As I said earlier, these two types of association are not completely distinct; associations arrange themselves on a spectrum from narrowness and precision to width and suggestiveness.

What has this to do with graduate economic education? A lot. A great deal of education is the formation of associations; and the spectrum ranges from collections of narrow but precise theories on one side to wide but suggestive and imprecise pictures on the other. We need both types of association to function successfully as human beings.

In economics, graduate education at least in the first year or two consists in mastering 20 or 30 theoretical economic models—thin associations. These include the principal–agent model, the overlapping generations model, the prisoner's dilemma model, and so on. The idea is that these theoretical metaphors will later become useful associations. We hope that if the student is later employed say at the World Bank, she will be able to look at a situation and say, "This problem in African agriculture is partly a principal–agent problem. It does have some overtones of overlapping generations, and it's also got this game theory component. So I can put together a hybrid version of the three models to get insight." All this is fine. It is fine that economics has recognized recurring structures that it has rendered into theories. We can hope and expect that a well-educated student will use these as association components later.

But models cannot be all that we teach. There's been a tendency in many graduate schools to increase teaching in theory at the expense of teaching in economic history and in case example. Students of course can still choose to study the experience-details of the economy; but they are aware that this may not enhance their graduate careers. In 1990 Colander and Klamer asked students how important having a "thorough knowledge of the economy" was to succeeding as an economist. Three percent thought it very important, and 68% thought it unimportant. Important was: "Being smart in the sense of being good at problem solving," and "excellence in mathematics." With this bias toward theory and away from experience, we eliminate the wider metaphors that come from history-experience—the thick associations. These allow students to put their models into perspective; they provide the vocabulary, so to speak, where theory provides the grammar; they provide a richness of thought and a breadth of association that theory cannot possibly match.

When a decision maker faces a situation of high complexity, say Bosnia in the mid-1990s, applying theory prematurely—a set of precise but narrowly applicable metaphors—can be dangerous. Let's say he is in the State

Department looking at Bosnia and has been in graduate school in political science, doesn't have much experience and is full of theories. His reaction may be to shoehorn Bosnia into a pre-constructed framework. But in this situation it is better to wait and observe. And in observation to invoke a variable set of pictures on which he may conjure up a richer set of associations. Such free association comes from a study of history, not theory. "Well, it could be a bit like the Bosnian crisis of 1908, but it's not unlike the situation under Turkish rule in 1831 when Husein seized power. On the other hand there are elements of the ethnic rivalries of 1875 that resulted in the Austro-Hungarians taking over." What's of use is to have thousands of such pictures from history, available for pondering and perusal. Eventually from such pondering and perusal—from dreamlike association—a composite set of hypotheses or composite picture may emerge. It's at this stage that theory might apply. Premature association without going through the richness of a wide set of pictures may be disastrous. Where I come from, Belfast—another complicated situation—we say: "If you're not confused, you don't know anything."

I am saying here that students need experience—details as well as theory. That is, they need economic history, not as an adjunct to theory, but as a supplier of cognitive understanding in its own right. What about teaching the history of economic thought—another threatened discipline in economic education? From the cognitive point of view, the history of economic thought bestows on us an awareness of the associations we make. Without such awareness, associations can be unconscious and poorly suited to the case in hand. Consider the English painters who came to Australia in the late 1700s or early 1800s. These artists depicted trees in Australia as they would have depicted English trees; they were well trained in English art schools and knew how to paint trees. But in Australia the leaves of most trees—often eucalyptus trees—are thinner, and the sun shines through them. Trees there look different—lighter, more airy. It took a generation of Australian-born painters before the trees in paintings started to look like Australian trees. Before that European painters were unconsciously making European associations and imposing these upon Australia. Similarly Europeans depicted aboriginals in this early period as Europeans with dark skins. This is not to criticize artists. It is to be aware that the actions we take are built upon our unconscious associations. We need to be conscious of our associations and where they come from. We need to be suspicious of them. We need a Zen-like standing back and seeing from beginner's mind. We need an awareness that theories aren't exogenous—they were constructed by people with agendas from other times sometimes suited to the purposes of other times. We need knowledge of the history of economic thought to be fully aware of the associations we make in economics and their provenance.

So what in graduate economics education do we really want? We certainly need theory. As a theorist I'm all for theory. But we also need the rich pictures given by the study of history and institutions. We need both types of association: the theoretical, quantitative, precise frameworks and the case-based, vivid pictures in their tens of thousands. To teach only theory is equivalent to training doctors by teaching only endocrinology and pathology, and not the wide diagnostics doctors learn on grand rounds. To operate only with theory—think of driving a car—makes us beginners. It's not until we can seamlessly integrate theory and vivid pictures—theory and experience—that we become expert. I believe we are currently turning out students who lack those pictures. And in doing so, we're doing them a disservice.

DO ISSUES OF COGNITION MATTER?

Perhaps in asking my fellow economists to think about the implications of cognition, I am asking for something useful but not necessary—a luxury? I don't believe so. Consider just one example. The Soviet Union in 1990–91 decided to go capitalist. And from us economists it got much advice. But our natural bias, given the current development of economics, was to concentrate upon a worthy, but imagined, general-equilibrium outcome where institutions would be in place and markets would work smoothly and incentives would be correct.

A cognitive view of economics might have balanced this ideal view with an awareness that Russians were not arriving with empty minds to their version of capitalism. Not only did they possess old structures both economic and political, they harbored from their 70 years of communism and earlier czarist past old associations too—of what business means, of how one interacts with authorities, of how one organizes if one wants to make money, of what one does with economic power and wealth. More enlightened advice would have built upon an understanding of how these embedded structures and understandings would play out given the new possibilities. The subsequent history of Russia's experiment with capitalism showed that these matters of cognition had great importance.

Economic agents bring to their actions not just their preferences and endowments, but also their understandings—the associations and meanings they have derived from their history of previous actions and experiences. In many of the small, standard problems of economics, we can ignore this. In the larger issues of development and reconstruction, and in constructing an economics for problems of complication and ill-definition, we cannot. We need to take cognition seriously.

REFERENCES

Arthur, W. B. (1994), "Complexity in Economic Theory: Inductive Reasoning and Bounded Rationality," *American Economic Review*, 84(2), 406–411.

Arthur, W. B., J. H. Holland, B. LeBaron, R. Palmer, and P. Tayler (1997), "Asset Pricing under Endogenous Expectations in an Artificial Stock Market," in W. B. Arthur, S. Durlauf, and D. Lane (eds), *The Economy as an Evolving Complex System II,* Reading, MA. Addison-Wesley.

Clark, A. (1993), *Associative Engines,* Cambridge, MA: MIT Press.

Jaynes, J. (1976), *The Origin of Consciousness in the Breakdown of the Bicameral Mind*, Boston: Houghton Mifflin Company.

Laxness, H. (1935), *Independent People*, New York: Vintage.

Rust, J. (1987), "Optimal Replacement of GMC Bus Engines: An Empirical Model of Harold Zurcher," *Econometrica*, 55(5), 999–1033.

Sargent, T. J. (1993), *Bounded Rationality in Macroeconomics*, New York: Oxford University Press.

CHAPTER 11

The End of Certainty in Economics

W. BRIAN ARTHUR

In the mid-1980s deterministic and rationalistic thinking dominated theoretical economics, yet many economists, including myself, felt profoundly uneasy with it. This essay is a reaction to this narrow form of high-rational thinking and it points out a fundamental indeterminacy in the economy. We act on our forecasts or expectations, and so our expectations create the world—the outcome—our expectations are trying to predict. Without knowledge of others' expectations, or knowledge that everyone has knowledge of others' expectations, an agent's expectations become impossible to formulate logically and so do others' expectations. Rational expectations thus become dubious and fragile assumptions, and the real world is subject to fundamental uncertainty. This indeterminacy means that economic behavior builds from subjective beliefs; these arise, co-evolve, change, mutually reinforce, mutually negate, and decay. I argue that economics should recognize and accept such subjective reasoning as its basic premise.

This essay was given as a talk at the conference Einstein Meets Magritte, in Brussels, in 1999, and some of its examples repeat ones used elsewhere in this book. The essay appeared in the volume *Einstein Meets Magritte*, D. Aerts, J. Broekaert, and E. Mathijs (eds.), Kluwer Academic Publishers, Holland, 1999.

The story of the sciences in the 20th century is one of a steady loss of certainty. Much of what was real and machine-like and objective and determinate at the start of the century, by mid-century was a phantom, unpredictable, subjective, and indeterminate. What had *defined* science at the start of the century—its power to predict, its clear subject/object distinction—no longer defines it at the end. Science after science has lost its innocence. Science after science has grown up.

What then of economics? Is economics a science? Well yes, I believe so. For sure it is a body of well-reasoned knowledge. Yet until the last few years it has maintained its certainty, it has escaped any loss of innocence. And so we must ask: is its object of study, the economy, inherently free of uncertainties and indeterminacies? Or is economics in the process of losing its innocence and thereby joining the other sciences of this century?

I believe the latter. In fact, there are indications everywhere these days in economics that the discipline is losing its rigid sense of determinism, that the long dominance of positivist thinking is weakening, and that economics is opening itself to a less mechanistic, more organic approach. In this talk I want to show my own version of this loss of certainty. I want to argue that there are major pockets of uncertainty in the economy. I want to show that the clear subject/object distinction in the economics often blurs. I want to show that the economy is not a gigantic machine, but a construct of its agents. These are not "anomalies" to be feared, they are natural properties of the economy, and if we accept them, we will have a stronger, not a weaker science.

Let me start from the beginning. The fundamental ideas in economics stem from the thinking of the 18th century, in particular from the thinking of the English and Scottish Enlightenment. In 1733, at the height of the intoxication of enlightenment thinking, Alexander Pope condensed its essence in one stanza of his *Essay on Man*:

> All Nature is but Art unknown to Thee
> All Chance, Direction, which thou canst not see
> All Discord, Harmony, not understood
> All partial Evil, universal Good:
> And, spite of Pride, in erring Reason's spite
> One truth is clear, "Whatever *is*, is *right*."

In this context "Art" means artifice. It means technique or mechanism. And so, all the intricate wonders we see in nature, says Pope, are in fact a gigantic machine, an artifice like the mechanical automata figures of his time. All that looks unkiltered really has direction behind it. All that looks complex and discordant, like the movements of planets before Kepler's and Newton's times, has a hidden simplicity. All that affects each of God's creations adversely, in some unspoken way works to the good of the whole. Quoting Socrates, "Whatever is, is right."

These were not merely the ideas of Pope. They were the ideas that filled the intellectual air when Adam Smith was growing up. Smith went on to enshrine them in *The Wealth of Nations,* that magnificent work that uncovered the hidden simplicity behind the traffickings of traders and manufactories and butchers and bakers. The economy was indeed Art, and its principles were now unhidden. The selfish interests of the individual were guided as by an invisible hand to the common interest of all. Whatever was, was right. Two centuries later, the philosopher of science, Jacob Bronowski, was to comment glumly that economics never recovered from the fatally rational structure imposed on it in the 18th century. But we inherited more than Smith's rational structure. Deep in some recess of our minds, we inherited the thinking that the economy is but Art, a gigantic machine, that if we merely understood its parts, we could predict the whole. Certainly when I was studying economics in Berkeley 25 years ago, many economists hoped (as I did) that a Grand Unified Theory of economics was possible. From the axioms of rational human behavior, a theory of the consumer could be constructed. From this and a corresponding theory of the firm a consistent microeconomics could be constructed. From this, somehow, an aggregate theory of the economy, macroeconomics, could be constructed. All this would constitute a Grand Unified Theory of the economy.

There have always been two embarrassments to this hope of constructing a theory of the economy from its reductionist parts. One is that the economy relies on human beings, not on orderly machine components. Human beings with all their caprices and emotions and foibles. The second embarrassment is technology. Technology destroys the neatness because it keeps the economy changing. Human behavior was finessed in economics by the device of Economic Man, that perfectly rational being who reasons perfectly deductively on well-defined problems. Technology change was not so much finessed as ignored, or treated as exogenous. And so to make an orderly, predictive theory possible, Economic Man (the subject) needs to operate on well-defined Problems (the object). There should be no blurring of agent and problem. The well-defined Problems should have well-defined Solutions. And the solutions would comprise the building blocks for the next aggregated level of the theory.

This approach works. But it runs into difficulties when problems start to involve more than one decision maker and any degree of complication. Then heroic assumptions must be made. Otherwise well-definedness unravels, agent and problem become blurred, and pockets of uncertainty start to bulge.

Let me show you what I mean in the context of a typical microeconomic situation in modern economics. (I have chosen it from the late-1970s literature on industrial organization.[1]) Consider this problem: We have a circle that we might think of as a 24-hour clock. A number of firms, say 20 airline companies, have to decide in which time slot of this clock their planes will take off in, for example from La Guardia Airport to go to Washington. Of course the different airlines have different preferences when to take off. They know their preferences and are going to book suitable takeoff slots. The choices will be

1. The example is based on the approach used in "Sequential Location among Firms with Foresight," E. C. Prescott and M, Visscher, *Bell Journal of Economics*, 8, 2, 378–393, 1977.

made once and for all. There is a trade-off (in every decent economic problem there is always a trade-off) between where they really want to take off versus not being too close to other airlines' choices of their time slots. So, given the airlines' preferences, which time slots will they choose? This is the problem.

We might feel uneasy about saying much with certainty here. But I want to show you the modern version of the Enlightenment approach, where we find the Harmony of a solution within the Discord of the situation. This High Modern approach is called rational expectations. I will first spell it out, then shine a bright light of realism on it, so that it starts to unravel and pockets of uncertainty appear. Let's go ahead.

In the rational expectations approach, we begin by supposing we know the order in which the airlines will submit their choices. Now imagine airline number 20 reasons like this: knowing where the first 19 airlines are going to be, I will know where I want to be. So regardless of any arbitrary choice of the first 19 airlines, I will know which time-slot to choose. This is an easy problem for me as the 20th. What about airline number 19? Well, airline number 19, when choosing, will know the arbitrarily chosen positions of the previous 18 airlines and can figure what it should do, given that the 20th will choose an optimal position given the positions of the 18 other airlines and 19's choice. What about the 18th? Well, the 18th, knowing where the previous 17 will be, arbitrarily can solve the problem of selecting an optimal placement knowing what the 19th will do, given that the 19th makes his optimal choice, given what the 20th will do as a result of 19's choice. Getting complicated? Yes. But you can work the whole logic in reverse order by backward deduction, or more properly by dynamic programming, and deduce how all 20 firms will place themselves.

Notice the properties of this procedure. The problem is well defined, by making it sequential and assuming the firms use logical backward deduction. The solution is precise and clean in a mathematical sense. The problem becomes a mathematical one. (Indeed all such problems become mathematical. Economics in turn becomes mathematics.) Another property that we normally have in this kind of problem is that the individual act comes to good of the whole, that is, partial evil is universal good. It is not quite true in this case, but nevertheless this is a generic property that often holds in economics.

But the Solution comes with a lot of fine print. Airlines must know exactly their preferences. Not only that, they must know the preferences of all other airlines. Further they must know that every other airline accurately knows the preferences of every other airline. They also must know that every airline knows that every airline knows the preferences of every other airline, and so on in an infinite regress. Also, each airline must be rational enough to work out the solution. Further, each airline must believe that every other airline is rational and will use perfect rationality to work out the solution. Further, each airline must know in an infinite regress that every other airline is using this rational way to work out the problem, because if one of these airlines messes up, it messes the solution up for every other airline. Further, the optimal placement of each airline using this backward deduction must be unique. If any link of this network of requirements breaks, the solution ceases to exist. In the spirit of being in Belgium, my comment on this is: "C'est magnifique, mais ce n'est pas la guerre."[2]

This type of multi-agent choice problem is pervasive in economics. So let us take this solution approach seriously. What if we are airline number 3 and we feel uncertain as to what airline number 17 is going to do? As airline number 3, we might say: I don't think the people of airline number 17 are that super bright, and I'm not sure whether they are going to solve this problem by this rational method. If they don't work it out in this way then I am not sure what my optimal choice would be as the third chooser in the process. This is sufficient to upset the situation. But worse, airline number 3 may communicate its uncertainty to other airlines and they may no longer rely on number 3 or number 17. The entire solution is starting to unravel. In fact the Solution as created is a function of airlines' expectations or predictions of what other airlines are going to do. So the problem is that if I am a representative airline I am trying to figure out what my expectations ought to be—I am trying to predict a world that is created by the expectations of myself and everybody else. There is a self-referential loop here. The outcome each airline is trying to predict depends on the predictions it and others might form. In other words, predictions are forming a world those predictions are trying to forecast. Barring some coordinating device, by which an airline can logically determine the predictions of others (such as the tortured solution-reasoning above), there is no logical way it can determine its prediction.

There is a logical indeterminacy. So in the economy, people are creating a world that forms from their predictions, but if they try to form these expectations in a perfectly logical deductive way, they get into a self-referential loop. There is a logical hole in standard economic thinking. Our forecasts co-create the world our forecasts are attempting to predict. Without knowing how others might determine their forecasts, mine are indeterminate. There are some cases in economics where it is pretty obvious that everyone can figure out what to do, where something like the above given scheme does work. Otherwise the problem is fundamental. The agents in the economy are in a Magritte world. When our ideas and preferences co-create the world they are trying to forecast, self-reference renders the problem indeterminate. The idea that we can separate the subjects of the economy—the agents who form it—from the object, the economy, is in trouble. Pockets of indeterminism are present everywhere in the economy. And the High Modern form of economic determinism fails.

2. Marshal Canrobert's remark on the charge of the Light Brigade at Balaclava.

There are two questions we want to ask. One question is: Does it matter? Maybe all of this happens on a set of measure zero, maybe this difficulty is confined to some trivial examples in economics. The second question is: If there is a real difficulty, how should we proceed?

I want to show you an argument taken from the field of capital markets, from asset pricing theory. And I want to show you this theory lands in the same trouble as the theory that explained the airlines' choices.

The only difference is that this is a theory that matters.

In 1991, I was hired by Citibank in Hong Kong as a consultant to develop sophisticated neural-network models to predict prices in foreign exchange markets. My initial reaction as an economist was skepticism. I believed the standard theory, and one of its implications is that there is no way to predict the financial markets. But soon I discovered that traders in the foreign exchange market disagreed. They believe they *can* predict price movements—at least to the degree they can make money. But first let me quickly outline the standard theory. The standard efficient markets theory says that all information coming in will be used by speculators and investors and anything in that information hinting about the future changes of the price will be used. In other words, by an argument very much like the airline argument, that I will show you in a moment, each stock's price is bid to a unique level that depends on the information currently available. Using past patterns of prices to forecast future prices (technical trading), in this view, cannot lead to further profits. Otherwise the information inherent in past prices could be used to make further profits, and by assumption investors have already discounted all information into current prices. So the standard theory says investors use all information available to form expectations. These will determine stocks' prices, which on average will uphold these same expectations. Rational expectations again. Thus there is no way to make any money, and the market is efficient. Traders, on the other hand believe that the market is forecastible. They believe they can spot patterns in past prices helpful in prediction—they believe in technical trading. They believe the market is anthropomorphic, that it has a psychology, that it has motives. "The market was nervous yesterday. But it shrugged off the bad news and went on to quiet down." Economists are skeptical of this. I remember hearing one famous economist remark: "If technical trading could make money, there would be a lot of companies and banks getting rich." This puzzled me. Because there *are* a lot of companies and banks getting rich using many forms of technical trading.

The standard theory is wonderfully successful. It has its own logic. This logic is complete and has desirable properties like mathematical uniqueness. But the standard theory must face some unexplained phenomena. It calls these empirical anomalies. (The basic notion is that there is something wrong with these phenomena because they don't fit the theory, rather than that there is something strange with the theory because it doesn't explain these phenomena.) So if there is a crash in the October 1987 stock market and the market loses 23% of its value, this is called a "correction." Yet there is no news in October '87 that calls for this crash. Another anomaly is "bubbles," like the famous Dutch tulip bubble where the prices stay high without any apparent reason. Additionally the volume of market trades is orders of magnitude higher than theory predicts. Several economists (Brock, Lakonishok, and Le Baron, notably) have shown that technical trading is indeed profitable statistically. Another puzzle is so-called GARCH behavior, (GARCH means Generalized Auto Regressive Conditional Heteroscedasticity), which means there are periods of high volatility in stock prices interspersed randomly with periods of quiescence.

In sum, there are at least half a dozen major statistical anomalies that are not explained in the standard theory. This has led to a great deal of more modern and ingenious theorizing, some using ad-hoc behavioral observation, some more sophisticated theorizing.

Let me show you now, as in the airline problem, how the standard theory breaks down and leads to pockets of indeterminacy. Suppose investors can put some portion of their money in a single stock that pays a dividend every time period (a day, a year, say) that investors cannot perfectly predict. The investors are buying the stock for this dividend plus any capital appreciation (tomorrow's price), and they face the problem of forecasting these. To make the standard solution work, we assume homogeneous, identical investors—clones—who have identical forecasts of the dividend at the end of the period and identical forecasts about the stock's price in the future. Forecasts that are on average unbiased and are therefore rational expectations. A little economic reasoning then shows today's price is equal to the common expectation of tomorrow's price plus dividend (suitably discounted and weighted). This yields a sequence of equations at each time, and with a pinch or two of conditional-expectation algebra, we can solve these for the expectations of future prices conditioned on current information, and wind up with today's price expressed as a function of expected future dividends. Problem solved. But it is only solved, providing we assume "identical investors who have identical forecasts of the dividend at the end of the period and identical forecasts about the stock's price in the future." But what if we don't? What if we assume investors differ?

Let us look at the same exercise assuming our investors agents are not clones—not homogeneous. Note that the standard theory's requirement of identical "information" means not just the same data seen by everyone, but the same interpretation of the data. But imagine yourself in a real setting, like the Hong Kong foreign exchange market. Information then consists of past prices and trading volumes, moves made by the central banks of New Zealand or the bank of Singapore or the central bank of China, rumors, CNN, news, what your friends are doing, what they are telling you by telephone, what somebody's aunt thinks is happening to the market. All of these things comprise actual information and it is reasonable to assume that, even if everybody has identical access to all this information, they would treat this information as a Rorschach inkblot and would interpret it differently. Even if we assume that the people interpreting this information are arbitrarily intelligent (they may be infinitely smart) and they are all perfectly trained in statistics, they will *still* interpret this data differently because there are many different ways to interpret the same data.

So there is no single expectational model. Each individual investor can still come up with an individual forecast of the dividend. But tomorrow's price is determined by this investor's and other investors' individual forecasts of the dividend and of next period's price. And there is no way for the individual investor to fathom the forecasts of the others—to figure "what average opinion expects the average opinion to be" (to use Keynes' words). To do so brings on a logical regress. "I think that they might think, but realizing that I think that, they will think this." Unless we assume identical investors, once again our agents are trying to forecast an outcome (future price) that is a function of other agents' forecasts. As before with the airlines problem there is no deductive closure. Expectations become indeterminate, and the theory fails.

Worse, expectations become unstable. Imagine a few people think that prices on the market are going to go up. If I believe this and I believe that others believe this, I will revise my expectations upward. But then I may pick up some negative rumor. I will reassess downward, but realizing that others may reassess and that they too realize that others, I may further reassess. Expectations become fugitive, rippling up or down whether trades are made or not. Predictions become unstable. This is the way price bubbles start. If somehow people expect prices to go up, they will forecast that other people will forecast that prices will go up. So they will buy in. A bubble starts. People can see prices go up and their expectations of upward motion fulfilled. Therefore prices may continue to go up. The bubble is self-fulfilling.

Similar logic applies to "floors" and "ceilings." If, for example, the price is 894, many investors believe that at 900 there is some sort of membrane, a ceiling, and when the price reaches this ceiling it will bounce back down with a certain probability or it may "break through." My first reaction to hearing about floors and ceilings was one of disbelief. Then I started to realize that many investors may have sell orders at 900, simply because it is a round number. So expectations that the price will fall if it hits 900 are likely to be fulfilled. Ceilings and floors emerge as partially self-fulfilling prophecies, held in place by their being convenient sell and buy places. We are now a long way from homogeneous rational expectations. Under the realistic assumption that traders may interpret the same information differently, expectations become indeterminate and unstable. And they may become mutually self-fulfilling.

To summarize all this: if we look at a serious branch of economics, the theory of capital markets, we see the same indeterminacy as we saw in the airline problem. Agents need to form expectations of an outcome that is a function of these expectations. With reasonable heterogeneity of interpretation of "information," there is no deductive closure. The formation of expectations is indeterminate.

And yet... and yet... in every market, in every day, people *do* form expectations. How do they do this? If they cannot do this deductively, then should we model their behavior in this area?... In 1988, John Holland and I decided that we would study situations like this by forming an artificial stock market in the computer and giving the little agents—artificially intelligent computer programs—some means by which they can do the reasoning that is required. This was one of the very earliest artificial, agent-based markets. Later we brought in Richard Palmer who is a physicist, Paul Tayler who is a finance expert and Blake LeBaron who is a financial theorist in economics. When we started, John Holland, the renowned computer scientist who devised the genetic algorithm, could program only in BASIC. And I could only program in BASIC. However, Richard was a sophisticated programmer and we rapidly progressed. We designed our artificial stock market within the machine (first on a Macintosh then a NeXT) and got it working.

In this market there was no feed-in from the real stock market. It was an artificial world going on inside the machine. The artificial agents, the little artificial investors, are all buying and selling a "stock" from one another. The computer could display the stock's price and dividend, who is buying and selling, who is making money and who is not, who is in the market and who is out, and so on. The price is formed within the machine by bids and offers. Another little program—a specialist—sets the price to clear the market, as in actual stock markets.

The modeling question was: If the agents cannot form their expectations deductively, how are they going to form them? We decided to follow modern cognitive theory about how actual human beings behave in such situations. So we allowed our artificial agents looking at the recent history of the stock's price to posit multiple, individual hypothetical models for forecasting and test these on a continual, ongoing basis. Each of these hypotheses has a prediction associated with it. At any stage each agent uses the most accurate of its hypotheses, and buys or sells accordingly. Our agents learn in two ways: they learn which of their forecasting hypotheses are more accurate, and they continually toss out ones that don't work and replace these using a genetic algorithm. So they are learning to recognize patterns they are collectively creating, and this in turn collectively creates new patterns in the stock price, which they can form fresh hypotheses about. This kind of behavior—bringing in hypotheses, testing them, and occasionally replacing them—is called induction.

Our agents use *inductive rationality*. And this is a much more realistic form of behavior.

Alright then. But now the key question is: Does our market converge to the rational expectations equilibrium of the academic theory or does it show some other behavior? What we found to our surprise was that two different regimes emerged. One, which we called the *rational expectations regime*, held sway when we started our agents off with sets of predictive hypotheses close to rational expectations. We could plot the parameters of all the predictive hypotheses on a chart, and in this case, over time, we could watch them getting gravitationally pulled into the orbit of the rational expectations solution, forming a "fuzz" around this point, as they made occasional predictive forays away from rational expectations to test different ideas. It is not hard to see why rational expectations prevailed. If the overall mass of predictions is near rational expectations, the price sequence will be near rational expectations, and non-rational expectations forecasts will be negated. So the academic theory was validated.

But there was a second regime, which we called the *complex regime,* and it prevailed in a much wider set of circumstances. We found that if we started our agents with hypotheses a little removed from rational expectations, or alternatively, if we allowed them to come up with hypotheses at a slightly faster rate than before, the behavior of the market changed. Subsets of mutually reinforcing predictions emerged. Imagine we have 100 artificial agents each using 60 different prediction formulas, so that there is a universe of some 6,000 predictors. Some of these predictors that emerge are mutually reinforcing, some are mutually negating. Suppose many predictors arise that say the stock price cycles up and down over time. Such predictors would be mutually negating because they will cause agents to buy in at the bottom of the cycle, and sell at the top of the cycle, mutually negating profits, and therefore eventually disappearing from the population of predictors. But if a subset of predictors emerged by chance that said "the price will rise next period if it has risen in the last three periods," and there were enough of these, they would cause agents to buy, which on average would cause the price to rise, reinforcing such a subpopulation. Such subsets could then take off, and become embedded in the population of predictors. This was what indeed happened in the complex regime, endowing it with much richer set of behaviors. Another way to express this is that our artificial traders had discovered forms of technical trading that worked. They were using, with success, predictions based upon past price patterns. And so technical trading was emergent in our artificial stock market. This emergence of subsets of mutually reinforcing elements, strangely enough, is reminiscent of the origin of life, where the emergence of subpopulations of RNA in correct combinations allows them to become mutually enforcing.

Another property that emerged in the complex regime was GARCH behavior—periods of high volatility in the stock price followed by periods of quiescence—another property unexplained in the standard model. How did GARCH become an emergent property? What happens in our artificial market is that every so often some number of investors discover a new way to do better in the market. These investors then change their buying and selling behavior. This causes the market to change, even if slightly, causing other investors in turn to change. Avalanches of change sweep through the market, on all scales, large and small. Thus emerge periods of change triggering further change, periods of high volatility, followed by periods when little changes and little needs to be changed, periods of quiescence. This is GARCH behavior.

Let me now summarize. What we found in our artificial stock market is that, providing our investors start near the rational-expectations academic solution, this solution prevails. But this is a small set of parameter space. Outside this, in the complex regime, self-reinforcing beliefs and self-reinforcing avalanches of change emerge. A wider theory and a richer "solution" or set of behaviors then appears, consonant with actual market behavior. The rational-expectations theory becomes a special case.

In the standard view, which has come down from the Enlightenment, the economy is an object. It is complicated but can be viewed mechanistically. Subject and object—agents and the economy they perform in—can be neatly separated. The view I am giving here is different. It says that the economy itself emerges from our subjective beliefs. These subjective beliefs, taken in aggregate, structure the micro economy. They give rise to the character of financial markets. They direct flows of capital and govern strategic behavior and negotiations. They are the DNA of the economy. These subjective beliefs are a-priori or deductively indeterminate in advance. They co-evolve, arise, decay, change, mutually reinforce, and mutually negate. Subject and object cannot be neatly separated. And so the economy shows behavior that we can best describe as organic, rather than mechanistic. It is not a well-ordered, gigantic machine. It is organic. At all levels it contains pockets of indeterminacy. It emerges from subjectivity and falls back into subjectivity.

CHAPTER 12

Complexity and the Economy

W. BRIAN ARTHUR

This essay summarizes my thinking on complexity and the economy in 1999. It is a precursor to (and heavily overlaps) the introductory chapter of this volume, but I include it here because it introduces the term "complexity economics" for the first time. The article appeared in *Science*, April 2, 1999, 244: 107–109.

Common to all studies on complexity are systems with multiple elements adapting or reacting to the pattern these elements create. The elements might be cells in a cellular automaton, ions in a spin glass, or cells in an immune system, and they may react to neighboring cells' states, or local magnetic moments, or concentrations of B and T cells. Elements and the patterns they respond to vary from one context to another. But the elements adapt to the world—the aggregate pattern—they co-create. Time enters naturally here via the processes of adjustment and change: As the elements react, the aggregate changes; as the aggregate changes, elements react anew. Barring the reaching of some asymptotic state or equilibrium, complex systems are systems in process that constantly evolve and unfold over time.

Such systems arise naturally in the economy. Economic agents, be they banks, consumers, firms, or investors, continually adjust their market moves, buying decisions, prices, and forecasts to the situation these moves or decisions or prices or forecasts together create. But unlike ions in a spin glass, which always react in a simple way to their local magnetic field, economic elements (human agents) react with strategy and foresight by considering outcomes that might result as a consequence of behavior they might undertake. This adds a layer of complication to economics that is not experienced in the natural sciences.

Conventional economic theory chooses not to study the unfolding of the patterns its agents create but rather to simplify its questions in order to seek analytical solutions. Thus it asks what behavioral elements (actions, strategies, and expectations) are consistent with the aggregate patterns these behavioral elements co-create? For example, general equilibrium theory asks what prices and quantities of goods produced and consumed are consistent with (would pose no incentives for change to) the overall pattern of prices and quantities in the economy's markets. Game theory asks what moves or choices or allocations are consistent with (are optimal given) other agents' moves or choices or allocations in a strategic situation. Rational expectations economics asks what forecasts (or expectations) are consistent with (are on average validated by) the outcomes these forecasts and expectations together create. Conventional economics thus studies consistent patterns: patterns in behavioral equilibrium that would induce no further reaction. Economists at the Santa Fe Institute, Stanford, MIT, Chicago, and other institutions are now broadening this equilibrium approach by turning to the question of how actions, strategies, or expectations might react in general to (might endogenously change with) the aggregate patterns these create (*1, 2*). The result—complexity economics—is not an adjunct to standard economic theory but theory at a more general, out-of-equilibrium level.

The type of systems I have described become especially interesting if they contain nonlinearities in the form of positive feedbacks. In economics, positive feedbacks arise from increasing returns (*3, 4*). To ensure that a unique, predictable equilibrium is reached, standard economics usually assumes diminishing returns. If one firm gets too far ahead in the market, it runs into higher costs or some other negative feedback, and the market is shared at a predictable unique equilibrium. When we allow positive feedbacks, or increasing returns, a different outcome arises. Consider the market for online services of a few years back, in which three major companies competed: Prodigy, Compuserve, and America Online. As each gained in membership base, it could offer a wider menu of services, as well as more members to share specialized hobby and chat room interests with—that is, there were increasing returns to expanding the membership base. Prodigy was first in the market, but by chance and strategy America Online got far enough ahead to gain an unassailable advantage. Today it dominates. Under different circumstances, one of its rivals might have taken the market. Notice the properties here: a multiplicity of potential solutions; the outcome actually reached is not predictable in advance; it tends to be locked in; it is not necessarily the most efficient economically; it is subject to the historical path taken; and although the companies may start out equal, the outcome is asymmetrical. These properties have counterparts in nonlinear physics where similar positive feedbacks are present. What economists call multiple equilibria, nonpredictability, lock-in, inefficiency, historical path dependence, and asymmetry, physicists call multiple metastable states, unpredictability, phase or mode locking, high-energy ground states, non-ergodicity, and symmetry breaking (*5*).

Increasing returns problems have been discussed in economics for a long time. A hundred years ago, Alfred Marshall (*6*) noted that if firms gain advantage as their market share increases, "whatever firm first gets a good start will obtain a monopoly." But the conventional static equilibrium approach gets stymied by indeterminacy: If there is a multiplicity of equilibria, how might one be reached? The process-oriented complexity approach suggests a way to deal with this. In the actual economy, small random events happen; in the online services case, events such as random interface improvements, new offerings, and word-of-mouth recommendations. Over time, increasing returns magnify the cumulation of such events to select the outcome randomly. Thus, increasing returns problems in economics are best seen as dynamic processes with random events and natural positive feedbacks—as nonlinear stochastic processes. This shift from a static outlook into a process orientation is common to complexity studies. Increasing returns problems are being studied intensively in market allocation theory (*4*), international trade theory (*7*), the evolution of technology choice (*8*), economic geography (*9*), and the evolution of patterns of poverty and segregation (*10*). The common finding that economic structures can crystallize around small events and lock in is beginning to change policy in all of these areas toward an awareness that governments should avoid both extremes of coercing a desired outcome and keeping strict hands off, and instead seek to push the system gently toward favored structures that can grow and emerge naturally. Not a heavy hand, not an invisible hand, but a nudging hand.

Once we adopt the complexity outlook, with its emphasis on the formation of structures rather than their given existence, problems involving prediction in the economy look different. The conventional approach asks what forecasting model (or expectations) in a particular problem, if given and shared by all agents, would be consistent with (would be on average validated by) the actual time series this forecasting model would in part generate. This "rational expectations" approach is valid. But it assumes that agents can somehow deduce in advance what model will work and that everyone "knows" that everyone knows to use this model (the common knowledge assumption.) What happens when forecasting models are not obvious and must be formed individually by agents who are not privy to the expectations of others?

Consider as an example my El Farol Bar Problem (*11*). One hundred people must decide independently each week whether to show up at their favorite bar (El Farol in Santa Fe). The rule is that if a person predicts that more that 60 (say) will attend, he or she will avoid the crowds and stay home; if he predicts fewer than 60, he will go. Of interest are how the bar-goers each week might predict the numbers of people showing up, and the resulting dynamics of the numbers attending. Notice two features of this problem. Our agents will quickly realize that predictions of how many will attend depend on others' predictions of how many will attend (because that determines their attendance). But others' predictions in turn depend on their predictions of others' predictions. Deductively there is an infinite regress. No "correct" expectational model can be assumed to be common knowledge, and from the agents' viewpoint, the problem is ill defined. (This is true for most expectational problems, not just for this example.) Second, and diabolically, any commonalty of expectations gets broken up: If all use an expectational model that predicts few will go, all will go, invalidating that model. Similarly, if all believe most will go, nobody will go, invalidating that belief. Expectations will be forced to differ.

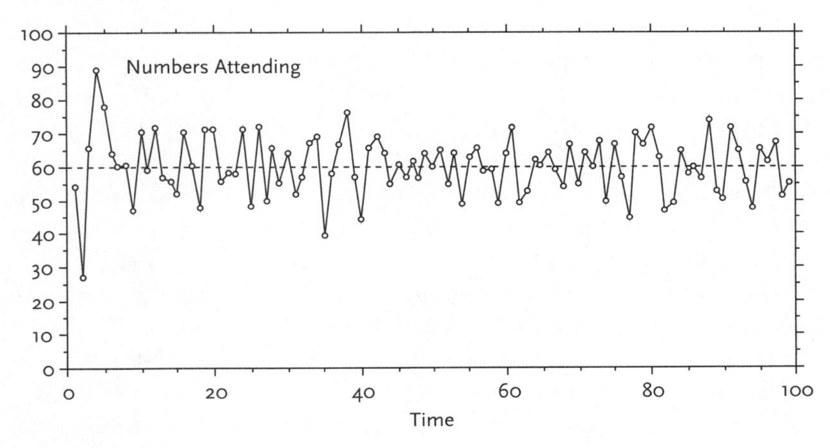

Figure 1:
Bar attendance in the first 100 weeks.

In 1993, I modeled this situation by assuming that as the agents visit the bar, they act inductively—they act as statisticians, each starting with a variety of subjectively chosen expectational models or forecasting hypotheses. Each week they act on their currently most accurate model (call this their active predictor). Thus agents' beliefs or hypotheses compete for use in an "ecology" these beliefs create.

Computer simulation (Figure 1) showed that the mean attendance quickly converges to 60. In fact, the predictors self-organize into an equilibrium ecology in which, of the active predictors, 40% on average are forecasting above 60 and 60% below 60. This emergent ecology is organic in nature, because although the population of active predictors splits into this 60/40 average ratio, it keeps changing in membership forever. Why do the predictors self-organize so that 60 emerges as average attendance and forecasts split into a 60/40 ratio? Well, suppose 70% of predictors forecasted above 60 for a longish time, then on average only 30 people would show up. But this would validate predictors that forecasted close to 30, restoring the ecological balance among predictions. The 40%/60% "natural" combination becomes an emergent structure. The Bar Problem is a miniature expectational economy with complex dynamics (*12*).

One important application of these ideas is in financial markets. Standard theories of financial markets assume rational expectations—that agents adopt uniform forecasting models that are on average validated by the prices these forecast (*13*). The theory works well to first order. But it doesn't account for actual market anomalies such as unexpected price bubbles and crashes, random periods of high and low volatility (price variation), and the heavy use of technical trading (trades based on the recent history of price patterns). Holland, LeBaron, Palmer, Tayler, and I (*14*) have created a model that relaxes rational expectations by assuming, as in the Bar Problem, that investors cannot assume or deduce expectations but must discover them. Our agents continually create and use multiple market hypotheses—individual, subjective, expectational models—of future prices and dividends within an artificial stock market on the computer. These "investors" are individual, artificially intelligent computer programs that can generate and discard expectational hypotheses and make bids or offers based on their currently most accurate hypothesis. The stock price forms from their bids and offers and thus ultimately from agents' expectations. So this market-in-the-machine is its own self-contained, artificial financial world. Like the bar, it is a mini-ecology in which expectations compete in a world those expectations create.

Within this computerized market, we found two phases or regimes. If parameters are set so that our artificial agents update their hypotheses slowly, the diversity of expectations collapses quickly into homogeneous rational ones. The reason is that if a majority of investors believes something close to the rational expectations forecast, then resulting prices will validate it, and deviant or mutant predictions that arise in the population of expectational models will be rendered inaccurate. Standard finance theory, under these special circumstances, is upheld. But if the rate of updating of hypotheses is increased, the market undergoes a phase transition into a complex regime and displays several of the anomalies observed in real markets. It develops a rich psychology of divergent beliefs that don't converge over time. Expectational rules such as "if the market is trending up, predict a 1% price rise" that appear randomly in the population of hypotheses can become mutually reinforcing: If enough investors act on these, the price will indeed go up. Thus subpopulations of mutually reinforcing expectations arise, agents bet on these (therefore technical trading emerges), and this causes occasional bubbles and crashes. Our artificial market also shows periods of high volatility in prices, followed randomly by periods of low volatility. This is because if some investors discover new profitable hypotheses, they change the market slightly, causing other investors to also change their expectations. Changes in beliefs therefore ripple through the market in avalanches of all sizes, causing periods of high and low volatility. We conjecture that actual financial markets, which show exactly these phenomena, lie in this complex regime.

After two centuries of studying equilibria—static patterns that call for no further behavioral adjustments—economists are beginning to study the general emergence of structures and the unfolding of patterns in the economy. Complexity economics is not a temporary adjunct to static economic theory but theory at a more general, out-of-equilibrium level. The approach is making itself felt in every area of economics: game theory (*15*), the theory of money and finance (*16*), learning in the economy (*17*), economic history (*18*), the evolution of trading networks (*19*), the stability of the economy (*20*), and political economy (*21*). It is helping us understand phenomena such as market instability, the emergence of monopolies, and the persistence of poverty in ways that will help us deal with these. And it is bringing an awareness that policies succeed better by influencing the natural processes of formation of economic structures than by forcing static outcomes.

When viewed in out-of-equilibrium formation, economic patterns sometimes fall into the simple homogeneous equilibria of standard economics. More often, they are ever changing, showing perpetually novel behavior and emergent phenomena. Complexity therefore portrays the economy not as deterministic, predictable, and mechanistic but as process dependent, organic, and always evolving (*22*).

REFERENCES AND NOTES

1. P. Anderson, K. J. Arrow, D. Pines, Eds., *The Economy as an Evolving Complex System* (Addison-Wesley, Reading, MA, 1988).
2. W. B. Arthur, S. N. Durlauf, D. A. Lane, Eds., *The Economy as an Evolving Complex System II* (Addison-Wesley, Reading, MA, 1997).
3. W. B. Arthur, *Sci. Am.* 262, 92 (1990).
4. W. B. Arthur, *Increasing Returns and Path Dependence in the Economy* (Univ. of Michigan Press, Ann Arbor, Ml, 1994).
5. I have avoided exact definitions of "complexity" and "complex systems." Technically, the systems I have described are referred to as adaptive nonlinear networks (J. H. Holland's term), and typically if they exhibit certain properties that have to do with the multiplicity of potential patterns or with the coherence or propagation of substructures, they are said to be "complex." Definitions vary widely.
6. A. Marshall, *Principles of Economics* (Macmillan, London, ed. 8, 1920), p. 459.
7. E. Helpman and P. R. Krugman, *Market Structure and Foreign Trade* (MIT Press, Cambridge, MA, 1985).
8. W. B. Arthur, *Econ. J.* 99, 116 (1989).
9. W. B. Arthur, *Math. Soc. Sci.* 19, 235 (1990); P. R. Krugman, *J. Polit. Econ.* 99, 483 (1991); in (2), p. 239; *Geography and Trade* (MIT Press, Cambridge, MA, 1991).
10. S. N. Durlauf, in (2), p. 81; *J. Econ. Growth* 1, 75 (1996).
11. W. B. Arthur, *Am. Econ. Rev.* 84, 406 (1994).

12. J. Casti, *Complexity* 1 (no. 5), 7 (1995/96); N. Johnson *et al., Physica A* 256, 230 (1998); D. Challet and Y.-C. Zhang, ibid. 246, 407 (1997); ibid. 256, 514 (1998).
13. R. E. Lucas, *Econometrica* 46, 1429 (1978).
14. W. B. Arthur, J. H. Holland, B. LeBaron, R. Palmer, Paul Tayler, in (2), p. 15; W. B. Arthur, *Complexity* 1 (no. 1), 20 (1995).
15. See K. Lindgren's classic paper in *Artificial Life II,* C. G. Langton, C. Taylor, J. D. Farmer, S. Rasmussen, Eds. (Addison-Wesley, Reading, MA, 1991), p. 295; H. P. Young, *Econometrica* 61, 57 (1993); L. E. Blume, in (2), p. 425; B. A. Huberman and N. S. Glance, *Proc. Natl. Acad. Sci. U.S.A.* 90, 7716 (1993).
16. R. Marimon, E. McGrattan, T. J. Sargent, *J. Econ. Dyn. Control* 14, 329 (1990); M. Shubik, in (2), p. 263; W. A. Brock and P. de Lima, in *Handbook of Statistics 12: Finance*, G. S. Maddala, H. Rao, H. Vinod, Eds. (North-Holland, Amsterdam, 1995).
17. T. J. Sargent, *Bounded Rationality in Macroeconomics* (Clarendon Press, Oxford, 1993); D. A. Lane and R. Maxfield, in (2), p. 169; V. M. Darley and S. A. Kauffman, in (2), p. 45.
18. D. C. North, in (2), p. 223.
19. Y. M. loannides, in (2), p. 129; A. Kirman, in (2), p. 491; L. Tesfatsion, in (2), p. 533.
20. P. Bak, K. Chen, J. Scheinkman, M. Woodford, *Ric. Econ.* 47, 3 (1993); A. Leijonhufvud, in (2), p. 321.
21. R. Axelrod, *Am. Pol. Sci. Rev.* 80, 1095 (1986); K. Kollman, J. H. Miller, S. E. Page, in (2), p. 461.
22. I thank J. Casti and S. Durlauf for comments on this article.

AN HISTORICAL FOOTNOTE

The table below is an entry from my research notebook from November 5, 1979. I include it because it has been much cited in the last few years, and because the thoughts here were the basis from which the papers in this volume arose.

In 1979 I was working at the International Institute for Applied Systems Analysis in Austria. I had been reading a lot of biology, especially the work of Jacques Monod and Francois Jacob, and much of the work of the Brussels and Stuttgart groups on self-organizing systems. Given these ideas, and my own predilections, it gradually became clear to me that economics would be different in the future—it would be based on different principles. I wrote what I thought these principles would be in my notebook. The table includes thoughts on demography, which was one of my chief interests at that time, and is reproduced in whole (complete with haphazard punctuation).

ECONOMICS OLD AND NEW

Old	New
Decreasing returns	Much use of increasing returns
Based on marginality (neoclassical)	Other principles possible (e.g. accounting principles)
Maximizing principles (profit motive)	Order principles
Preferences given	Formation of preferences becomes central
Individuals selfish	individuals not necessarily selfish
Society as backdrop	Institutions come to the fore as a main decider of possibilities, order and structure

(continued)

Old	New
Technology given or selected on economic basis	Technology initially fluid, then tends to set
Essentially deterministic, forecastible	Non-deterministic. Unforecastible because of fluctuations and strange attractors (and suchlike)
Based on 19th-century physics (equilibrium, stability, deterministic dynamics)	Based on biology (structure, pattern, self-organization, life cycle)
Time. Treated not at all (Debreu)	Time. Becomes central
Treated superficially (growth theory)	Closely tied to age
Age. Very little done	Individual life comes to center. Age begets time.
Emphasis on quantities, prices and equilibrium	Emphasis on structure, pattern, and function (of location, technology, institutions, and possibilities)
Elements are quantities and prices	Elements are patterns and possibilities. Compatible structures carry out some functions in each society (cf. anthropology)
Language: 19th-century math and game theory, and fixed point topology	Language more qualitative. Game theory recognized for its qualitative uses. Other qualitative mathematics useful
Generations not really seen	Generational turnover becomes central. Membership in economy changing and age-structure of population changing. Generations "carry" their experiences
Heavy use of indices People identical	Focus on individual life. People separate and different. Continual switching between aggregate and the individual. Welfare indices different and used as rough measure. Individual lifetime seen as measure
No real dynamics in sense that everything is at equilibrium. Cf. Ball on string in circular motion. No real change happening: just dynamic suspension	Economy is always on the edge of time. It rushes forward, structures constantly coalescing, decomposing, changing. All this due to externalities, increasing returns, transactions costs, structural exclusion, leading to jerky motion

Old	New
If only there were no externalities and all had equal abilities we'd reach Nirvana	Externalities and differences become driving force. No Nirvana. System constantly unfolding.
Most questions unanswerable. Unified system incompatible	Questions remain hard to answer. But assumptions clearly spelled out.
"Hypotheses testable" (Samuelson) Assumes laws exist	Models are fitted to data (as in [exploratory data analysis]) A fit is a fit is a fit. No laws really possible. Laws change.
Sees subject as structurally simple	Sees subject as inherently complex
Economics as soft physics	Economics as high complexity science.
Exchange and resources drive economy	Externalities, differences, ordering principles, compatibility, mind-set, family, possible lifecycle and increasing returns drive institutions, society and economy.

OTHER PAPERS ON COMPLEXITY AND THE ECONOMY BY W. BRIAN ARTHUR

The following papers, not included in this volume, may be of interest to the reader.[1]

"Complexity, the Santa Fe Approach, and Nonequilibrium Economics," in *History of Economic Ideas*, 8, 2, 149–166, 2010.

"The Structure of Invention," *Research Policy*, 36, 2, March 2007.

"Agent-Based Modeling and Out-Of-Equilibrium Economics," in *Handbook of Computational Economics,* Vol. 2, K. Judd and L. Tesfatsion, eds, Elsevier/North-Holland, 2006.

"Time Series Properties of an Artificial Stock Market," with B. LeBaron and R. Palmer, *Journal of Economic Dynamics and Control*, 23, 1487–1516, 1999.

"Beyond Rational Expectations: Indeterminacy in Economic and Financial Markets," in *Frontiers of the New Institutional Economics*, 291–303, J. N. Drobak and J. V. Nye (eds.), Academic Press, San Diego, Ca, 1997.

"Artificial Economic Life: A Simple Model of a Stockmarket," with R. Palmer, J. Holland, B. LeBaron, and P. Tayler, *Physica D*, 75, 264–274, 1994.

"Economic Agents That Behave like Human Agents," *Journal of Evolutionary Economics,* 3, 1–22, 1993.

"Why Do Things Become More Complex?" Essay in *Scientific American*, May 1993.

"Learning and Adaptation in the Economy," Santa Fe Institute Paper 92-07-038, 1992.

"Designing Economic Agents That Act like Human Agents: A Behavioral Approach to Bounded Rationality," *American Economic Review* (A.E.A. Papers and Proc.) 81, 353–359, 1991.

"The Economy as a Complex System," in *Complex Systems*, D. Stein (ed.), Wiley, New York, 1989.

1. So may some of my papers on positive feedback (often seen as part of complexity). These appeared in the earlier collection, *Increasing Returns and Path Dependence in the Economy*, W. B. Arthur, University of Michigan Press, 1994.

INDEX

academic theorists, compared to market traders, 40
active predictors, 35, 185
active repertoire, 126, 127f
adaptation, 92, 154
adaptive complex system, 37
adaptive nonlinear networks, 92–93
adjacent probable, 128
adopters, 71n4, 80–82
adoption, 71–72, 72t
adoption process, 75, 80
agent-based models, xv, 24, 39, 95, 99, 102, 112–113, 115
agent homogeneity, 53, 101
agents, 2–3. *See also* economic agents
  acting as market statisticians, 96
  adapting forecasts, 42
  affecting other players' well-being, 110
  arriving inductively at a homogeneity, 53
  basing actions on expectations, 95
  choosing between technologies, 70
  entertaining more than one market hypothesis, 60
  evolutionary selection of via wealth, 66
  expectations, 42–43, 49, 78
  exploring their way forward, 7
  facing not a problem but a situation, 159
  finding out what works, 115
  forecasting outcomes, 178
  gaming the criteria, 108
  generating contingent actions or rules, 114
  hypothetical patterns, frameworks and associations, 164
  imposing meaning on problem situations, 165
  inhabiting a world they must cognitively interpret, 93
  inside information, 110
  interacting through impersonal markets, 94
  introducing heterogeneity, 43
  keeping strategies in mind, 115
  learning from each other, 98
  learning which hypotheses work, 33, 49, 165
  making sense of their problems, 93
  not knowing, 5
  optimizing allocation, 47
  recognizing different states of the market, 49
  remembering what happened before, 50
  showing uncertainty in choice, 16
  subjective beliefs, 32
  taking over part of the machinery of a system, 108
  "tested" for survival, 7
  testing forecasting parameters, 52
agent space, emergence of structure in, 99
aggregate patterns, 3, 99
"AI-complete" problems, 116
aircraft designers, knowing causes of failure, 110
air transport, problem of worldwide spread of infections, 142

algorithm
arriving at complicated circuits, 125
behind the computation, 8
building a library of functionalities, 124
comment on, 131
for the formation of the economy, 19, 137
working best where needs are ordered, 129
algorithmic model, rewriting in equation form, 11n15
algorithmic parse trees, 150
alife approach, 102
Allen, Peter, xxi, xxiii
allocation
within the economy, 22
mathematical analysis of, 23
problems, 22, 70
process, 75, 84
in the three regimes, 73–75
alternating current, 81
alternative expectations, 53
alternative explorations, 54
alternative technologies, 78
Anderson, Phil, 89, 101
anthropomorphic market, 176
anticipation, by adaptive nonlinear networks, 92
anticipative models, 93
arbitrage pricing model, 43–46
Arrow, Kenneth J., x–xii, xv, xxiii, 30, 89, 107
Arthur, W. Brian, 79, 90, 193
Arthur-Ermoliev-Kaniovski theorem, 80, 86
artificial agents, 179
artificial evolution contexts, 147
artificial intelligence, 116
artificial markets, 66
artificial stock market, 179–181
artificial traders, 180
assemblies, of technologies, 18
asset composition, 47
asset markets
models of, 47
reflexive nature of, 62
asset pricing, 11, 42, 96, 176
associations, cognitive, 160, 163, 168
associative engines, brains as, 162
asymmetric information, 107
atomic power, problem of disposal of waste, 142
attractor, in the bar problem, 37
autocorrelated volatility, 57n14
autopoiesis, 20, 120n2
avalanches
of change, 15, 59, 122, 181, 186
of collapse, 130, 130f
Axelrod, Robert, 111
Axtell, Robert, xxi, xxiii, 2n3

Bailey, James, xxiv, 11n16
Bak, Per, xvi
Baker, W., 99
bar problem. *See* El Farol bar problem
Barrett, Chris, xxiii
base of a system, collapse near, 151
behavior. *See also* exploitive behavior
adjusting to appear virtuous, 108
assuming to make models realistic, 6n8
depending on exogenous characteristics, 100
economic, 171
human, 173
inductive, 30–38, 164, 185
intelligent, 6, 44–46, 64
behavioral economics, ix, 6
behavioral noise-trader literature, 41
Beinhocker, Eric, xxiii, 2n2, 8n11
belief-models, each agent tracking, 33
beliefs. *See* subjective beliefs
Berra, Yogi, 35n3
binary decision diagrams (BDDs), 132
biological organisms, built from modules, 155
biologists, doubts about linkage between evolution and complexity, 145
biology
intermediate structures in, 122
as theoretical but not mathematical, 21
black box, getting from problem to solution, 159
Blume, Larry, xxiii, 61, 98, 101
Boldrin, Michele, 90
bounded rationality, 6n9, 31
Braudel, Fernand, 101
Bray models, 61

breakdown, in engineering designs, 110
British railways, narrow gauge, 81n9
Brock, William, 90, 96
Bronk, Richard, xx, xxiii, 6
Bronowski, Jacob, 173
Brownian motion, 6, 7, 16–17
bubbles, 13, 40, 43, 54, 177. *See also* price bubbles
building blocks, 120, 126
build-out of technology, modeling, 121
bull-market uptrend, prolonged, 60
Buss, Leo, 98

California, freeing of its energy market, 104
Cambrian explosion, 148, 152
Campbell's law, 108
capital markets, 176
capturing software, 152–156
carbon-based fuel technologies, 142
Carlson, Rob, 133
Cassidy, John, 4n4, 117
causes, of exploitive behavior, 105–109
certainty, end of, 171–181
Chaitin, Gregory, 11n16, 25
Challet, Damien, xvi, 30
chance, 72, 140
change. *See also* structural change
  "avalanches" of cascading through the system, 59
  begetting change, 141
Ch'eng Hao, 163
Ch'eng Yi, 163
chess playing, inductive behavior in, 32
Cheung, Sai Hung, 103n1
choice process, deriving properties of, 75
circuits
  constructing from simpler ones, 124
  constructing new, 132
  "invented" for simple goals, 125f
  novel, 123
circular causalities, inherent, 148
Clark, Andy, 97, 162
classical game theory, 3
clustered volatility, 13
coevolutionary diversity, 145–148, 152
coevolutionary environment, 152
coevolutionary world, 33
coevolving systems, 145
cognition, 95–98
  as black box of economics, 158–169
  implications of, 169
  between the problem and the action, 160
cognitive foundations, 93–94
cognitive process, modeling, 164–166
cognitive reasoning, mirroring actual, 49
cognitive science, 6, 160
Colander, David, xxii, xxiii, 24, 167
collapses, near the base of the dependency hierarchy, 147
collective technology, 18, 20
combination, as the key driving force of formation, 18n25
combinatorial chemistry, 124
combinatorial evolution, 119
combinatorics, for an 8-bit adder, 125
common knowledge, cannot be assumed, 94
competing standards case, 84
competition
  causing complexity to increase, 150
  commodity, 78n7
  under increasing returns, 83
  between technologies having multiple potential outcomes, 70
  two-party, 100
complex features, creating, 119
complexity
  associated with nonequilibrium, 7
  consequences of interactions, 14
  described, 3
  economy and, 182–187, 193
  evolution of, 144–156
  in the form of greater diversity, 146
  increasing via generation of new niches, 148
  properties of, 15, 17
complexity economics
  compared to equilibrium economics, 24–25
  described, 183, 187
  different framework for economic thought, 1–25
  exploring the world of formation, 23
  variants of, 2n2
Complexity: Metaphors, Models, and Reality, 144
complexity outlook, adopting, 184
complexity perspective, in economics, 90

The Complexity Vision and the Teaching of Economics, 158
complex or rich psychological regime, 54–59
complex patterns, 40, 54
complex regime, 39, 43, 55f, 62, 180
complex systems, as systems in process, 182
complicated goals, 129
complication
dealing with, 32
increases in, 144
simplicity and, 151
computation, 8, 11
computer
generating new circuits, 122
revealing a new world, 25
computer experiments
constructing, 36–37
showing emergence of two market regimes, 51–59
computer industry, increase in diversity, 146
computerized market, phases or regimes, 186
computer laser printer, 18, 147
computer models, 112–115, 123
concrete economic problems, identifying, 95
concurrent behavior, massively parallel system of, 3
condition array, matching or recognizing current market state, 49
condition/forecast rule, 49
connected network, structures arising in, 99
connectionist models, 32n1
constant returns, 74, 76, 77
consumers, gaming Massachusetts' 2006 health insurance law, 107
contextual explanations, 100
continual adaptation, 92
conventional economics, studying consistent patterns, 183
correct meaning, determining, 164
correlated effects, 100
coverage, doing without, 113
Cowan, George, xxiii
Cowan, Robin, 69, 82–83
crashes
causes of, 13
damaging economists' beliefs, 40
evidence of temporary, 54
herd effects causing, 40
occurring from time to time, 43
in the October 1987 stock market, 177
unexpected, 186
creative formation, 22
credit default swaps, 109
cross-correlation, of trading volume with volatility, 59f
cross-cutting hierarchical organization, 92

Darley, Vince, 95, 96
Darwin, Charles, xvii, 21, 119, 148
data
different meanings imposed on the same, 162
interpretation of, 95, 178
mind as a container holding, 160
David, Paul, 69, 81
Davis, John, 4n4
"dead" behavior, 17
deductions, making local in chess, 32
deductive logic, not used by early man, 163
deductive rationality, 5–6, 31
deductive reasoning, 43–46
derivatives, financial, 109, 154, 156
descendant technologies, 130
descriptors, summarizing the state of the market, 51
designers, multiple working in parallel, 111
design sophistication. *See* structural depth
determinism, 172
development, locking-in a regrettable course of, 83
diagnostic tests, on a model, 52
diminishing returns, 75–77, 183
discovery
including in a model, 114
of structure, 93
displaced technologies, 137
disruptions
drivers of, 6
ongoing waves of, 7
scale and duration of, 13

distress, cascading, 14
distributions, with extreme tails, 101
diversity
collapsing, 152
loss of, 146
of strategies increasing, 152
tending to grow in a self-reinforcing way, 145
"Down by the Salley Gardens" (W. B. Yeats), 161–162n1
dream-like world, 167
Durlauf, Steven, xxiii, 89, 91, 95, 98, 99
dynamical systems approach, 91
dynamic model, constructing, 35
dynamic programming, 174

early adopters, imposing externalities on later, 82
early-start technology, as already locked in, 77
Easley, David, 61
ecological balance, among predictions, 185
ecology
active hypotheses forming, 35
of agents' beliefs or hypotheses, 185
of beliefs co-evolving over time, 40
emerging computationally, 10
economic agents. *See also* agents
adjusting to situations, 182
forming internal models, 6
looking for ways to frame the situation, 164
as rational optimizers, 93
economic behavior, building from subjective beliefs, 171
economic crises, of the last 25 years, 24
economic disasters, warnings having little effect, 104
economic elements (human agents), reacting with strategy and foresight, 182
economic entities, recursive structure, 94
economic historians, view of new technologies, 137
economic history, students needing, 168
Economic Man, 173
economics. *See also* complexity economics; equilibrium economics
complexity perspective in, 90
different principles for the future, 191–192
end of certainty in, 171–181
as high-complexity science, 192
as inherently difficult, 158
inhibiting economists from seeing future potential exploitation, 104
two great problems in, 22
economic safety, not improved in the last five decades, 117
Economics Program, at the Santa Fe Institute, xi, xxiii, xxvi, 39, 89, 90
economic structures, crystallizing around small events, 184
economic theory, 93–95, 160
economic thought, history of, 168
economists, education of, 166
economy
complexity and, 2–4
constructed from its technologies, 136
defined, 19, 135
different way of seeing, 2
emerging from its technologies, 136
evolving as technologies evolve, 134–143
as an expression of its technologies, 135–137
features presenting difficulties for traditional mathematics, 92
in formation, 17–21
fundamental indeterminacy in, 171
interpretations of changing constantly, 143
locked-in to inferior technology paths, 71, 81, 134–135
as path dependent, 23
proceeding from its instruments of production, 19
process and emergence in, 89–102
readjusting, 19, 137
showing organic behavior, 181
studying process and emergence in, 95
The Economy as an Evolving Complex System, 90
The Economy as an Evolving Complex System II, 89, 90
ecosystems, becoming more complex, 151

efficient-market financial theory, assumptions of, 40–41
Eigen, Manfred, 98
elements. *See also* novel elements, adapting to the aggregate pattern, 182
El Farol bar problem, 10n14, 34–37, 36f, 166, 184–186, 185f
emergence
  determining, 52
  modeling, 112
  of new cognitive and social things, 94–95
empirical anomalies, 176
enabling technologies, 130
encryption systems, beta testing of, 111
endogenous expectations, agents' becoming, 42
endogenous-expectations market, exploring computationally, 51
endogenous-expectation theory, 61
engineering, failure mode analysis, 107, 109–110
enlightenment thinking, 172
entities, appearance of new, 147
enzymes, doing the programming, 155
Epstein, Joshua, xxi, xxiii, 11n15
equations, doing poorly with new categories, 21
equilibrium
  conception of becoming untenable over time, 23
  by definition, 4, 24
  dynamical process "selecting" from multiple candidates, 83
  not the natural state of the economy, 5
  patterns in, 3
  remaining useful as a first-order approximation, 25
equilibrium approach, 91
equilibrium economics
  compared to complexity economics, 24–25
  not primed to look for exploitation of systems, 24, 104
equilibrium finesse, price for, 4
ergodicity, in constant and diminishing returns cases, 76
ergodic property, 73, 84
Ermoliev, Yuri, xi, xxiii, 79
Erwin, Douglas, xxiii
Essay on Man (Pope), 172
evolution
  of complexity, 144–156
  in its phylogenetic sense, 145
  strategies competing for survival, 10
  of technology, 142
evolutionary market, exhibiting turbulence followed by quiescence, 59
evolutionary models, of Blume and Easley, 61
The Evolution of Complexity (Bonner), 148
expectational architecture, 50
expectational models, 96
expectational system, implementing, 49
expectations
  adjusting, 42
  commonality getting broken up, 34–35
  economic agents forming, 93
  endogenous, 96
  forced to differ, 185
  formed on anticipations of others' expectations, 62
  forming by deductive reasoning, 43–46
  forming by inductive reasoning, 46–47
  indeterminate and unstable, 45, 178, 181
  individuality emerging over time, 49
  modeling the formation of, 48–51
  more successful discovered, 58–59
  recursive character under heterogeneity, 42
  self-fulfilling, 85
  sources of, 95–96
  system of temporarily fulfilled, 33
  treating as hypotheses, 62
expectations case, 84–85
experience, as thick association, 166–167
experimental design, 51–52
experimental results, 124–126
experimental system, 122–124
experiments
  arriving at complicated circuits, 125
  with a computer model, 52–53
exploitation
  emerging in real life, 114
  by a few well-positioned players, 24
  generic categories of, 106

happening on every scale, 106
modeling, 112–115
exploitive behavior
automatic pre-discovery, 115–116
building into a model, 113
causes and mechanisms of, 105–109
classes of, 103
in economic and social systems, 103–117
injecting foreseen into the computer model, 112
not happening at equilibrium, 24
not rare, 106
at a smaller scale than the overall system, 110
exploitive-mode analysis, 117
exploratory actions, 6
explosive behavior, 17

factory, as a means of organization, 138–139
factory discipline, 140
failure-mode analysis
for assessing policy systems, 106
in engineering, 107
needed by economics, 103
failure modes, anticipating, 109–112
failure-mode studies, 117
failures, of economics in the practical world, 24
families, of related phenomena, 20
Farmer, Doyne, xxiii, 2n3, 14
Farrell, Joseph, 69
fast pattern completer, mind as, 162–164
feelings, triggering, 160
financial derivatives. *See* derivatives
financial instruments, 101
financial markets
characteristics of actual, 57
standard theories assuming rational expectations, 186
financial time series, patterns of nonlinearity in, 91
fixed points, 79
flexibility property, 73, 76, 84
floors, as self-fulfilling prophecies, 178
focal models, 34, 165
focal predictors, 35
Fontana, Magda, xxiii, 24
Fontana, Walter, 98
forecasting beliefs, 14
forecasting methods, 13
forecasting sequence, 84
forecasts, 52, 56
foresight horizons, shrinking of, 97
formation
within the economy, 22–23
economy in, 17–21
founder effect mechanism, 83
framework, providing, 2
framing
a problem, 159–160
a situation, 164
free association, 168
free markets, unwarranted faith in, 117
fuel economy standards, for motor vehicles, 109
functionalities
creating a toolbox of useful, 131
new ways of executing, 129
fundamental uncertainty, 5
future, imagined by each man, 6
futures contracts, of associated underlyings, 154

"gales of destruction," 120, 122, 130, 130f
game theory, 94, 183
gaming, 105, 105n4
GARCH (Generalized Auto Regressive Conditional Heteroscedasticity) behavior
characteristic of actual market data, 43, 62
in the complex regime, 57
emerging in the complex regime, 181
gas-cooled reactor, given equal development, 82
gas-turbine (or jet) aero engine, evolution of, 149–150
Geanakoplos, John, xiii, 101
Gell-Mann, Murray, xi, xxiii
gene-expression "grammar," 155
general equilibrium theory, 3–4, 183
general framework, 78–81
genetic algorithm, 150, 151f
discarding and creating predictors, 49–50
generating "smarter models," 34
in Santa Fe Market, 63–64
varying rate of invocation of, 53n10
genetic code, not changing easily, 156

genetic material, available for "adaptive radiation," 148
genetic programming, 37
genetic sequence, changing easily, 156
genotype, of a technology, 123
geographical segregation, emergence of, 99
Gintis, Herbert, xxiii
global controller, none, 92
Goldman Sachs, package of mortgage-linked bonds, 107
Goodhart's law, 108
Goodwin, Brian, 156
governments, nudging hand of, 184
gracefulness, in the learning process, 50
graduate economic education, cognition and, 166–169
grammar level, adaptation of, 154
Grand Unified Theory of economics, hoping for, 173
greedy algorithm, 73n6
growth, in coevolutionary diversity, 145–148

Haldane, Andrew, 14
Halley, Edmond, 166
hand craft, mechanization of, 140
Hanson, Ward, 69, 78
Hausmann, Ricardo, 18n25
Hayek, Friedrich, 23
health care, opening market forces, 106
health care industry, prone to information asymmetries, 107
health insurance, basic model of, 112–113
heavy tailed probability distributions, 15
herd effects, causing bubbles and crashes, 40
heterogeneous agents, 32, 42, 47, 92, 165
heterogeneous price expectations, as indeterminate, 45
heterogeneous traders, assuming, 45–46
hierarchical organization, 92
high inflation, as a situation of institutional break-down, 97
High Modern approach, 174
high stress, looking for in a proposed system, 110
historical events, 70, 72, 73, 81
historical footnote, 191–192
historical small events, 71, 72, 74
Hobbesian marketplace, 106
Holland, John, xi–xiii, xv, xxiii, 30, 35, 92n3, 133, 147, 150, 179, 186
Hommes, Cars, 14, 60
homogeneous agents, adoption payoffs for, 74t
homogeneous equilibrium, 64
homogeneous investors, assuming, 44–45
homogeneous rational expectations, 53
homogeneous rational-expectations equilibrium (h.r.e.e.) values, 52, 64
horse-drawn transportation industry, "niche firms" in, 147
human behavior, finessed by the Economic Man, 173
human language, evolution of, 153
human rationality, bounded, 31
Hutchins, E., 97
hypotheses
  forming for bar problem, 35
  sources of, 33–34
hysteresis, built-in, 165

Iceland, banking system in 2008, 104, 109
ideas, containing the mind, 163
ill-definedness, dealing with, 164
ill-defined problem, 34, 185
imagination, using, 6
implication primitive, as starting point, 124–125
incentives, 105
increasing returns
  adoption, 75f
  with agents of one type only, 73–74, 74t
  allowing, 183
  competition between economic objects, 83
  driving the adoption process, 71
  dynamics of allocation under, 70
  flexibility not holding, 76
  leading to multiple equilibria, 69
  many outcomes are possible, 82
  path-efficiency and, 77
  process of, 17
Increasing Returns and Path Dependence in the Economy (Arthur), 193n1

increasing-returns case, 74–75, 75f
ergodicity and, 77
laissez-faire giving no guarantee about "superior" technology, 82
predictability lost, 76
increasing-returns economics, 69
increasing-returns problems, 184
increasing-returns properties, 70
indeterminacy, 1, 24, 43–44, 72, 96, 171, 175, 184
pockets of, 175, 177, 181
individual behaviors, 3
individuals
within ecosystems become more complex, 151
finding optimal solutions to complex questions, 159
induced expectations, market with, 47–51
induction, 6, 32–34, 179
inductive behavior, in chess playing, 32
inductively rational agents, 46, 61, 62
inductive rationality, agents using, 180
inductive reasoning
defined, 46
humans using, 38
reasons for, 43–46
in situations complicated or ill-defined, 31
industrial cities, growth of, 139
industrial mutation, process of, 141
inflexibility property, 71
information, people interpreting, 178
insignificant circumstances, become magnified by positive feedbacks, 82
institutions, 21, 100
insurance, 113
intelligent behavior, bootstrapping itself up, 64
intelligent search device, generating "smarter models," 34
intelligible patterns, imposed, 162
interaction, of dispersed agents acting in parallel, 92
interaction networks, sociological literature on, 98n6
interactions, self-reinforcing behavior in, 16
interaction structure, importance of, 97–98
interactive grammar, 152, 155
intermediate needs, necessary to produce complex circuits, 128
Internet IP security protocol, 111
interpretation, of data, 95, 178
invention, order of making a difference, 126
invention machine, 116
investors, in computer programs, 13
investors agents, as not clones, 177–178
Ioannides, 95, 98–99

Jacob, François, 191
Jaynes, Julian, 161
Jeopardy quiz show, computer answering questions, 116
jet aircraft designs, improving significantly, 70n2
Judd, K., 2n2

Kaempffert, W., 120n1
Kaniovski, Yu, xxiii, 79–80, 86
Katz, M., 78
Kauffman, Stuart, xi, xii, xxiii, 95, 96, 133, 147, 148
Kepler-Newton version, of the Copernican theory, 151
key building blocks, appearance of, 126
key mechanisms, constructing computer-based models of, 22
Keynes, J. M., xxi, 5n6, 17, 45, 143, 178
Kindleberger, Charles, 69
Kirman, Alan, xxi, xxiii, 61, 95, 98
Klamer, A., 167
Kollman, K., 95, 99, 102
Koppl, Roger, xxiii
Koza, John, 37, 150
Krugman, Paul, 91, 95, 99
Kupers, R., 4, 24
kurtosis, evident in the complex case, 54, 56t

labor laws, 139
Landes, David, 140
Lane, David, xi, xv, xxi, xxiii, 30, 89, 91, 97, 98
Langton, Chris, xxiii
language, as programmable software, 153
Lansing, J. S., xxiii
laser printer, 18, 147

lattice, arraying agents on, 96
lattice network, structures arising in, 99
Laxness Haldór, 160
learning, 50–51, 165
"Learning by Using," 70n2
LeBaron, Blake, xxiii, 66, 179, 186
Leeuw, Sander van der, xxiii
Leijonhufvud, 91, 96–97, 100
Lenski, Richard, 133
Liar's Paradox, 30
libraries of objects, building, 131
Lindgren, Kristian, 9–10, 11f, 99, 152
linear forecasting models, 48
lock-in, 17, 69, 78, 81
logical hole, in standard economic thinking, 175
logical indeterminacy, 175
logical needs, artificial world having, 121
logic circuits, 121
logic functions, 122t, 132
long correlations, 15
long-term adoption shares, examining, 75
losses, taking early on, 78
Louça, F., 4
low volatility, 13
Lucas, Robert, xiv, 49n2
Lyapunov function, 86

machine-language programs, 147
Maglio, Paul, 103n1
Manski, Eric, 95, 100
manufacturing laborers, working conditions, 139
Marengo, L., 66
Margarita, S., 66
market(s)
  careening out of control, 24
  entering an evolutionarily stable, rational-expectations regime, 53
  as forecastible, 176
  heterogeneity of preferences in, 84
  increasingly locked-in to an inferior choice, 74
  self-organizing, 60
market anomalies, 186
market hypotheses, creating multiple, 46
market psychology, 40, 43, 47
market realities, alternative theories explaining, 41–42
market signals, 60
market statistician, each agent acting as, 46
Marshall, Alfred, 23, 184
Martin, Henri-Jean, 161
Marx, Karl, 22, 135
mathematical and computational techniques, 93
mathematical models, leaving important questions unanswered, 101
mathematics
  facilitating theory, 10
  shifting, 25
Maxfield, Robert, 97
McShea, Daniel, 148n1, 156
meaning
  different imposed on the same data, 162
  emerging, 160, 161
  residing in associations, 164
  as a set of associations, 160
Medicare system, costs tripled within five years, 106
medium-exploration-rate experiments, 53
mental models, 33–34, 37
meso-economy, properties of, 16
meso-layer
  in the economy, 16, 25
  between micro and macro, 2
meso-level phenomena, 12, 16
metabolic chemical pathways, grammar consisting of, 155
metaphors, as a form of pattern association, 163
microeconomic situation, in modern economics, 173–174
micro level, breakdown of a structure starting at, 110
microprocessors, creating niches, 146
Microsoft, Point-to-Point Tunneling Protocol (PPTP), 111–112
Mill, J. S., 22
Miller, John, xv, 99, 102
mind
  as fast pattern completer, 162–164
  notions of, 160–162
Minority Game, 30
Mirowski, Philip, xxiii, 4n4
Mitchell, Melanie, xxiii

model(s)
filling the gaps in our understanding, 32
relaxing rational expectations, 186
modeling
cognitive and structural foundations for, 95
the cognitive process, 164–166
induction, 32–34
molecules, universal across all terrestrial life, 155
Monod, Jacques, 191
Morowitz, Harold, 156
mortgage-backed securities market, in 2008, 104
multi-agent choice problems, pervasive in economics, 175
multi-arm bandit problem, 83
multiple equilibria, static analysis locating, 70
mutation and crossover, genetic algorithm procedures for, 64
mutually reinforcing expectations, subpopulations of, 186
mysterious alchemy, 161

NAND primitive, as starting point, 124–125
Nash equilibrium, 37
The Nature of Technology: What It Is and How It Evolves (Arthur), 119, 134
needs
number of, trade-off with creation of new technologies, 127
represented by truth tables, 123
satisfied by simple technologies first, 120
satisfying, 123
negative feedbacks, system containing only, 17
Nelson, Richard, 69
neoclassical allocation model, simple, 72
neoclassical economics, handling time poorly, 23
neoclassical economy, living in a Platonic world, 4
NetLogo, 112
network(s)
emerging from initially random patterns of dyadic interaction, 98
literature on, 14n19
mutually stabilizing or destabilizing, 14n19
properties of, 129–130
network-based structures, 94
network externalities, 81n9
network structures, of agents, 94
neural-network models, predicting prices, 176
neural systems, 155, 163
new circuits, constructing, 121
new technologies. *See* novel technologies
no global controller, 92
noise traders, 41
nonequilibrium
assuming, 1, 4, 105
connecting with complexity, 12, 15
endogenously generated, 4–7
natural state of the economy, xix, 5
theorizing under, xx, xxi, 7–11
nonequilibrium systems, pre-analysis of qualitative properties, 9
non-ergodicity (or path-dependence) property, 71
nonlinear dynamics, 90
nonlinear effects, requiring nonlinear inferential techniques, 100
nonlinear increasing returns, with a continuum of adopter types, 80–81
non-predictability property, 70
non-r.e.e. beliefs, subsets of not disappearing rapidly, 56
North, D., 91, 97, 100
"noticing," building into a model, 114
noun-based science, economics as, 25
novel actions, constructing randomly from time to time, 114–115
novel circuits, created from existing ones, 123
novel combinations, creation of, 141
novel elements
becoming available, 19, 137
constructed from existing ones, 120
creating, 18
novel technologies
calling forth novel arrangements, 137
causing further opportunities, 20
constructed by randomly wiring together existing ones, 121
constructed from components, 120n1

novel technologies *(cont.)*
entering in groups, 20
entering the active collection, 137
forming from existing technologies, 20
making possible other novel technologies, 6–7
not constructed by random combination, 130–131
setting up a train of technological accommodations and new problems, 141
steps following the appearance of, 137–138
triggering a cascade of further events, 134
novelty, perpetual, 92
nuclear industry, 81–82

objects, creating a growing collection of, 131
Ogburn, William Fielding, 120n1
opportunity niches, forming and disappearing, 19
optimal course of action, not definable, 93
options, associated with contingent events, 154
organizations, changing as the economy changes, 21
origin of life, 56, 155, 180
outcomes, collectively re-forming, 7
out-of-equilibrium dynamics, 92
outside changes, adjusting equilibria to, 6
overlapping generations model, 167

Packard, Norman, 91n2
Padgett, John, 98
Page, Scott, 99, 102
Palmer, Richard, xi, xiv, xv, xxi, xxiii, 66, 85, 179, 186
PARC (formerly Xerox Parc), xvii, xxiii
partial evil, as universal good, 174
parts, of technologies, 18
path-dependence, ix, 17, 71, 90, 183
theorem on, 80
path-efficiency, in constant--and diminishing-returns cases, 77
path-efficient process, 73
path-efficient property, of the allocation process, 84
pattern-cognition, mapping directly in action, 32n1
patterns, recognizing, 31, 179
Paulson, John A., 107
payoff, total or aggregate, 73n6
Perez, Carlota, 20
perfect or deductive rationality, 31
performance criteria, tailoring behavior to conform to, 108
perpetual novelty, 92, 95, 101
petrol-versus-steam car case, 82
phase transition, 14
phenomena
harnessed into use, 120n2
simpler toy models of, 9
phenotype, of a technology, 123
phoneme or simple element level, adaptation of, 154
Pines, David, xxiii, 90
Planck, Max, 158
pluralistic cognitive foundation, 93
Polak, Wolfgang, xviii, xxiii, 22n30, 119
policy implications, of complexity, 23–24
policy systems
injecting foreseen exploitive behavior in a simulation, 113–114
looking for weak points in, 111
probing computer-based models of for possible failure, 112
questioning the outcome of, 106
political economy, 2, 23, 187
Pope, Alexander, 172
population games, providing a class of models, 98
positive feedback(s)
allowing, 183
causing nonequilibrium, 16–17
inherent, 148
literature in economics on, 17
in models, 91
nonlinearities in the form of, 183
theory of, 90
positive-feedback trading strategies, seen as rational, 41
possible actions, generating families of, 115
potential inefficiency property, 70
power law(s), 15, 122, 129, 130

predictability, 76
property of, 73, 84
predictions
becoming unstable, 178
subsets of mutually reinforcing, 180
predictor accuracy, 59, 63
predictors
"alphabet soup" of, 36
clustering in the more visited parts of the market state space, 50
forecasting part of each, 49
forming for bar problem, 35
luck in finding good diverging over time, 61
multiplicity of, 50
needing to "cover" the available prediction space, 37
recognizing many states of the market, 49
self-organizing, 36, 37, 185
subjective expectational models represented by sets of, 49
turning off the condition part of all, 57
premature association, as disastrous, 168
preventive medicine and disease control, looking to future prevention, 107
price
driven endogenously by induced expectations, 42
as a function of expected future dividends, 177
price bubbles, 178, 186. *See also* bubbles
price statistics, in the complex regime, 54
price volatility, 40, 57
principal-agent model, 167
principles, of the new economics, 191–192
prisoner's dilemma
model, 111, 167
strategies meeting randomly and cumulate profit by playing, 152
privileged information, profiting from, 107
probabilistic cloud, surrounding existing technologies, 128
probability, of each technology's being chosen, 78
problem and solution, what constitutes, 101–102
problems, as the answer to solutions, 140–143
procedural theory, 21–22
procedure, properties of, 174
process-and-emergence viewpoint, 95
processes
through which structure emerges, 93
triggered by other processes, 21
process-oriented complexity approach, 184
profitable expectations, discovering, 42
program output level, adaptation of, 154
propagations, of events causing further events, 15
properties, definitions of, 84
psychological behavior, emerging, 61
psychological change, structural change causing, 140
psychology, market possessing, 47
Ptolemaic astronomy, collapse of, 151

qualitative phenomena, associated with the complex regime, 59
QWERTY typewriter keyboard, 81, 81n9

radio broadcasting, elements making possible, 120
railway locomotive, construction of, 19
random events, allowing the possibility of, 70
random predictors, agents initialized by seeding with, 64
random walks, 75, 76, 85
rating agency's models, gaming, 108
rational expectations, 30, 78, 171, 174, 176
rational expectations economics, 3, 183
rational expectations equilibrium, 14, 52, 53n11, 84
rational-expectations regime, 42, 53, 180
rational-expectations theory, as a special case, 181
rationality
arguing against conventional notions of, 96
not well defined, 5–6
perfect or deductive demanding much of human behavior, 31

rational solution, accomplishing, 159
Ray, Tom, 147
realism, shift in attitude in the direction of, 24
reality, idealized, rationalized world distorting, 4
real phenomena, understanding of, 100
real world, subject to fundamental uncertainty, 171
reasoning, depending on the past experiences of the reasoner, 164
recombination, of predictor arrays, 50
recursive loop, connecting with complexity, 3
reflexivity, 5n7, 62, 62n17
regimes
  properties of, 75–77, 76t
  two different, 53
regime transitions, from equilibrium to complexity to chaos, 14
Reisman, David, xxiii, 5n5
replacement
  avalanches of, 122
  causing the collapse of technologies backward, 130
research directions, emerging, 95–102
research program, building, 95
returns, affecting predictability, efficiency, flexibility, and ergodicity, 71
returns regimes, interpretation of economic history different in different, 82
reversals, 150
Ricardo, David, 143
rich psychology, market settling into, 96
Rieck, C., 66
risk-free bonds, 47
Robinson, Joan, 23
Rosenberg, Nathan, xxiii, 69, 70n2
Rosser, J. B., 2n3
Rothmaier, Daria, 103n1
rules of the game, 100
Rumelhart, David, 30
Russell, Bertrand, 158, 162–163
Russia, players seizing control of state's newly freed assets, 104
Russians, not arriving with empty minds to their version of capitalism, 169
Rust, John, xv, xxiii, 159
Samuelson, Paul, 4–5, 69
"Santa Fe approach," emerging within economics, 91
Santa Fe Artificial Stock Market, 13, 39, 42, 63–65, 66, 166
Santa Fe Institute, x, xxiii, 2, 89, 183
Sargent, Tom, x, xiv, xxiii, 6, 46n7, 166
Scheffer, Martin, 14n19
schemata, 31, 150
Schumpeter, J. A., xxi, 6, 18, 23, 120, 130, 141
Schuster, Peter, 98, 133
sciences, becoming more procedural and less equation-based, 25
securities, backed by the underlying, 154
self-creation, perpetually in a process of, 141
self-referential character, of expectations, 62
self-referential loop, 175
self-reinforcing asset-price changes, 13
Shackle, 5, 6, 23
Shapiro, Carl, 78
Shepard, Roger, 30
short memory/short foresight adaptive mode, 97
Shubik, Martin, xxiii, xxiv, 69, 95, 100, 101
signaling, driving the observed patterns, 57
simple regime, corresponding to rational-expectations equilibrium, 62
simplicity, bursts of cutting through growing complexity, 151
Simpson, D., 4n4
simulations, future dipping into history, 116
single-technology dominance, theorem on, 80
slow-learning-rate experiments, 53
small-event history, determining the tipping process, 77
small events outside the model, influencing adoptions, 78
Smith, Adam, xxi, 3, 22, 143, 172, 173
Smolin, Lee, xxiii, 23
social and economic systems, incentives inducing further behavior, 117

social character, of human interactions, 98
social dimension, of cognition, 97
social interactions, recurring patterns of, 98
social roles, economic action is structured by emergent, 94
social system, stress testing a design for, 110
Solow, Robert, 18
solution-formulation, 150
solutions
  in economics, 25
  imagining, 116
  needing to be generated by computation, 166
Soros, George, 5n7, 13n18, 40n4, 62n17
Soviet Union, going capitalist in 1990-90, 169
spatiotemporal structures, forming of, 99
sponsoring firms, appropriating later payoffs, 83n12
spontaneous onset, of a phenomenon, 12
standard efficient markets theory, 176
standard finance theory, 186
standards, 78
standard theory, facing unexplained phenomena, 176
standing reserve, 126, 127f
stasis, economy never quite at, 141
states of the economy, aggregate-level, 91
state space, changing with time, 91n2
state variables, emergence of new kinds of relevant, 91
static equilibrium approach, stymied by indeterminacy, 184
static outlook, shifting into a process orientation, 184
statistical anomalies, explained in the standard theory, 177
Stiglitz, Joseph, 41, 47
stochastic dynamic programming, 159
stochastic process(es), 11, 47, 78, 85, 93, 184
stock market, asset pricing in an artificial, 39–66
stock returns, containing small, but significant serial correlations, 40
strategic agents, 111
strategic market games, 101
strategic options, constructing for the agents, 110–111
strategies
  ecology of, 10
  evolving in a game-theoretic setting, 152
strategy modules, soliciting, 111
stress testing, policy designs, 117
structural change, 4, 21n27, 22, 134, 137–141, 143
structural deepening, 148–152
structural depth, 149, 151f
structural foundations, 94
structure
  creation and re-creation, 18
  of the economy, 136
  emerging, 20, 56, 93
  formation of, 3
  of human interactions, 98–101
sub-assemblies, of technologies, 18
subjective beliefs
  about subjective beliefs, 31
  changes in rippling through the market, 186–187
  differing among agents, 32
  economy emerging from, 181
  forming, 5
subjective expectations, repeated iteration of, 45
subschemas, hierarchy of collapsing, 150
subsystems, 149
sudden percolation, 14
sun, never at equilibrium, 9
symbiotic clusters, of entities, 147
syntax, understanding of, 160
synthetic biology, 124
systems
  capturing simpler elements, 156
  with multiple elements, 182
  outcomes for highly interconnected, 8
  taking partial control of, 108–109

Tabb, William, xxiii, 21n27, 23, 117
Tayler, Paul, xxiii, 39, 95, 179, 186
technical analysis, 57
technical trading, 176
  emerging, 42, 54
  heavy use of, 186
  signals, 57
  test for the emergence of, 51

technological change, as a driver of disruption, 6
technological disruption, compared to Brownian motion of uncertainty, 7
technology (technologies). *See also* novel technologies
building itself out of itself, 119
build-out of, 126–129
competing for a "market" of potential adopters, 70
constructed from components, 120
creating, 120n2, 121
defined, 18, 120, 136
demand for, 19
destroying neatness, 173
displaying increasing returns to adoption, 70
each containing the seeds of a problem, 142
encountered by industries, 20
evolution within a simple computer model, 119–133
expression of, 19
gaining self-reinforcing advantage, 80
key used heavily to directly construct new, 129f
locking in to one technology only, 75
as main agent of change in the economy, 18
putting in the foreground, 18
as self-producing or autopoietic, 120n2
simple model of two new, 71
sponsored by firms, 77–78
technology-based evolution, 131
technology change, 173
technology-creating-the-economy-creating-technology, 137
temporal phenomena, 9, 12–14, 16
Tesfatsion, Leigh, xxi, xxiii, 95, 98–99, 102
textile factory or mill, as a higher level organizational arrangement, 137
thematic challenges, calling forth novel solutions, 21
theoretical limits, to the predictability of the economic future, 83
theories
applying prematurely as dangerous, 167–168
becoming the understanding of mechanisms, 25
as metaphors with entailments, 166
not consisting of mathematics, 10
as thin associations, 166
theory of the firm, 98
thick associations, 166–167
thin associations, 166, 167
thinking
associatively, 163
inductively, 31–34
Tierra system, 147
time, rethinking the issue of, 23
timing, in the market, 48
Tordjman, H., 66
trade, motivation to, 60
traders
seeing markets as offering speculative opportunities, 40
view justified by invoking behavioral assumptions, 62
trade unions, 139
trading volume
in real markets, 40
showing persistence or autocorrelation, 57
traffic flow, simple model of, 12
transfer process, 34
transient phenomena, 94–95
truth tables, 123
Turing, Alan, 8, 11n15, 25

uncertainty, 5, 7, 93, 172–175
fundamental, ix, xx, xxi, 5, 158, 171
unconscious associations, 168
underlyings, 154, 156n3
uninsured, opting in and out of coverage, 113
unitary cognitive foundation, of neoclassical economic theory, 93
unstable equilibrium, positions of, 4–5
user technologies, each technology linking to, 129
US invasion of Iraq, generated insurgency, 106

Veblen, Thorstein, 23
verb-actions, economics shifting toward, 25
Victorian industrial economy, emergence of, 139
volatility, 13, 58f
von Ohain, Hans, 149

Vriend, Nick, 30

Waddington, C. H., 148
Waldrop, Mitchell, 2n2
Wall Street firms, getting better ratings, 108
Walras, Léon, 5n5, 94
Watts, Duncan, 14
The Wealth of Nations (Smith), 172
Whittle, Frank, 149
Whittle's jet engine, 151
Wolfram, Stephen, 8
working class, demanding a larger share of the wealth, 139
Wright, Gavin, 69

Yeats poem, 161–162

Zhang, Yi-Cheng, xvi, 30
Zurcher, Harold, 159